My Supernatural Dad and Me!

From Natural to Supernatural!

By John Jackson

Publisher's information:
John Jackson
P.O. Box 153
Ada, OK. 74821
jjackjr3@gmail.com
Charitable donations are accepted.

ISBN: 978-1-7348949-0-5 (E-Copy)
ISBN: 978-1-7348949-1-2 (Paperback)
ISBN: 978-1-7348949-2-9 (Hardcopy)

Library of Congress Control Number: 00000000000

Any references to real people, or real places, are used as named, or a name of author's choice. Names, characters, and places are products of the author's life memories, and are true and correct to the best of the Author's recollection.

Front and Back cover design by Elaine Grutas Derilo.

Book design by John Jackson.

Printed by Kindle Direct Publishing, in the United States of America.

First printing edition 2020.

Author's Website:

www.saymakeaway.com

DISCLAIMER:

All Scripture references used within this writing are from the New American Standard Bible, unless otherwise noted.

I did not seek permission from every person whom I have desired to write about within this book; and the people I did ask to use their names or their deceased parent's names denied me permission. Therefore, any names mentioned herein, will be by initials or author's nickname preference only.

To some, the writing within this book may not seem appropriate for your reading. The fact is, it is a part of my life; I cannot deny the truth. I believe that what I have written within the pages of this book is exactly what my Father God wanted me to write. There may be something in this book that God can use to set people free from issues they may be dealing with in their own lives. On the other hand, maybe you know someone who may be battling the dark side without hope and what I write may bring them hope enough to believe that there is freedom in Jesus Christ.

I pray that this book will bring the people of Jesus Christ to a place more of an understanding that just because "life happens" the Heavenly Father will never leave, nor forsake us (Hebrews 13:5). Nothing can ever separate us from the Father's love (Romans 8:38-39), which He showed for all mankind when Jesus Christ gave His life as a ransom for those who will believe in His sacrifice, and in His Name (John 3:16). From the Holy Bible, the Apostle Paul said, "…I have become all things to all men, so that I may by all means save some." (First Corinthians 9:22). That does not mean that Paul experimented with anything and everything just so he could have common ground with other people in hopes of winning souls for Jesus Christ. It simply means that Paul lived life as it came, which gave him experience in areas of life that bring people down and make them hopeless. Paul went through some things by the Lord's will so that Paul could be experienced in areas where he related to certain people; some things were not Paul's own will for his life.

Things happen in life that we are not happy about; we do not want to accept what is happening, but it is happening; things we wish would have never happened, but they happened.

Please read this book at your own risk. That does not mean that you will agree with everything I write here. You are entitled to your own opinion. Please read with an open mind, knowing that life happens.

DEDICATION

This writing is dedicated to my dearest friend and his lovely misses, Estell and Stephanie Kauffman.

Estell and I became friends sometime around 2016. I was a door greeter at one of the biggest churches in Ada. As well, Estell attended the same Sunday school class as me.

One needs only to take one look at Estell and you know you're in the presence of a genius. I mean, if I had time to list this guy's accomplishments within this Dedication, I would not be able to finish the book!

Among other things, Estell is a singer. Besides singing in the Sunday Choir, he travels around and sings with a big bunch of other men.

Estell has a body that looks like Arnold Schwarzenegger because he lifts weights religiously. He has inspired me to have my own weight-lifting time on a regular basis.

My true friend is a survivalist as well. I have no doubt that if it came to us living in the wild, I would learn a whole lot about living off the land.

I was thoroughly impressed with Estell's intelligence. He has a brilliant mind for investing. Just listening to him speak teaches you volumes.

I too, figured out late in life, that I have a knack for investing in stocks. There is just something about a penny stock that excites me. I know there is money to be earned in the proper investments. However, I am not a tech savvy individual; thus, I needed some help. I was praying for God to send someone who could teach me about trading stocks. Thus, God sent Estell.

With that in mind. one Sunday morning, when I was greeting at a door of the church, I saw Estell and his Misses Stephanie strolling down the hallway towards me, while on their way into the sanctuary for the main service (Estell was heading to sing in the Choir). As they approached, Estell had a big radiant smile on his face that drew me to him. We began conversing, one thing led to another, and we found ourselves talking about trading stocks and crypto currencies. Before our conversation ended, I knew Estell was Godsend to help me learn about trading stocks; I commented to Estell of that fact.

Estell and I began meeting at his office on a weekly basis in order to visit and encourage each other in our pursuits of life. I remember being very fascinated with the wealth of knowledge Estell brought to the table. I had a healthy fear of trading stocks, but during our visits, my fears were calmed and I began trading stocks with real money.

Estell inspires me with his mannerism, dedication, simplicity, kindness, sternness, and unfailing love. He is a prime example of what a true man of God looks like.

As well, Stephanie has been such a blessing to me with her humble kindness. Her humble dedication to her husband is a Proverbs 31 example for other women to follow.

I dedicate this book to Estell and Stephanie because there is not a doubt in my mind that God is using these two precious souls to provide the necessary shelter and time in order for me to complete this writing.

Thank you Estell and Stephanie for your unfailing, unconditional love that you have shown me over these past few years.

I pray that God blesses you with over and above all that you can ask or think, in this life, and the life to come, and that you continue to rise and shine for many years to come.

INTRODUCTION

The book you hold in your hands has not been written by a super Christian, but just a mere man who has had many of the same struggles in life that you have had. That is one reason, among other reasons, that God wants this book published and in your hands—to show you that He is a God who works supernaturally in an ordinary person's life. Hence, God is "super", and we are "natural"; and when God uses us as witnesses, it's "supernatural". God wants you to know, that no matter how big an idiot you may think you are, He can still use you to confound those who are the so-called "experts".

When I was a child growing up, my mother sent my little brother and me to church. I remember being as young as four or five years old walking down the front porch steps holding my little brother's hand while we walked to the awaiting church bus. I went to church until the time I was about fifteen years old, yet, I had no idea who God was, nor what He was capable of doing until He decided to reveal Himself to me later in my life, supernaturally.

For me, going to church as a child, and then a teenager, was not about worshiping Jesus Christ during the "praise and worship" session. Neither was it about hearing a preacher talk about the God of the Holy Bible. When I went to church, it was about obeying my mother; about the loving feeling I felt as I rode the church van, making the stop at a blind man's house to pick him up so I could guide him to the church pew. Then, back to his front door after church was dismissed. The fact is, I really did not listen to the preacher talk about the God of the Holy Bible; his words just did not sink into my brain; I never made the connection with the God of the Holy Bible, until…

CHAPTER ONE: Birth

"For You formed my inward parts; You wove me in my mother's womb." (Psalm 139:13).

I was born, not hatched (laughter). Before I was conceived and brought into this world, my mother had complications with her first two conceptions; she had two miscarriages before conceiving me and going through the birth pangs. My mother does not like to talk about it (and I understand why), but she has hinted to me that my natural father, John Sr., punched her in the stomach while she was pregnant with the first two conceptions of pregnancy. Now, you can draw your own conclusion as to why my mother had two miscarriages from that information. I feel as if my natural father had a hand in on the results of the miscarriages. Moreover, it stands to reason, because my mother told me that the man chosen to conceive me, hated babies; more specifically, crying babies. In quoting my mother, "Your father hated crying babies. He could not stand being in the same house with a crying baby. If there was a crying baby in the house when we went to visit my relatives, your father would sleep outside in the car." Therefore, when I was conceived in my mother's womb, God must have had His hand upon my life in order for me to make it to live birth.

My natural father abandoned my mother and me before I was born; he joined the army and then went AWOL, leaving my mother a single parent.

My mother called her father, CT, who lived in Sulphur, Oklahoma at the time, and told him she was in the state of Texas alone, pregnant, scared, and she wanted to come home. My grandfather sent her a bus ticket, and she went home.

I was born a short time after on November 25, 1967.

CHAPTER TWO: Growing Up

"Your eyes have seen my unformed substance; and in Your book were all written the days that were ordained for me, when as yet there was not one of them." (Psalm 139:16).

My mother did not drag me to church, she sent me to church. One of my first memories is of me holding the hand of my younger brother while we stepped down some steps that were in front of a mobile home we lived in so we could take a seat on the awaiting church bus. I could not have been over five years old, which meant my brother was about three years old. I do not have any more memories of going to church until I was in my teens, but I am sure my mother sent me to church more than that one time.

It was also about this time when I began wearing eyeglasses. Back in the '70s, technology was not as advanced as it is today, so I had to wear what was called "pop-bottle" eyeglasses. Moreover, I hated it! The eye doctor said that I had a lazy eye, and his attempt to correct the eye was to prescribe me to sit about five feet from the television in hopes of strengthening the eye; it did not work.

MR. AND MRS. GONE

My mother divorced my natural father and married another man named Jimmy Gone. My mother conceived by Mr. Gone and gave birth to my half-brother CJ. I consider CJ my big brother because he is a genius in his mind; the man is highly intelligent, a mastermind to me.

Jimmy's family roots began in the state of Arkansas, so they lived there until my mother and Mr. Gone were divorced. From there, my mother moved to Little Rock, Arkansas. Although I never believed my mother, she told me that I wanted to live with Mr. and Mrs. Gone. I was about five years old when I went to live with them.

Jimmy was an officer in the United States Air Force, and was on active duty most of the time, which took him away from home for months at a time. I remember how Mr. Gone taught me how to mow grass with a push lawnmower, and how to ride a bicycle. Jimmy was an okay father figure to me, while Missu was mean to me in the absence of her husband.

Mrs. Gone was one of those "mean step-mothers". Of course, I was the outcast because I was the child of the first marriage, causing me to be the one who caught all of the frustration through abuse from the stepmother. I remember coming home from school and as soon as I stepped inside the door of the house, Missu would give me a mean look and point towards my bedroom with her index finger and arm stretched out. I knew what that meant, "Go to your room and don't come out until I call you for supper!" Thus, off to my little 5x8' foot bedroom I would go, not to come out until my dinner plate was full of food and sitting on the supper table. After I had eaten dinner, I was made to go back to the "dungeon".

Mrs. Gone did spiteful things to me as in the time when I broke my eyeglasses and left them at school so I would not get into trouble at home. Missu saw that I did not have my eyeglasses on my face and decided to allow me and CJ write a letter to our mother. I could not see the lines on the paper well enough in order to write between the lines. When Missu saw the letter I wrote and how it was sloppily written out of the lines, she asked me where my eyeglasses were. After I told her about breaking the eyeglasses, she gave me a whipping because I did not bring the eyeglasses home.

There were happy times when Mr. Gone was at home on leave from the Air Force. Mrs. Gone would be as nice as any other loving mother would be while Mr. Gone was at home. We would play ball, ride bicycles, eat cookies, watch television, mow grass, and go watch movies at the drive-in theatre. However, just as soon as Jimmy left home to go back to active duty, Missu turned into the wicked witch of the house again, at least towards me.

The abuse was not Mrs. Gone's fault. Later in life, after I was an adult, my brother told me that Missu was diagnosed with schizophrenia and taking medicine, and that she was a very different person after she began taking the medicine. I was happy for her, and by that time, I had forgiven her for the way she treated me; holding no hard feelings towards her.

I pray that her soul is resting in peace.

GRANDMA AND GRANDPA G

There were other happy times with other family members as well. There was Saturday nights when we would go to Grandma G and Grandpa G's house and watch movies on the television. Watching a movie back in the early 1970's was a big deal for us children. My most favorite part about "movie night" was when we would get to go to the shop building and get a soft drink to drink with our popcorn. We had a choice between Pepsi, Mountain Dew, Dr. Pepper, Sprite or Orange Crush. I loved getting a Mountain dew. During the movie, someone would always be churning butter the old style way, with a jug and plunger. Sometimes, that "someone" was me! I liked churning butter. The process fascinated me at that tender age.

There are other memories at CJ's grandpa and grandma's house. Like, every day for lunch was the same menu: Brown beans, fried taters, and biscuits.

I also remember when Grandma G. would say, "Go get me a chicken." That did not mean for someone to drive to the grocery store and buy a chicken already processed and cut into pieces. No, that meant to go out into the yard and chase a live, squawking chicken around the yard until you caught the chicken (lol... I had to "corner" the chicken before I could catch it), and then take the chicken by the head and spin its body around and around until the body separated from the head, which left the head in your hand; and yeah, blood slinging everywhere and running out of your hand, down your arm. Yeah. Yuck! Then, you picked the chicken up and hung it by its feet until all the blood drained out of the body. After most of the blood dripped out, you plucked the feathers out of the chicken's body by hand, at which time you took the chicken to grandma so she could prepare it for the meal.

There were other times where us children had fun but would get us into trouble with Grandma G. For instance, CJ's youngest uncle and I would try to "rope" CJ with rubber a car tire; that was until Grandma G. saw us and hollered at us to quit because we could hurt CJ. We did not listen very well, which made Grandma G. angry. Then, she would say, "Go cut me a switch!" That meant it was time for a whipping. Someone had to go to a tree and cut Grandma G. a small limb from the tree in order for her to be able to give us some lashings for not obeying her commands. We would usually run away from

Grandma G, but that did not do us any good. We thought that she might forget about whipping us with the switch, until we showed up tired, hungry, and ready to eat; then, Grandma G. had us cornered, and we got a worse switching than we would have if we would just have stood still the first time, instead of running around like chickens with our heads chopped off (Lol. That is what a chicken's body will do if you put it on the ground after plucking or chopping its head off; it runs around as a chicken with its head chopped off).

Grandma taught us children a lot about life. I will never forget how Grandma G. taught me how to get a speck of dust out of my eye. She said to tilt your head forward and look at the ground. Then, use your thumb and index finger, or your index finger and middle finger to spread your eyelid apart while blinking your eye. That remedy has worked for me countless times throughout my life.

Grandpa G. was cool. I liked Grandpa G. because he had a harelip; he sounded funny when he talked. Sometimes, what Grandpa G. said was difficult to understand. Some of us children would talk as if we had a harelip so we would sound like grandpa; now, I feel bad about mocking Grandpa G's harelip. Grandpa G. had a heart of gold, and was a smart man. He had a mechanic/welding shop across the highway from their house. Grandpa would work on automobiles, weld on farm equipment, fix flats, and whatever else needed affixing for other people who lived around town.

One of my last memories of living in Berryville is a memory that has puzzled me ever since. I tell this here because I feel I should. Most men have a sexual battle raging inside their soul. Whether that battle is just to fantasize about a woman's body, only to masturbate about the visual fantasization, or by acting upon the fantasization and raping a woman. It does not matter the case; what really matters is that the "act" of fantasizing and all that follows is of the devil. The devil uses this fantasization method to build a stronghold in the man's life, especially a Christian's life, causing the Christian to be defeated in the spirit realm. I too have battled this fantasizing method of the devil for many years. I have yet to understand exactly where the devil was able to get his sexual stronghold locked in on my life. I mean, did the overly strong sexual desires come from my natural father's genes, or was it by some other means? I do not ever remember being molested by any adult in my childhood. Unless you consider the story I am about to tell you an actual "molestation". I do not consider it to be so. While I lived with Mr. and Mrs. Gone, I remember them having at least three daughters; but we never "played" with each other sexually; maybe talked about sexual things once or twice, but nothing like what I am about to share with you. Without further ado, here follows the story:

I had to be about eight years old at the time. I remember being in the back bedroom of Grandpa and Grandma G's house. Half of the house contained a "great room" where we watched television, and the other half contained the beds where everybody would sleep. The kitchen was in a separate building, as well as the outhouse was separate for bathroom use.

One particular summer day, all the children were going to a swimming hole to swim. (We did not have a city pool to swim in). I was in the bedroom putting on my swimming trunks when a girl came into the room wearing a two-piece swimming suit. It is my guess that she was about sixteen years old at the time. She took off the bottom part of her swimming suit and then told me to take off my swimming trunks. Then, she told me to lie on top of her, while the both of us were naked. I do not remember penetrating her vagina with my penis, but I definitely remember lying on top of her naked body. I would like to say that the sexual stuff stopped there, but I cannot. I would even like to leave the sexual stuff out of this writing, but I would be in disobedience to the Lord Jesus Christ.

As with life, things change. I have heard it said, "One thing you can count on is change." The following story is just one of those changes.

I'M GOING ON A TRIP?!

Change they did! As I wrote on a previous page, Jimmy Gone was in the United States Air Force; thus, Mr. Gone got an active duty call where he was being stationed overseas in England. I still remember to this day how both Mr. Gone and Mrs. Gone came into my room one night as we were bedding down. I slept in a top bunk and they talked with me, telling me that Mr. Gone was being sent to England, and the whole family was going. They asked me if I wanted to go with them on the trip and live in England for the next three years. My other choice was to go live with my mother in Little Rock, Arkansas. I was about nine years old at the time. I was afraid (Get this. Do not laugh!) I would not understand the language over in England, so I opted out for going to live with my mother.

I do not remember exactly how long of a span of time it was before my trip to live with my mother, but what a trip it was! One day Mrs. Gone came to me and told me to pack my belongings, because this was the day I was leaving to go live in Little Rock. As we got into the old red Ford pickup, I was not sure what to expect about the trip. I remember being very excited to be going to live with my mother, and, for a young, nine-year old boy, what happened next was even more exciting! Mrs. Gone took me to a Greyhound bus station and put me on a big, grey bus. I sat directly behind the man who drove the big bus to my ending destination—Little Rock, Arkansas. I still remember sitting in the first seat, looking out of the big front glass of the bus, waving at Mrs. Gone very big, with a great big smile across my face. Nevertheless, part of my excitement was turned to disappointment because Mrs. Gone never waved back; she just looked out the back glass of the pickup at me as the pickup drove away, with that all too familiar scrawl on her face. Then, Mrs. Gone was gone.

MY SON IS WHERE?!

Looking out the big front windshield of the big grey bus is about all I remember of the bus ride to Little Rock until I arrived at the bus station about two o'clock in the morning. I remember walking up to the counter and not being able to see over it. The attendant asked me some questions with one particular question being "Do you have a phone number for your mother?" I happily said "Yes! It's in my shoe!" My mother would come and visit my brother and me while we lived with Mr. and Mrs. Gone. One time, she said, "Johnny. I wrote my phone number on this piece of paper so you can call me in case you have an emergency." Well, a nine year old arriving at a bus station in the wee hours of the morning, and in a big city as Little Rock, seemed to be an emergency to me. I got the piece of paper out of my shoe and gave it to the attendant.

While I waited for him to contact my mother, he bought me a Pepsi and a Zero candy bar. It was the first Zero candy bar I had ever had the pleasure of eating; I fell in love with Zero candy bars. The attendant contacted my mother. The only thing is, the phone number was the number of my mother's neighbor. When my mother's friend knocked on the door of my mother's house, at what had to have been three o'clock in the morning to tell her that her nine-year old son was at the bus station, my mother did not believe her. Finally, my mother was convinced, and came to pick me up. Mrs. Gone did not alert my mother of my potential arrival in Little Rock; it was a total surprise for my mother.

At that time, my mother was married to a man who came from Puerto Rico. He did not want me to stay there and wanted my mother to send me back to Berryville where I had come from. My mother denied his request. I cannot say this to be the truth, but it is my belief that the reason my brother and me lived with Mr. and Mrs. Gone was that my mother's husband did not want us there. My arrival and my living there would eventually cause trouble; even being part of the reason my mother divorced him in the end.

NOW THIS IS THE LIFE FOR A NINE YEAR OLD!

My mother treated me like a king for some time after my arrival. She bought a bedroom suit for $200.00. It was a very nice bedroom suit containing a queen size bed, a dresser with mirror, Chester drawers, and a nightstand. I slept in heaven for a while. The bed is gone now, and my mother either still has, or had the dresser and Chester drawers up to a few years ago. I had a tiger lamp on my nightstand that my mother has continued to use for her nightstand lamp to this day.

My mother was a lot of fun. She worked for the Maybelline cosmetic company and earned a good income; thus, I was allowed to do fun stuff every week, like go roller-skating, and eat at McDonalds where my mother would give me the pickles from her burger every time we went in to eat a burger. My mother bought model airplanes so that I could glue them together; then, she hung the airplanes from my bedroom ceiling. It was my mother who introduced me to Chips Ahoy chocolate chip cookies, of which I still eat at least three cookies with my lunch just about every day (Unless my mother bakes some snicker doodle cookies and sends them home with me. ...hehehe). I remember my mother bought a Dodge Dart Light automobile brand spanking new. It was gold in color with white pinstripes down the side. Later in this story, I will tell you the crying shame of what happened to my mother's new car.

ABUSE OVER BUT A TROUBLESOME FREEDOM

As written previously, Mrs. Gone was abusive to me between the ages of five and eight years old. As well, she was not at fault.

I was normal like any other young boy. However, my mother gave me total freedom when I went to live with her. Freedom like leaving me sleeping at six o'clock in the morning when she went to work. Then, she would call me on the telephone and wake me up in time to get up and get ready for school. I was able to go outside and play when I wanted to; I could go over and play at my friend's house; I caught crawdads from the creek; I played baseball with a team; I burned holes in a paper bag with the sun using the pop-bottled eyeglasses I was forced to wear; different things like that.

However, trouble came because of having too much freedom. I acted out in a very negative way towards authority figures and fellow classmates. For instance, one day, my mother's now-ex-husband, took me to baseball practice as he did several times each week. This particular day, I was in one of those rebellious moods, and I was late for baseball practice. I got out of the car and walked onto the field to see the coach, when I got to the coach, he said, "Jackson! You go play outfield!" I snapped and said, "You (blankety- blank) coach! Don't tell me what position to play! I will play whatever position I want because I own this team!" It need not be said, but the coach showed me just "whose" team it was because he kicked me off the team. My mother's ex-husband was very angry, and embarrassed at the same time.

Another time, and the "straw that broke the camel's back" so-to-speak, came one day when I was at school. The students were standing in a line waiting to go into the gymnasium for some sort of presentation. As we stood in the line, I felt someone push me from behind, and again, something in me snapped and I spun around with my elbow outstretched, knocking the person behind me in the side of the head. Then, I blacked out.

When I came back to consciousness, two teachers were pulling at me from behind, trying to pull me off the chest of a student whose face I was pounding into the ground with my fists.

When the school officials notified my mother, she was shocked and took me to see a psychiatrist. The doctor played some psycho games with me and then prescribed a medicine for me to take called Ritalin. I do not remember having any more trouble with the rebellious attitude afterwards, until I was a teenager.

WHAT IS THAT SMELL?!

Here is where the story goes on the sexual stronghold trail again.

My mother's ex-husband had a daughter named Marcel who was a year or two younger than I was. One summer, this girl came to visit us. I remember thinking about how cute she was, but I never thought of her in a sexual way, until…

One night, I was sleeping sound in my bed when I awoke to an awful smell. After becoming alert, I saw that it was the Chloraseptic spray from the bottle I kept by my bed for a sore throat. With further investigation, I discovered that the bottle was being waved under my nose by the cute stepsister.

Yeah. Mmmhmm; this girl was awakening me with the Chloraseptic spray because she wanted me to get naked with her so we could lie in my bed and "play" with each other.

Marcel did this night after night. Her sexcapade did not stop until one morning her father opened the door to tell us breakfast was on the table and ready to eat. Marcel and me had "played" with each other during the night and then fell asleep naked.

After her father startled us to life for breakfast, we went to the bathroom together to brush our teeth and freshen up. While in the bathroom, Marcel suggested we tell her father the truth, but I insisted that we tell him we were not doing anything. Sure enough, after we seated ourselves at the breakfast table, her father asked us if we were "...doing anything in the bedroom last night?" I blurted out "No!", while Marcel sheepishly said "Yes." I looked at Marcel and said, "No we were not!" I do not remember her father disciplining us for our bedroom sexcapades.

I remember a time when Marcel and I were down by the creek with some other neighborhood friends when she said, "Hey Johnny! Let's get naked and 'do it' so our friends can see us doing it!" I told her that I did not think our friends wanted to see us "do it", but she insisted, I relented, and we commenced to "getting it".

Marcel was not finished with me sexually. I remember another completely different time where I went to visit her and her father. I am not sure what the circumstances were surrounding the why I was visiting, but we almost were caught in the bed naked by her father again. He stepped out to go to the convenience store and when he came back, we were in the bed naked. We jumped out of the bed and ran in different directions; I ran to the closet and began getting dressed while she ran into the bathroom dragging the bed sheet's end into the bathroom with her, leaving the rest of the sheet lying across the floor to the bed. Once again, her father questioned us about our actions, only to hear both of us say "No daddy! We were not doing anything!" I am quite sure he did not believe us, nor did he trust us.

MOTHER! WHAT HAPPENED TO YOUR EYE?!

I do not remember seeing Marcel again after that.

What I do remember is seeing my mother with a black eye.

My mother and her ex were arguing, so she sent me to a friend's house and told me to stay there until she came to get me. I remember wondering why she had sent me to the friend's house; I found out later that it was a sad reason. Her and her ex got into a fight. The details are sketchy, but he had a .22 rifle in his hands and my mother went to wrestle the gun out of his hands when the butt of the gun hit my mother in the eye, blackening her eye. When my mother came to get me, I saw her black eye and lost my emotions; I was very upset.

It was at this point that my mother divorced her ex-husband. I never saw him nor Marcel again.

CALIFORNIA! HERE WE COME!

Although the caption seems a bit excited, the trip to California was not a fun trip.

It was just my mother and I after she divorced her ex. CJ was still in England while his father continued active duty with the Air Force.

My mother met another man. This man was a tall and big man; about 6'2" and weighing in at 250-275 lbs. or so. This guy was a different type of guy than I had been used to. For instance, when we would stop and eat at a restaurant, he would order the food for us in a deep voice, but he would talk to us in a normal tone. As a young boy, I thought that was weird.

We did not stay in one place for very long. There were times when he would leave for work in the morning only to return quickly, telling us to "Pack up! We gotta go!" I thought that was weird as well, until later when we found out that he was a wanted man by the FBI. The Feds would be waiting for him at his workplace, looking to arrest him, for what charge I do not know.

WHAT THE...!!!

It was during this trip to California when my mother's car was destroyed by this guy on the run from the Feds.

I remember lying down in the back seat of the Dodge Dart Light, so I could sleep, when all of a sudden, I was awaken by loud banging noises! Once awake, I discovered that the outlaw was swerving from one guardrail to the other on the highway, banging the sides of the car in like a big wrecking ball. The problem was that he was falling asleep because he could not stop and rest from fear of arrest. I remember being sad because the car was a very nice car. Later in life, I wanted to restore the car, but never got the chance.

After that trip, the car looked horrible! The passenger side door was so difficult to shut that the outlaw had to slam the door after my mother and me were in the car; even then, the door had a tendency to come open without warning.

MOM! MY PUPPY!

My mother allowed me to have a puppy dog. I do not remember what type of dog it was, but it was a cute brown puppy.

The puppy liked to sleep on the floor between the seat and the passenger side door.

After the sides of the car were demolished, we were driving through another town when the outlaw took a hard left turn into a convenience store parking lot. At that moment, the passenger door went flying open and my puppy went rolling out of the car.

Thankfully, my mother had time to grab a hold of the hem of my shirttail before I went rolling out into the street as well.

Sadly, as I was hanging out of the car door by the hem of my shirt, I watched in horror as my puppy rolled underneath a women's car. Then, the woman opened her car door, reached out of her car and picked up my puppy. The woman never did bring my puppy back neither.

WHAT'S KIND OF BEAST IS THAT?!

Considering how the outlaw could not stay in one place for a very long period of time from fear of being arrested by the Feds, I was moved from school to school. There was one town in California (I believe it to be Los Angeles) where we stayed for about two weeks. We lived close enough to the school where my mother enrolled me that I could walk to school.

Each day, I had to walk by one particular residence that had a huge dog in a chain link fence, which, to a ten-year old boy, the animal seemed to reach the sky.

The first day I walked to school, this huge dog came running and barking at me. The dog was taller than I was and it startled me! I am sure my eyes got as big as saucers when I saw this beast of a dog!

From that day and until the last day I walked by the dog, I walked on the opposite side of the street. Since then, I have learned that the breed of dog was a Great Dane.

THE GLASS BLOWN FIGHT

I do not recall the name of the last town we stayed in while we were in California, but I liked living in this place. We lived in an apartment complex where there was a playground outside, and the school I attended was just about two blocks away.

One night, as I lay in the bed sleeping, I was awoken by my mother hollering and the breaking of glass. I did not dare come out of the bedroom to see what the commotion was because I could hear the outlaw hollering back at my mother and knew that it was another one of their arguments.

The next morning, I came out of the bedroom to see little pieces of glass all over the living room floor. The glass came from little glass blown animals from some sort of amusement park that we had visited; my mother bought several little sculptured animals that she displayed on glass shelves in the living room. They were nice and very pretty.

OH! WHY DOES THAT FEEL SO GOOD?!

Again, discretion is advised with reading of what I write. I cannot help but prayerfully tell the truth in hopes that this writing will set someone free from any stronghold that the devil may have on their life.

The act of masturbation began in that very same bedroom where I was awoken by the breaking of the glass animals, and it seems as if the "act" began that very same night of the big argument; I was a mere ten years old at the time. I had a yellow satin pillow about twelve inches square in diameter. One night as I lay awake in the bedroom, I began rubbing the pillow against the head of my penis. It was immediate gratification, and it would be the start of a very long sexual/lust battle that would eventually get me into some serious trouble, along with the help of alcohol.

WHEWWW! I AM GLAD THAT IS OVER!

The day came for my mother I to escape from the outlaw. I walked to school on this particular day as I did every morning. A couple of hours later, while the outlaw was in the shower, my mother grabbed the only thing she could in the spur of the moment (Her alarm clock radio, and of course the car keys) and came to the school to get me.

The school secretary came, called me out of the classroom, and took me to the office. I thought I was in trouble until I saw my mother; she had a serious, scared look on her face.

From the office window of the school, my mother saw the outlaw walking down the road toward the school and alerted the school secretary that he was the man she was avoiding.

The school officials allowed us to hide in an inner office, and while we were hiding, the outlaw came into the school, and in his silly deep voice, asked the school officials if I was in the building. The secretary told him I was not there, but that my mother had already come and taken me from school.

The outlaw exited the school and proceeded to walk down the road looking for my mother and me.

My mother had hidden her beat-up car across the street behind some storage buildings because she knew he would come looking for us. After the outlaw was out of sight, my mother and I ran to the car, high tailing it out of there.

My mother borrowed some money from her stepmother who lived in Bakersfield, California so we could buy the fuel necessary to get back to Oklahoma with. My mother did not waste time in getting us out of town. We were on the highway headed home in a flash of time.

I remember being so happy to be away from the outlaw. Finally, it was over.

THAT'S A BIG 10-4 THERE CUDDLES

All I remember of the trip back to Oklahoma was my mother talking to the truck drivers on the CB radio she had in the car. Back in the '70s, CB radios were very popular. People who used CB radios usually chose what was called a "handle". Their handle was a nickname to be used on the CB instead of their real name. My mother chose "cuddles" to be her handle on the CB radio.

As well, my grandmother had a base CB radio setup in her home so she could talk to people in the area; she gave truck drivers area information, and directions. I remember my grandmother's handle being "Shorty", because she was short (laughter). We made it back to my grandmother's house in Sulphur, Oklahoma at what seemed to be in the middle of the night. How relieved we were to be back in a familiar place.

MY SWEET GRANDMOTHER V

I would not do this writing justice if I did not pay tribute to my grandmother. I loved my grandmother very much. I was very hurt and sad when she passed away in 2005; I have cried many times since her passing.

Grandmother V was stern, yet a sweetheart.

My first memories of my Grandmother V are after my mother and I returned from California. My brother and I would visit, staying several nights at a time.

I first saw the sternness of my grandmother one night after we came home from her friend's home. Before we went to the home of her friend, Grandmother V asked my brother and me if we wanted something to eat while we were at the house; we both said "No grandma. We are not hungry." In my grandmother's sweetness, she said, "Okay. Don't you ask for anything to eat while you are at my friend's house."

While at her friend's home, the lady asked us boys if we were hungry. Guess who spoke up and said, "Me!" The nice lady fixed ME something to eat, and I ate it.

After returning back to my grandmother's home, grandmother entered the door of the house first followed by me. I no sooner got through the front door than I began feeling something stinging my face; it was my grandmother's hands slapping my face! It was not just one hand of my grandmother slapping me up one side of my face, but each of her hands slapping each side of my face at the same time! As she slapped, she was saying, "Don't you ever embarrass me in front of any of my friends ever again! Do you understand me?!" "Yes grandma!" All CJ could do was duck and get out of the way. As you progress further in reading this book, you will read where I was a kleptomaniac as a child; at times, I stole just to be stealing. One such incident happened while I stayed with my grandmother in her home.

I played with another little boy who lived down the street. He had a mini motorbike that he was riding; he would not let me ride the mini bike. Therefore, after dark, I went and stole his mini bike and went joy riding with it. After taking the mini bike to a field with overgrown tall weeds, I stashed it in the field, then, I went to my grandmother's house and got into the bed to sleep for the evening.

Sometime later, the police came knocking on the door; they wanted to ask me some questions about the mini bike. My grandmother would not allow them into the house in order so that they could wake me up.

My grandmother moved from there to the country outside of another small town. I went and stayed a summer or two with her there.

My grandmother did not live with a plumbed water supply in the mobile home she lived in. I had collar length hair then and needed a place to wash my hair. In asking my grandmother about a place to wash my hair, she replied, "Take a 5-gallon bucket down to the pond and wash your hair with pond water." I was reluctant, but I had no choice.

My grandmother was very good to me; there was never a day when she did not ask me if I was hungry and wanted something to eat.

As well, she taught me several things. Among those things were how to spade the ground with a shovel for gardening, and how to dig a posthole for a fence post. She also gave me some advice saying, "Johnny. When you go into a public place and sit down; always sit with your back to the wall so that no one can jump you from behind while you are not looking." To this day, just about every time I go into a public place, I can hear her voice telling me to sit with my back to a wall.

One summer, when I was helping my oldest uncle haul hay, I passed out standing up on the back of the hay truck, leaning against the cab. We were finished for the day and headed home when my uncle, who was driving, took a sharp curve to the left. The force of the turn pulled me off the back of the truck and I landed on the pavement with the back of my headfirst; it knocked me out cold. When I came back to conscientiousness, the first person's face I saw was my grandmother's face. She told me that my mother was on her way to get me and take me to the hospital. My grandmother was a certified nurse at one time; therefore, she would not let me go unconscious again. I was thankful for her.

In my grandmother's later years, she had a couple of strokes. My mother took me to visit my grandmother when she had her first stroke. While I sat with my grandmother, my main concern was whether or not my grandmother was saved and going to Heaven. Thus, I asked her if she was saved by Jesus Christ. She could not talk, so she shook her head violently in a forward and backward motion as to say "Yes!" My heart was relieved.

My grandmother was placed in a nursing home here in Ada. I visited her a few times in my coming and going. I could hardly stand to visit her because of the shape that her health had become. It just broke my heart to see her not be able to walk or talk. I remember how she would argue with my mother because my mother wanted to limit her cigarette smoking; that seemed to be all she wanted to do, was smoke cigarettes.

I miss my grandmother so much. Now, it is breaking my heart to see my mother aging.

My grandmother and grandfather did not remain together, but ended their marriage.

GRANDFATHER C

Grandfather C, my mother's father, was an entrepreneur. When he passed away, he was able to leave his remaining three children with some valuable assets. I watched my mother spread $5,000 dollars out on the kitchen table after the distribution of grandfather's will. I have not known any other family member to have such wealth since Grandfather C (I am not familiar with the Jackson side of the family).

Grandpa got his start with his ability to operate heavy machinery.

During his early twenties, my natural father worked for my grandfather as a dirt laborer. John Sr. worked on the end of a shovel cleaning out the ditches that my grandfather dug with his backhoe. After I met my natural father, I learned that he could operate any piece of heavy equipment on the market, thanks to my grandfather.

There is a family story told about my natural father that is funny. The story says that my natural father would talk to himself as he worked the shovel each day. I'm told he said things as, "Self, self oh boy. We are going to dig this ditch today. Aren't we self?" I am not sure if he answered his "self", as well, I am not sure if I want to know neither. Yet, later in life, I talked to myself. However, it took me a long time to figure out that I was saying the wrong things.

I met my grandfather when I was about twelve years old. After mother moved us to Ada, we would make the drive to a one-horse town called Calvin in order to visit grandpa.

Grandfather was cool. He loved to laugh. I do not ever remember my grandfather having a sad moment or countenance.

Grandfather owned a country store with gasoline station, along with a liquor store. One of my favorite things to do was go visit grandfather, because when we arrived, my brother and I would hug granddad's neck, then, we would await our cherished command, "You boys go on over to the store and get you some candy." I remember how mother would argue saying, "Daddy. They don't need any candy." Grandfather would say, "Oh. Let them get whatever they want." We wasted no time in booking it over to the goldmine for our strike of riches.

Grandfather was the first person who ever took me hunting. He would load up his .22 rifle and take us out to hunt squirrels and rabbits. I am not sure what part I liked most—shooting the gun, hitting my target, or eating the kill.

Then, there are the mountain oysters. When granddad introduced us youngsters to these pieces of meat, he did not tell us what exactly mountain oysters were, or what part of the bull they were cut from. For some people, that might just be a bunch of bull (hahaha... pun intended). The only thing grandfather said was, "Just try it! You might like 'em" Granddad was right! I loved the taste of the mountain oysters! They are good!

Then, my grandfather tricked me. Granddad enjoyed traveling to other cities in order to dine at a nice restaurant of his choice. At one such restaurant in McAllister, granddad said, "Here Johnny, try some of this salsa." I declined his offer stating, "No grandpa. I don't like hot stuff." My grandfather persisted in my obedience to him saying, "Oh. It's not hot."

To appease my grandfather, I took a chip and dipped it in the salsa; it was a mistake, for as soon as the salsa was in my mouth, it burned like a fire. As I hurriedly reached for the glass of water sitting on the table in front of me, my grandfather let out a laugh that I have never forgotten. Although I got over it, I was angry with him for that.

I want to tell of an accident that I was a passenger of when I was a teenager.

My grandfather had a big old tank of a car—a Lincoln Continental boat.

Granddad decided that he wanted to drive a town over and pick up some lunch for the family from one of his favorite places. My uncle rode in the passenger seat while I had the boats back seat.

The weather was that of a misting rain; the roads were freshly wet.

As my granddad drove, he applied the cruise control of the auto on about sixty miles an hour and settled into his autopilot mode of conversing with my uncle as he navigated down a rode he had driven many times before.

Suddenly, without warning, the car began fishtailing. Instinctively, my uncle reached over, grabbed the steering wheel, and attempted to help his father correct the vehicle. I can still hear my grandfather saying, "Let go of the steering wheel T! I got this!" My uncle said, "No you don't dad! You are all over the road!"

About that time, the car took a hard left and streaked off the road, at sixty miles an hour, towards a barbed wire fence; we were headed straight for a railroad tie that was being used as a fence post. The driver's side front bumper clipped the railroad tie, killing the cruise control. That spun the back-end of the car around to the right side, causing the back passenger panel to catch a huge tree. In turn, this spun the car back straight and sent it rocketing into an empty field. As the car came sliding to a stop, my uncle was the first one out of the vehicle to make sure we were all okay.

As we sliced through the barbed wire fence, I felt a prick on my right shoulder; I can only attest this to a barb that may have been flung as the wire of the fence was broken.

There were also times of water events. I can remember going out on a lake with my grandfather at the controls. The adventurous skiers of the family took advantage of their father's water navigation skills. My uncle carried on the boating tradition later as well.

It was at one such boat outing where I learned how to swim real quick. After traveling out to a dock in the middle of a lake, one of my uncles thought it would be funny to throw me off into the water that was about 15 feet deep. It was either swim, or get saved from drowning. I quickly learned how to dog paddle!

My grandfather, as with my grandmother, smoked cigarettes. My grandfather enjoyed menthol cigarettes. As a result, he developed lung cancer later in his life. Even with the money my grandfather had, he did not beat the cancer. He underwent chemotherapy, lost all his hair, and his life... My grandfather was 59 years of age when he died.

I remember how my mother loved her father till his dying day. From my observations, I believe my grandfather appreciated his daughter's help during his later years.

In the short time that I knew my grandfather, he inspired me more than he knew.

I remember how I loved seeing grandfather keep control and peace in the family. His decisions were always respected by the rest of the family. Grandfather C was always jolly. I do not remember anytime when he had to raise his voice to anyone. Grace flowed out from around him. He had a natural way of making sure everybody around him was taken care of. Just as with my grandmother's home, I never had to worry about food when we visited my grandfather.

I am thankful for how he took the time to teach me how to shoot a rifle.

I am thankful for having seen his example of what true prosperity looks like—heart.

HOME SWEET HOME!

We lived with my grandmother in Sulphur for a few months. My mother got a job at the hospital in Ada, Oklahoma, which was about a thirty-minute drive from Sulphur.

My mother saved the money she earned at the hospital and rented a house in Ada. About 1978, we made Ada our home for the rest of my childhood, and beyond.

MEMORIES, MEMORIES, MEMORIES

There are many, many memories I have from living in Ada. I will share a few here and then move on with the story.

One of my first memories in living at our first location in Ada is a sad memory of a white poodle I had named Sam. Sam was a fun dog. He always made me laugh with his quirkiness. Sam was so full of spunk and energy. However, as with some animals, Sam ran out in the street and died when a car hit him. I was very sad when I found Sam dead in the roadway.

I shot my brother in the leg with a bow and arrow during our days at this first place of residence. Our mother had previously thrown the bow and arrow in the trash, but I pulled it out of the trash and shot CJ in the leg with it. Our mother was not happy with me; it would be the start of many, many times where I disappointed my mother.

My mother kept the side-bashed-in Dodge Dart auto for some time. The car had an eight-track player radio in it that I would listen to when I was feeling sad; I loved listening to Elvis Presley.

It was at this particular house where I almost burned down the house without knowing it. I was asleep on the couch next to a heater when my pillow slipped out from under my head, and became lodged in the flames. I was awakened by someone telling me to get out of the house because the house was full of smoke.

My mother worked the graveyard shift at the hospital for a time. She used a hasp and padlock to lock the front door with when we all would leave and go somewhere. One night while she was at work, someone came by the house and locked the padlock in the hasp; locking CJ and me inside. We called our mother and she came and unlocked the door. We learned a valuable lesson then. From then on, my mother would lock the lock on the hasp until she needed to lock the front door again.

I went to church on a regular basis. I am not sure exactly why I went, whether the reason was that my mother wanted me to go, or because I got satisfaction from helping a blind man from his front door to the church van, to the pew, and back to his front door again.

I did not go to learn about God, Jesus, the Bible, or to learn the way a Christian was to conduct their lives.

I never made the connection between the God of the Bible, and the God that the preacher talked about; I was just there filling space.

I would go to the front when the preacher asked if anyone needed prayer and stand there with my arms stretched to heaven while listening to someone pray a prayer over me, but I never felt anything.

I always wondered just what the purpose was for me to go for prayer. I had asked my mother to go to church with me, only to hear her say, "Johnny. I don't feel right about going to church on Sunday morning after going to the bar on Saturday night." My mother loved to dance; therefore, she would go out to the dance hall on the weekend and dance to country music. I thought that if going to church was not good enough for my mother, it was not good enough for me; thus, I quit going to church.

It was about a month later when I met a guy at school named EC; and it would be EC who introduced me to marijuana on a school field trip.

This would also be the time I became hooked on alcohol; I was about fifteen years old. One of my mother's live-in boyfriends bought my first six-pack of Budweiser.

My brother was a movie geek; he loved Star Trek and a whole slew of other movies. He was the type who could read a five-hundred-page book in two days. The same book would take me months to read. Thus, my mother's boyfriend took CJ and me to the theatre to watch a movie one night; CJ went in to watch the movie, and I went to the back of the building to drink my first six-pack of beer. I drank five of the six beers that night.

The devil had me; I was hooked.

I will reiterate part of the disclaimer here—"Some of the writing within this book may not be deemed appropriate for your reading. The fact is, it is a part of my life, and I cannot deny the truth. I believe that what I have written within the pages of this book is exactly what my Father God wanted me to write. There may be something read in this book that God can use to set people free from issues they may be dealing with in their own life.

On the other hand, maybe you know someone who may be battling the dark side without hope, and what I write may bring them hope enough to believe that there is freedom in Jesus Christ.

I pray that this book will bring the people of Jesus Christ to a place of understanding that just because "life happens", The Heavenly Father will never leave, nor forsake us; and that nothing can separate us from the Father's love that He showed to all of mankind when Jesus Christ gave His life as a ransom for those who will believe in His sacrifice, and in His Name.

From the Holy Bible, the Apostle Paul said, "…I have become all things to all men, so that I may by all means save some." (1 Corinthians 9:22). That does not mean that Paul experimented with anything and everything just so he could have things in common with other people in hopes of winning souls for Jesus Christ. It simply means that Paul lived life as it came, which gave him experience in areas of life that bring people down and make them hopeless. Paul went through some things by the LORD's will, not Paul's will for his life.

Things happen in life that we are not happy about; we do not want to accept what is happening, but it is happening; things we wish would have never happened, but they happened.

Please read this book at your own risk. That does not mean that you will agree with everything I write here. You are entitled to your own opinion. Please read with an open mind, knowing that life happens."

THAT'S MY DAD?!

As mentioned in the first chapter, my natural father abandoned me in the womb. I spent my childhood into my teens not knowing who my natural father was. From time to time, I would ask my mother, "When can I meet my dad?" Her usual response was, "Why do you want to meet that SOB?" I would respond with, "Because he is my dad, and I want to meet him." My mother would let it go for a while until I asked again.

The last time I asked my mother when I could meet my dad, I was about 13 years old. She was not very nice with her response of "Why do you want to meet that SOB! Why can't you accept CJ's daddy as your father?!" My mother struck a nerve in me and I snapped back with an attitude and said, "Because I have a daddy, and I want to meet him!"

Not long after that, a man drove into the driveway, stopped and got out of his vehicle wearing a cowboy hat, button up short-sleeve western shirt, blue jeans, and cowboy boots.

My first impression was one of amazement; finally, I had met my natural father.

Unfortunately, for me, that amazement was turned to bitter anger one summer when I went to visit him at his home in Texas.

What was the cause of the anger?

My mother allowed me to grow my hair out to shoulder length. After I took a shower, I would part my hair down the middle and blow dry the sides into waves that wrapped around my ears; my hair looked like a 60's style wave, and it looked very good.

Yeah, you can imagine where I am going with this piece of the story; my natural father took me to the barbershop and had the barber cut off all my hair, giving me a "little boy's haircut". I was so angry with him; I could have spit in his eye!

It would be a few years later, but he got his reward with bitter embarrassment due to some of my own actions; not intentionally though. I will continue that story in a few pages.

A BRAND NEW HOUSE!

About 1980, my mother applied for a new home with a governmental self-help program. The program was one where the borrower helped in building the home. It took a year or so for the house to be completed. Then, about 1981, we moved into a brand new, two-bedroom, and one-bath home.

As of this writing, some thirty-nine years later, my mother continues living in the home.

I have a scar on my right cheek because I walked through two 2x4-wall studs as we were leaving the construction one day. I felt a slight ping on my face, but I had no idea that I was bleeding profusely until I got in the car and my mother saw the blood. She shrieked and took me to the hospital where the doctor put stitches in my cheek.

It was in the new house, and thanks to EC, where rock-n-roll music began shaping my taste. EC listened to the old classic rock-n-roll and he would question me to see if I could name the artist and song that was playing on the radio. Groups like CCR, ZZ Top, The Rolling Stones, Eric Clapton, and the like. My taste went a little harder, and I made my favorite group AC/DC. Although I am not proud of saying this, but I could sing most of AC/DC's songs by heart; it does not change the truth.

I now listen to Christian music only, and can sing Christian songs by heart now.

Let me say this about music. Before the devil became the devil, his name was Lucifer, meaning "shining one, light-bearer", or "bright and morning star". Lucifer's job in heaven was constantly to lead the music in worship of God. However, Lucifer became bitter with his job, and in pride of who he was, he became prideful.

In becoming jealous of God's position over him, he decided to shoot for the stars and make his position above Jesus Christ. That was a bad idea because God fired him from his worship position and kicked him out of heaven, along with a third of heaven's angels who followed Lucifer's haughty idea of overthrowing the Government of God.

Since then, the devil has used music to steer us away from the things of God.

Music can encourage us in the things of the Lord; helping us to stay focused and on track. On the other hand, music can cause us to fall away from God; making us think like the world; even causing us to chase after the lustful desires that is wrapped up in the world; namely, "…the lust of the flesh; the lust of the eyes; and the pride of life." (First John 2:16).

Be careful what you allow in by watching the idiot box (television), and the music that you listen to. The Bible teaches us this: "Watch over your heart with all diligence, for from it flow the springs of life." (Proverbs 4:23). Your eyes and ears are gates into your soul.

Control your mind by renewing your mind with the Word of God (Romans 12:2; Philippians 4:8). You have authority over your mind and should take EVERY thought captive and make it obey Jesus Christ (Second Corinthians 10:5).

It takes discipline.

It took me years to get the rock-n-roll songs out of my mind, but, by replacing the worldly music with Christian music, my mind is being renewed day by day.

Even at my place of employment where I work now, the other guys constantly play worldly music in the shop area where they work. The devil is constantly bombarding me with temptation to listen to their sickening music, but I combat him with a Bluetooth headset that I listen to Christian music with. I refuse to listen to the worldly music now.

That should be the same way every Christian, who claims to be a disciple of Jesus Christ, guards their heart. You should make it a priority today as well.

TYPICAL TEENAGER

The rest of my time in the new house as a teenager was adventurous to say the least.

I continued smoking marijuana with EC; he had become my main running buddy at school; we met in the eighth grade and hung out together all the time.

I would walk to his house in the mornings and his mother Beth, would give us a ride to school in her "smoking" red El Camino. No, I don't mean that the car was a "smoking hot" car, as in beautiful, I mean that the car engine smoked so bad, that the engine would smoke for a city block before the car got up enough speed to outrun the smoke. Then, when EC's mom would stop the car at a stop sign, the smoke would catch up with us and engulf the car in the smoke. I remember how we would just laugh, and laugh, and laugh about the car being engulfed in smoke. All of our friends knew we were coming down the road before they saw the car because of the smoke! Lol!

GET OUT!

My mother and I began having some bitter feuds. It seemed to me that after I met my natural father, she just could not stand me anymore. She treated me with scorn and repulsiveness. It seemed to me that I just could not please my mother anymore. I felt as if she was taking her bitter frustration for my natural father out on me. We argued constantly. I wanted nothing to do with my mother anymore due to how she was treating me; as well, it seemed as if her feelings toward me were mutual.

One day, we had a huge argument. I am not sure how it all came about. I believe that I told her that I did not want to live in her house anymore. In the heat of the battle, she told me to "Pack your stuff and get out!" I did just that, I packed my suitcase with some clothing, climbed on my 10-speed bicycle, and rode over to EC's house.

EC was happy to see me, and his mother had no problem with me living with them. I had no problem being away from my mother and living with my best friend neither. However, my mother had a problem with it; to my disappointment, she showed up a couple of hours later demanding that I come home. I told her that I did not want to go home but she would not relent. Thus, I sadly went back home with my mother. The relationship did not get any better from there. Of course, with a troublemaking son like me, it is no wonder why my mother had trouble with me.

The next time my mother kicked me out of the house was when I stayed out late partying with my friends; at least whom I thought were my friends. I was somewhere around sixteen or seventeen years old at this time. My mother and I had a big argument and once again, she told me to "Get out!" As a result, I packed my oblong tan suitcase, climbed on my bicycle, and rode away. I had no idea where I wanted to go.

I did not go to EC's house this time. Instead, I went to the man's house where the party was the night before. He welcomed me in and I told him how my mother and I had a huge argument, and how she kicked me out of her house, again. (Read the following at your own discretion) The man said I could stay with him with one exception—we get naked and have sex. I was not sure I wanted to "do it" with this man or not.

There had been a time or two before that, when I stayed the night with one particular male friend of mine, and we played around with oral sex. However, to allow another man to penetrate my behind with his penis was a very different thing.

Thus, I felt I had no choice this time.

Therefore, I gave in to the man's ultimatum and we had sex. I did not like his penetration. At that moment, I vowed never to allow another man to penetrate my behind ever again, even if I had to sleep in the street.

The next day, I told the man I had to find another place to stay, and I went to another man's house that I had met at a church function named Larkin.

Larkin was a comical type of guy. He resembled the comedian and actor Groucho Marks.

Larkin had a very beautiful eight-year old daughter named Sherri, whom he loved very much.

Larkin agreed to allow me to stay with him and Sherri as long as I kept the house clean.

Larkin enjoyed drinking beer as much as I did; he also stuck a needle in his arm and shot drugs into his system; when Larkin offered me the drug by needle, I declined because I hate medical needles.

Barbara was Larkin's mother who lived in town. Larkin and I lived with Barbara for a time.

It was during this time when I found the stories of the Bible absolutely fascinating.

Stories like Jonah and the big fish, God splitting the Red Sea, how the rods of Moses and Aaron became snakes, and Noah building the big boat. It seems like I spent six months straight just reading the Bible. I also attended some church services with Barbara and Larkin as well. Even then, I still did not know who the God of the Bible was; I only knew He did some very powerful things for non-deserving people.

I finally wound up sleeping on the couch at Beth's house, EC's mother. I was not attending high school at that time, and I was very depressed about life.

One day, Beth told me that I needed to go back to school, or regret it for the rest of my life. Thus, I went back to school and the teacher told me that I would need to make-up all the work I had missed. I completed the schoolwork required and graduated, but not with honors.

From the sixth grade until the ninth grade of school, I earned D's and F's for grades. Finally, in the ninth grade, the school got smart, and tested me for a learning disability. It was found that I did indeed suffer with a learning disability. The school placed me in special classes with a wonderfully sweet teacher who took the time to help me understand the schoolwork. It would be this teacher who would help me graduate from high school.

YOU ARE WHERE?!

Through childhood, and up until I was about nineteen years old, I was a thief. Thievery seemed to come natural to me. I stole money from women's purses, from the school locker room, and from my mother (among other things). I stole just to steal, kind of for the thrill of getting away with something wrong. This was before I knew the saying "What goes around comes around" and vise-versa. Later in life, things that I owned would just disappear, and I had no idea what happened to the things. I went out in the late night hours stealing toolboxes with tools, bicycles, lawnmowers, and car stereos.

Moreover, as a result of drunkenness, I even stole a car and took it for a joy ride. Sadly, I was so drunk that I could barely hold my head up straight enough to see over the steering wheel. Nevertheless, even then, God was watching out for me by His grace in my friend EC, because it was EC who asked me where I got the car. He told me that I "…better take it back before you get into some real trouble."

I did not make it back to the owner with the car, but I went and passed out cold.

I asked EC about the car the next day, and he told me that he took the car back himself.

I was very thankful.

As well, I also stole gasoline ten gallons at a time. I would steal enough gasoline to fill up EC's car, which afforded us the fuel to cruise around with; we would cruise the back roads around Ada, drinking beer, smoking pot, and listening to loud rock-n-roll music.

Although there was only one time when I nearly got caught stealing gasoline, at about age seventeen, I told EC that I would not be stealing any more gas. I suppose I just grew out of the bad habit. I am sure my conscience had something to do with it as well.

BUSTED

At age sixteen, I was caught shoplifting a carton of cigarettes. I had a habit to supply.

I also made money selling the cigarettes by the pack.

I ran out of the grocery store with the carton of cigarettes, but the store clerk caught me and called the police. In turn, the police took me to the juvenile center and called my mother. Amazingly, the police let me go home with my mother, without incident.

YOU DID IT AGAIN?!

At age seventeen, I got caught shoplifting again; this time the merchandise was a pouch of chewing tobacco from a different store. The store clerk called the police and back to the juvenile center I went. Once again, the police called my mother. This time, my mother had to pay $70 dollars to get me out of trouble.

YOU ARE ON YOUR OWN THIS TIME BUSTER!

Then, again at age seventeen, I broke into the business that employed me and stole a small amount of money. I will not disclose of the name or place because I never was charged with the crime. Although the statute of limitations has expired, I would rather keep quiet about the act of mischief.

However, that did not work on the second burglary I committed at age eighteen. Two of EC's friends talked me into breaking into a business that was supposed to house several thousands of dollars overnight. I was stupid enough to believe them.

After breaking the door lock and entering the building, I did not find any money, but I did find flashlights, with police officers behind them, looking for a crook, who was me. The building was wired with a silent alarm, which alerted the police.

The police took me to jail that night. The one calling and telling my mother was not the police, but myself using my "one free phone call" the jailer gives to one being booked into the jail.

I told my mother how much the bail was and she told me that I would have to sit there because she was not coming to get me. I had to find my own way out of jail.

I had bought a car with the money I got away with in the previous burglary. The water in the car engine froze and busted the block so the car was useless to me. Thankfully, the man I bought the car from gave the money back, which in turn paid my bail out of jail. I would like to say that this was the last time I would sit in jail, but it was not.

PROBATION BEGINS

The judge was kind and lenient in deferring the sentence with two years completed probation. All went well for about a year and a half until my foolishness got in the way. I continued to use marijuana.

One requirement of probation was for me to give a urine sample for drug testing; I failed one such test and the court revoked the probation.

As time went on, I was sentenced to more and more probation. When it was all said and done, I spent about the next nine years on probation before they let me go.

It would not be the last time I spent time on probation due to the stupidity of alcohol. In the book of Proverbs, chapter twenty-six, and verse eleven of the Holy Bible, it states, "Like a dog that returns to its vomit, is a fool who repeats his folly." That was me.

It would take years for this old dog to learn new tricks, or simply put, to allow the Bible to renew my way of thinking.

As a result of the initial probationary period, I moved back home and lived with my mother again.

Little did I know, she had a big surprise awaiting me upon my graduation from high school. It was a sad and horrible graduation present.

NO! I DO NOT WANT TO LIVE IN TEXAS!

I attended a woodshop class called CVET.

The instructor of the class had a tradition of taking his graduation class to Six Flags over Texas, an amusement park in Texas.

I was all hyped-up about going with the graduating class of 1986 to have fun, until once again, my mother told me to

"Pack what you want to keep because you are not coming back here."

Upon questioning her motives for such a demand, she told me that she and my natural father had made arrangements for me to live with him in Texas upon my graduation. I felt it quite unfair for my mother to make such a decision on my behalf without consulting me first.

I had every intention of getting a job in Ada and making my own way in life; unfortunately, she felt like she had the right to dictate my life after I became of age.

However, it backfired on both of my parents, and I went back to Ada.

I HAVE TO GET YOU OUT OF HERE!

My natural father was generous in accepting me into his home at age eighteen.

He did his best to help steer me down the right road of employment and sensible living; I was very hardheaded.

John Sr. got me a pickup on a loan note, which I was responsible to pay back to the bank; I faltered on the loan.

He also got me a job with the company he worked for; I was fired for not showing up for work on time.

It was here when I decided that stealing gasoline was just not worth the scared feeling I felt when stealing it. I was broke and in need of some gasoline so I could travel to work and home before payday. I went to the jobsite to steal some gasoline, and there and then decided that I was finished with stealing.

Now, if I even think about stealing an ink pen, my conscious bothers me too much to carry out the act. Now, I ask if I can have the ink pen.

Alcohol was a serious problem for me; it always caused me to make stupid decisions.

I got a job with a metal shop company grinding pickup bumpers and dipping them in acid.

A co-worker name Fred, invited me to his house for a big birthday party. Any time there was a "party", alcohol needed to be involved for me to enjoy it.

Fred lived about an hour and a half drive from where I lived.

When I drove up to the house where the party was being held, I locked eyes with a beautiful girl as she locked eyes with me. At the time, Fred was her stepfather, and he saw how the girl and I locked eyes. He expressed his concerns about us, but to no avail; it was too late, the love bug had struck.

Due to this drunken stupor, I landed in jail that very night.

The prosecutor was considering further charges stemming from my relationship with the girl.

Fortunately, for me, John Sr. was experienced with Texas law and he knew it would not go well for me in the long-run. Therefore, he cut a deal with the prosecutor promising that he would make sure I was shipped out of the state if they dropped all charges; they agreed.

Within the hour of being released from jail, John had me sitting at a bus station awaiting my exit from Texas.

Once again, I had no place to go, except back to my mother's house in Ada.

MORE TROUBLE IN GEORGIA!

It was along this time when my mother had a live in boyfriend, Mickey. Mickey was an Indian who liked to drink alcohol.

Mickey and I both needed employment. We looked and looked for work in Ada, but to our despair, we found no suitable work. Therefore, we headed to the state of Georgia to seek employment there. I believe it was Mickey, who was promised a job with an electrical outfit there in Savannah,

Georgia. I tagged along because my mother thought it was a good idea for me to go see if I could find work there as well.

When we arrived in Savannah, trouble was waiting for us. Mickey drank alcohol while driving. He decided to stop and ask a nice police officer for directions. The only problem with that was that the officer smelt alcohol coming from Mickey's breath. As a result, Mickey went to jail, and I spent the night sleeping on the street. My mother bailed Mickey out of jail, and we went to work.

I worked as a welder's helper building electrical power generating towers. It was a fun and interesting job; one I enjoyed.

Jobs in Savannah seemed to be a dime per dozen. The welder's helper position played out and I found another job working as a millwright's helper. That was a tedious job, which I liked a lot. I was fascinated at how precise the millwrights had to be in setting machinery. Everything from the ground up had to be very close to perfect or the machinery would not operate correctly; the balance of the machine would be thrown off, destroying the machinery.

Unfortunately, for me, I liked the effects of beer. It seemed that every time I got ahead in life, my carnal flesh felt like it should be rewarded, and I would begin drinking beer on a regular basis. Living in Savannah was no different from any other time.

Life in Savannah was just that—successful. I had a good job. I had a nice car. I even had a girlfriend who wanted to be with me.

For a short time, I even lived two city blocks from the Atlantic Ocean; there is nothing like being able to hear the waves come crashing in on the beach at sunrise.

Unfortunately, that amazing life came crashing down one night when I decided to go drive around and drink beer while enjoying my joy ride. I was not accustomed to big city driving. I attempted to make a left turn from the middle drive lane in downtown Savannah, only to have another automobile smash into the driver's side of my car. Then, even more unfortunate for me, there was a police officer sitting idle in his cruiser, who saw the whole thing; I was busted.

The officer allowed me to park my car in a nearby parking lot, and he took me to the jailhouse in order to give me a breathalyzer test. The officer was very nice about the whole situation, telling me that he would let me go if I was under the legal limit for alcohol. Fortunately, I was under the legal limit.

He had to let me go with one restriction, DO NOT go get the car until the next day. I did not listen very well; instead, I went and got my car from the parking lot that same night.

Did I go home and sleep it off? No. This dog returned to his vomit and I went drinking in another part of town only to be stopped by the police again. This time, I went to jail because I was over the legal limit for a person who has consumed alcohol.

When it came time to go to court and answer for my stupidity, I was scared.

Therefore, I skipped town and drove about eighteen hours straight, back to Ada, Oklahoma, only stopping for fuel.

LET IT SNOW, LET IT SNOW, AND LET IT SNOW…

Arriving late in the night, I went to the place I felt most comfortable in going, EC's house. I assure you, when I parked the car in the yard and fell asleep, there was not a flake of snow on the ground. Amazingly, when I woke up, there was snow on the ground up to the bumper of my car; it kept snowing until there was two feet of snow on the ground. Since that time, that is the last big snowfall I remember Ada having.

HOMELESS AGAIN

EC had a mean stepfather who weighed in at about 400 pounds name Kevin. Kevin's attitude would become extremely angry from time to time and he would hit EC, or Beth (or anybody else who got in his way), with his fists.

Later in life, I would become good friends with Kevin, but at that time, I did not feel comfortable staying with EC while his stepfather was there. Therefore, I slept in my car from night to night.

I remember how bitter cold it was, and how I could not get my feet to stay warm.

I ate what I could afford at that time—Vienna sausages. After a while, I went home.

CHAPTER THREE: I'm Getting Married!

"...a man shall leave his father and his mother, and be joined to his wife;..."

(Genesis 2:24).

I am a very loving man. When I love someone, I love the person. When someone crosses me, I get over it and love them anyway. Maybe you have heard the saying, "I am a lover, not a fighter." That fits me to the T.

After I took the Ritalin medication at nine-years old and calmed down, I was not one for a fight. One must back me into a corner before I will come out swinging. However, when I come out swinging, someone is getting physically hurt.

For one, I do not like feeling pain (Who in their right mind does?!)

For two, I do not like causing anybody else to feel pain (Emotionally or physically). Although I have caused many people to feel emotional pain, it usually comes back to make me feel more emotional pain than I like.

I am the quiet type of fighter, and deadly.

Therefore, I have no idea why I married my first wife, Linda (Ex-wife now for some twenty-eight years), except for the fact that I loved her and her two daughters.

When I met Linda, she was a single mother whom I felt compassion for in my heart.

Her two daughters were about the ages of eight (Angel) and five (Maggie) years old.

The house was a shambles. Angel tried to help her mother with the housework for some time after their father went away (I am not sure for what reason), but gave up helping her mother because the pressure from her mother became too much for Angel to handle at such a young age.

Maggie was a sweetheart, and she loved me as her daddy; we had a special kind of bond. Angel and I were not that close, because Angel was coming into the age of wanting to be her own person; having her own time and space.

As I said, the house was a mess. When I walked into the house, my mouth fell open, and my eyes got as big as half-dollars.

When I say mess, I mean a person could not walk into the garage. It was kind of like one of the hallway closets that a person stuffs full when company is coming, barely getting the door to close, and then everything falls out when they reopen the door.

The girl's bedroom was such a mess, their clean clothes were piled about two-feet high in front of the Dresser drawers; and, you could not see the rest of the floor because of all the toys and other collected junk.

With myself being an organizing freak, I went to work getting the house in order; beginning with the girl's bedroom.

VROOM, VROOM, VROOM...

It was happenstance when I met Linda because I lived in Ada with my mother. I could not find a job in Ada and had to venture out of the area to gain employment. Thus, I found a job in Sulphur, which was about thirty-minutes away from Ada, working for the local egg processing plant, MoArk Egg.

I purchased a motorcycle from a friend of mine, who lived in Ada, and began making payments on the bike so I could have a way to and from work in Sulphur.

One afternoon after I was relieved from work, I stopped at a convenience store to fuel the bike and head home. As I was getting the fuel for the bike, Linda caught my attention and we began talking with each other. I asked her if she wanted to go for a ride on the motorcycle with me and she accepted.

As a result, I asked Linda if she would marry me, she accepted that too! I do not remember the exact marriage date, but it was sometime in 1990 when we got tied the knot.

A SIMPLE WEDDING

We decided to keep the wedding simple; a few guests; some food, etc., etc...

Linda wanted a small wedding out in the wilderness, away from the city noise and commotion. Therefore, we walked down a dirt trail for about an eighth of a mile until we found the perfect spot for her satisfaction; it did not really matter to me where we got married, as long as we made it legit.

For whatever the reason, I felt it was best if we waited until after marriage before we had sex; it just seemed like the best thing to do. As well, I had to take the sex part of the marriage slow with Linda, because her ex-husband raped her at knifepoint just before he split, leaving her and their precious little girls high and dry.

HUH? WHAT? HUH?

Linda had a great percentage of deafness in her ears; usually more so in one ear than the other ear. It was quite annoying to me at the time, especially in the mornings, when she was almost totally deaf. As the day unfolded, Linda's hearing would get better, but until that point, it was very difficult to carry on a conversation with her.

I feel bad about it now, because I was not the perfect husband when it came to being patient with her loss of hearing.

Neither Angel, nor Maggie, had developed any hearing loss at that time. Now that I am older, I would have taken a different approach in conversing with Linda, either in the way of learning how to talk to her with sign language, or in writing on paper what I wanted to say to her, especially in the mornings when she was most deaf.

Of course, now, due to the process of learning from life's experiences, I understand a whole lot more about "how" to love someone, not just "loving" someone. As you read on in this book, I will share some of those "love-learning experiences" with you; of how God taught me about how He loves us, how to love others, and how to accept love from others.

THE MOVE

MoArk Egg made the business decision to close their plant operations there in Sulphur, Oklahoma. That meant I had one of two choices to decide between—resign from the plant in Sulphur with compensation, or transfer my employment, and family, to Neosho, Missouri where the company operated another egg processing plant. After discussing the matter with Linda and the girls, we thought the latter decision would be a good choice for all involved. The decision felt like a good one at the time, but as with time, only time would tell if it was a good decision, or not. At that time, it was good.

Let me just spit something out to you here and now, then, you can decide whether or not you agree with my reasoning. From my study of the Scriptures, although we think we are able to see the "big picture", the truth is, we just cannot "know it all", nor understand it all.

The God of the Holy Bible teaches us this: "'For My thoughts are not your thoughts, nor are your ways My ways,' declares the LORD. 'For, as the heavens are higher than the earth, so are My ways higher than your ways, and My thoughts than your thoughts.'" (Isaiah 55:8-9).

One thing about human beings is the fact that we want to know EVERYTHING. As well as, from time to time, we THINK we know everything, when the real truth is, if we will be honest with ourselves, we really do not know very much at all. God knows ALL (First John 3:19-20).

God's judgments and the way He has chosen to do something is past our understanding (Romans 11:33).

I say this because, as you may have seen in my writing by now, I tend to THINK I have made many mistakes.

However, I do not necessarily believe that we "make mistakes." We may think we are going down a wrong path, and do not understand how to get to the right path, but please, ponder this question: If King David is right in saying, (and he is), "O LORD, You have searched me and known me. You know when I sit down and when I rise up; You understand my thought from afar… and are intimately acquainted with all my ways. Even before there is a word on my tongue, behold, O LORD, You know it all… Where can I go from your Spirit? Or where can I flee from Your presence?... For You formed my inward parts; You wove me in my mother's womb… Your eyes have seen my unformed substance; and in Your book were all written, the days that were ordained for me, when as yet, there was not one of them (days)." (Psalm 139:1-16). If the LORD has all of our days written in His book before we live the days, can we really consider what we think we do wrong, a mistake? I cannot see it being so.

Consider this passage of Scripture—"and He made from one man every nation of mankind to live on all the face of the earth, having determined their appointed times and the boundaries of their habitation." (Acts 17:26).

I say all that to say this—if I had not moved to Missouri, I would not have a testimony of the first miracle the LORD performed in my life; on the other hand, would I?

MISSOURI! READY OR NOT, HERE WE COME!

Surely, you know this famous line from an old sit-com, "So we loaded up the truck and we moved to Beverly; Hills that is; swimming pools; movie stars…" In case you are not familiar with the sit-com, it is part of the theme song of The Beverly Hillbillies. I just thought I would throw that in here. There were hills in Missouri, but I never say any swimming pools or movie stars after we loaded up the car and moved to Neosho.

I got to where I could not make the payments on the motorcycle and my friend came and repossessed the bike. Therefore, we only had Linda's car as transportation after the move.

Things were going well for a while after we got to Missouri and rented a place to live in that was close to the egg processing plant. After a while, the manager of the plant asked me if I wanted to move into a small trailer house they had inside a local, little mobile home park just about a half of a mile from the processing plant. The manager said I would be the manager of the mobile home park, and the rent of the trailer house was included. That was a sweet deal, until…

NO WAY! TROUBLE AGAIN?!

The year was about 1992. Everything was going good.

I was working steady at the processing plant.

Linda and I were able to have some money in our savings account; we were living a comfortable, reasonable lifestyle.

We continued with one vehicle for a time due to the lack of finances, but after saving some money, I bought a 1949 model GMC pickup that needed some work.

The pickup would start and run, and it ran good.

The pickup had been sitting for some time and needed a bed, a tag, and some paint, but I liked it.

The only problem was that I let alcohol cloud my brain. The day I went and got it, I had been drinking beer. I decided to "try it out" on the way home and raced down the road as if I was in the Indianapolis 500.

My mistake—I raced by a police squad car that clocked me doing seventy miles an hour in a twenty-five mile an hour speed zone.

I jokingly say that is was my mistake, when we both know that my "mistake" was being an idiot in drinking and driving in the first place.

The pickup was not road ready in that it did not have an up-to-date tag, nor was it insured.

I had a list of charges as long as my arm so-to-speak, ranging from DUI to driving a motor vehicle under a suspended driver's license. Yeah. You can say that I was in some hot water with the law, and my now-ex-wife.

Life deteriorated from that point forward. For one, I had to come face to face with the fact that I was a full-blown alcoholic. I had to have alcohol every day. It was a thought that I never had to deal with up until that point.

The stint in Georgia did not hit me like a ton of bricks, because I had an escape from the truth that helped the idea of being an alcoholic elude my mind. There was no way of getting around the cold hard truth now; I had to face my fault every day after that, until God put a halt to the problem.

My obvious problem was that I liked the results that alcohol, namely beer, gave me; I loved the affects. The main problem was beer; it had a negative effect; a negative, lasting effect.

Rrrrrrr! MORE PROBATION!

I barely remember being in jail for the crimes I committed. What I remember about being in jail is the common jailhouse prayer that most criminals pray after they are locked up and desperate for a way out. Although I was not interested in living a life according to a God I did not know, I bowed my knees on the cold concrete floor next to the steal piece of metal they called a "bed." The prayer went something like this: "God. I don't know You, but if You will get me out of this jail, I will be very thankful; and, I will do my best to live right. Amen."

I have no idea how long I was in jail that time, but I do remember calling my mother who said something like, "I can't get you out."

The judge was very kind to me as the others were in times past; he dropped everything, reducing the crime down to a mere DUI and stacking more probation on top of what I was already serving.

As I wrote earlier, God has shown His love to me through His mercy and grace many times over; this was yet again, one of those "times."

One thing for you to ponder again—Proverbs, chapter 21, and verse 1 states: "The king's heart is like channels of water in the hand of the LORD; He (the LORD) turns it (the king's heart) wherever He (the LORD) wishes." I have often thought long and hard about that verse of Scripture. The verse tells us that the LORD God is in control of any "king" (judges, employers, landlords, peace officers, etc.) and how that "king" will decide our fate; ultimately putting God in control of our lives.

Now, that does not mean that you can just go and do anything you want, because, as well, those same judges and peace officers are in place to bring correction when we need it.

The Apostle Paul made that clear in the book of Romans, chapter 13, and verses 1-3: "Every person is to be in subjection to the governing authorities. For, there is no authority except from God, and those, which exist, are established by God. Therefore, whoever resists authority, has opposed the ordinance of God; and they who have opposed, will receive condemnation upon themselves. For rulers are not a cause of fear for good behavior, but for evil. Do you want to have no fear of authority? Do what is good and you will have praise from the same."

THE FIGHT

Along with the probation, the judge also sentenced me to attend Alcoholics Anonymous meetings in order to deal with the alcohol problem. To assure that I was attending the meetings, the judge made it mandatory for me to have a piece of paper signed by someone of authority within the meetings. Then, I was ordered to present the signed piece of paper to the probation officer who was put in charge of overseeing my progress.

I actually advance up the ranks in the meetings to the point of being a chairman.

I was given a key to the building, put in charge of making the coffee, setting up the room for the meeting, and opening the meeting.

I did that faithfully, but, I was still bound by the alcohol; I still needed to drink at least a six-pack of beer every day. Thus, I would drink two or three beers BEFORE I went and opened up for the meetings (Yeah. That is when you begin to understand that you might just have a problem with alcohol).

As well, the alcohol was being a problem within the marriage with Linda. Although she never actually complained about my drinking of alcohol, it finally came to a head one day.

It was most likely a Saturday; a beautiful, spring-summer day. I had drunk several beers that day (as I usually did on the weekends). I was standing at the kitchen counter while Linda and I was having a huge argument (maybe about the alcohol); as well, it was in front of the girls, when all of a sudden I snapped and slid the dish drainer full of clean dishes off the counter at Linda's feet, making quite the mess with the breaking of glassware; then, I went and passed out cold.

When I came to, Linda and the girls were gone. After I searched the house, I discovered that Linda had packed what she could of her and the girl's belongings into the only car we had and split town.

Some days later, I was told that she had driven back to Sulphur, and with the help of my mother, filed for a divorce. The marriage was over. That left me a foot, broke, busted, and disgusted. I was still required to attend the AA meetings; therefore, I had to walk to the meetings, and work. For that matter, I had to walk everywhere I went. Unfortunately, the walk to town took about thirty minutes each way.

It was not easy. How did I vent my frustration?

Soon after I knew Linda was gone, and not coming back, I got real drunk and mowed the yard naked; with a push mower nonetheless. It was amazing how nobody called the authorities.

THE FIRST SUPERNATURAL MIRACLE

Obviously, the LORD did many, many miracles for me up to this point (Even though I did not know it was Him), but the following testimony is of the first supernatural miracle God ever did for me, and in me.

In drinking a six-pack of beer every day, and even more on the weekend, I needed a twelve-pack every other day.

Considering I was walking to town every day, I needed to stop and buy alcohol at least every other day. So that I would not "look" like an alcoholic, or be burdened with carrying more than a twelve-pack of beer home, I would only buy a twelve-pack every other day because I was trying to quit drinking alcohol for obvious reasons.

Oh! But the fight within! When I walked to town, and needed to buy beer, I would hear a voice within myself say, "You need to stop and get beer today." Since I wanted to quit drinking, I would answer the voice saying, "No. I am not buying any beer today because I quit." and I would continue making my way to town. Nevertheless, the voice would continue, "You need to stop and get beer today."

The voice would begin when I was on my way to town. Even though I would argue and argue with the voice, it was to no avail. I would finally give in and stop to buy the beer.

This internal fight continued for what seemed like a month of Sundays (And most likely was that long or longer). One day, as I walked by the convenience store on my way to town, the voice started on me: "You need to stop and buy beer today." I came back with my usual, "No. I am not buying beer today because I quit drinking." "You need to stop and buy beer today." "No. I quit. So, I don't need to buy beer today." "You need to…" At that point, I had enough! I threw my arms and hands straight out to the sides as if I was hanging on a cross! I looked at the sky and screamed aloud, "You've got to help me!" At that precise moment in time, the desire for alcohol vanished, and I never heard the voice again.

As I have written on previous pages, I did not want anything to do with God, and I mean not one thing—no Bible reading, no prayer, and no church pew sitting. Therefore, when He supernaturally delivered me from alcohol on that beautiful summer day, it did not surprise me. I did not run and tell everybody what happened to me. I continued with life as usual—walking to the probation office, walking to the AA meetings, and walking to work. I just did not have the drinking problem anymore. I still did not want anything to do with Bible reading, prayer, or with going to church. I do not even remember stopping life for a moment to tell God "Thank You." I walked on as if I did not even know God.

By the way, I am sure that the statements I just made in the last few sentences seem cold to you, and they are. Nonetheless, it is the truth. That is not the case now. I am a devoted disciple of Jesus Christ. I have a mandate from Heaven to preach His soon coming return. I have every intention of finishing my race a winner so I can receive my crown when I get home.

In later pages, as the testimonies of miracles continue to unfold, I pray that you will understand my stance of faith in the Lord Jesus Christ.

FINALLY, LIFE GETS BETTER

With alcohol removed from my daily routine, of course, the situation progressively got better. I was hired by Tyson Foods Inc. chicken processing plant making more money.

I was able to rent a one-room cottage closer to town, only being a half of a city block from a major grocery store, fast food restaurants, and Tyson.

I began attending Narcotics Anonymous with a man name Steve. I met Steve while working for the chicken plant. This man was nice enough to stop at my cottage and give me a ride to work each day; he seemed genuinely to care for me. I was very grateful for Steve's concern of me; of how he went out of his way to make sure I was at work each day. Steve had a kind heart.

I remember how Steve would start the engine in his automobile, but would not move the car until the temperature gauge moved. You want to talk about patience! I squirmed!

Steve also invited me to his house for dinner on special occasions.

TIME TO MOVE

I worked for the chicken plant for a few months until I talked with my brother on the telephone. CJ informed me of how he was working for Tyson Foods as well; catching the chickens that Tyson processed and shipped out to the processing plants like the one I worked in.

After CJ told me how much money he earned catching the chickens, my ears perked, and I applied for a transfer within the company in hopes of being able to move to Arkansas where he lived.

It was about 1993 when the transfer was granted. Thus, I moved to Arkansas in order to catch chickens with my brother.

CHAPTER FOUR: This Is Not Working Out!

"...sin is crouching at the door; and its desire is for you, but you must master it." (Genesis 4:7).

pon arrival in Arkansas, I could not stay with my brother and his family, but we had a cousin who worked at the chicken plant as well; I shall refer to our cousin as TC. TC rented a small two-bedroom kitchenette that was about four miles outside of town. TC agreed to let me stay there with him, but the ultimate decision was up to the landlord.

THE LANDLORD

The landlord, whom I shall refer to as Danny, was a millionaire, to the tune of having a net worth of about three million dollars. Danny agreed to let me stay in the apartment with TC. The relationship that developed between Danny and I would turn out to be a bitter ending when it was all said and done.

Danny was a jolly man. He always, and I mean always carried a positive, upbeat attitude. Once Danny found out that I was a person who did not mind hard work, he utilized my ability to the extreme; in the end, among other things, his usury of me, as well as other people, was the one thing that turned me against him. I felt as if he "used" people to expand his business.

As well, I also saw some unfair business practices that I did not feel to be proper for him to be utilizing.

However, it is not my intentions to bash the man here in this writing; I just want to state the truth.

Danny helped me quite a bit; as well, he taught me a thing or two about life, people, and Christianity.

There is one thing I will never forget that Danny said to me—"John boy. It takes all kinds of people to make the world go around." I have passed that phrase on to several other people over the past seventeen years.

Danny owned a cattle ranch; raising about two-hundred and fifty head of cattle at any given time, on 800 acres of land. Thus, for a peasant like myself, I was prime beef to Danny (pun intended).

Danny said he got his start working at Tyson; saying that he walked about six miles one way to work and back home.

When I met Danny, he had several irons in the fire.

He operated a successful car lot in town, and had many people who owed him money for the vehicles they bought from him (My brother being one of those customers). I became one of his customers myself when I bought a Chevy Silverado 4x4 pickup, about a 1992 model. The pickup had a flatbed with fifth-wheel tow package installed.

When I was not working for the chicken processing plant, I worked for Danny, helping him work his cattle among other tasks.

THIS JOB STINKS!

(Laughing out loud) The job of catching chickens for a processing plant is no joke. In fact, the job is strenuous, hard, and nasty. If a person is not a hard worker, catching chickens is not the career choice to make. As well, as the caption insists, the job of catching chickens literally stinks.

During the process of raising the chickens, ammonia builds as a result from the chemical decomposition of uric acid in the droppings of the birds by a certain bacteria in the litter. The presence of the ammonia is higher in chicken houses where the same litter is used for more than one flock of chickens.

During the winter, when a crew arrives at a chicken house to begin the long process of gathering the chickens for shipping to the processing plant, the chicken houses are closed up tight, and the ammonia smell is ridiculously high. Unless the catchers wear a respiration mask, the smell of the ammonia will literally take their breath away. On top of that, some of the birds are dead, adding to the sickening smell. I cannot say that I ever got over the smell, and I caught chickens for Tyson for a period of about two and a half years.

THAT IS A NASTY HABIT

Back in 1982 or so, when I began experimenting with drugs and alcohol, I began the nasty habit of smoking cigarettes as well. When I started catching chickens, choking on the ammonia just about put a stop to that nasty habit. The ammonia would fill my lungs, and when I smoked a cigarette, I could barely breathe. Therefore, I could not smoke a cigarette for hours after getting off work. It would take more than the ammonia to make me quit smoking cigarettes; that story is next.

WOW! WHO IS THAT WOMAN?! WOE-MAN!

Soon after I moved in with TC, I saw Susan. TC was sitting at the kitchen table while I was standing in the doorway of the apartment smoking a cigarette. We were having a conversation when I heard a lawnmower buzzing by the doorway. I looked out the door and saw this beautiful woman in shorts and tee-shirt, riding a lawnmower, mowing the lawn. It was love at first sight! I looked at TC and asked with exuberating excitement in my voice, "Who is that?!!!" I can still hear TC laughing as he replied, "That is Susan. She works with Danny." I happily proclaimed, "I am going to get to know her better!" Continuing to laugh, TC warned, "If you are going to get to know her better, you will have to stop smoking those cigarettes, because she is a religious girl." I shot down his warning with, "I don't care! I will get to know her better! You watch and see!" Then, the heat was on!

I do not remember exactly how long it took, but I do remember setting a specific day to quit smoking the nasty, smelly cancer sticks; it was on a Saturday when I quit. Thus, the Friday night before, I put the cigarettes down, and I have never picked up the nasty habit since.

THE STRATEGY

In 1993, when I laid eyes on Susan and fell in love, the feelings were not mutual. She was very headstrong and determined to do only one thing—worship the ground Danny walked on. I did not fully understand how devoted Susan was to Danny, until later; at that moment in time, I did not really care, just as long as she would love me later.

Susan was thirty-two years old, and had never been married. That was one of the reasons I liked Susan; according to Danny, she was a virgin. She was also well on her way to being a millionaire just like Danny. When I met Susan, she had assets worth over one-hundred thousand dollars and counting. However, the money was not a factor in my decision to love Susan. In the beginning, I did not know she was worth that much money.

As mentioned earlier, I noticed Susan while she was mowing the lawn; she was also responsible for the upkeep of the car-lot lawn. Thus, I felt sorry for Susan, and began taking care of the lawn mowing for her.

Susan also had a laundry business that she operated. She was in contract with the local hospital to go pick up the laundry to wash and dry, then, she delivered the laundry to the hospital. As well, there was a tourist town about ten miles away where she seasonally contracted to do the laundry for the local motels and bed-n-breakfast places.

After I gained Susan's trust with the upkeep of the mowing, I advanced into picking up, helping wash, and returning the hospital's laundry; eventually, she trusted me to pick up and deliver the seasonal laundry as well.

It only took a couple of years to gain Susan's trust, but I kept my promise to my cousin, TC.

Susan and I jelled well together. Even when we would work cattle together, she and I had a good time laughing and such; we just seemed to click. It was as if we could read each other's minds, as if we knew what made each other happy.

At Danny's request, Susan began washing my weekly chicken catching clothes. I was extremely shocked that she was willing to wash my nasty clothes; trust me, the clothes were nasty! They were always caked with bird poop and drenched with sweat.

I was confident that I would marry Susan one day; so much so, I told my brother CJ of my plans. CJ is one of those who are opinionated, especially when he does not agree with the person, and, he did not agree with me about marrying Susan. In the end, if I had not gotten cold feet, I could have married Susan.

HAHAHA! HE WILL NOT DO IT!

I am one who sports a full facial beard. At that time, I had a beard, which I had not trimmed for seven years straight. The beard reached down to the collar on my shirt.

One Christmas Eve, the family was celebrating at Danny's house. As we sat at the dining room table playing games, the subject of my beard came into the conversation. Danny kidded with Susan about seeing my face clean-shaven (Danny shaved every morning).

I am not sure if Susan really wanted to see my face shaven or not, but I went to the apartment, cut the beard off, and shaved my face smooth. I then went back to the party with a bandana over my face like a bandit. I sat down to play games again and let them wonder if I had really shaved my face; then, I pulled the bandana off and showed them that I actually had shaved my face for Susan. I hated myself for shaving my beard. About four years into our relationship, while Susan and I were working in the laundry together, I told her of how I loved long hair on a woman, and how I would like for her to let her hair grow. To my surprise, she did let her hair grow. Keep this in mind, later, I will explain how Susan's hair played a key role in showing me how she indeed had fallen in love with me, and would have married me, if I had only asked her to do so; then, I would have proved John Sr. and my brother wrong.

THE TRUTH

Oddly enough, and to show you that God is working in our lives even with we don't realize it, I went through a phase of life where I would not read any material I did not think was the truth. I would not stand to read any fiction (and continue even now), sci-fi, or the like. I believed Reader's Digest to be good reading material, even paying for a subscription to the magazine for a time.

About this time, I also went through a spell of attending a church, even though I was not saved at this time; it turned out to be a "religious" phase of life as well. I was seeking the truth, but I did not find the truth in this particular church setting.

Later in life, I would learn that "religion" is nothing but following a set of rules; a way that seems right to man, but in the end is the way of death.

The truth is only found in Jesus Christ, and He requires a "relationship" with Him; a life of mercy and compassion, not a life of harsh regulations.

A BRUSH WITH THE DEATH ANGEL

By this time, I had quit catching chickens due to a recurring back injury; Tyson would not allow me to catch chickens anymore.

Therefore, I transferred inside the processing plant and worked the graveyard shift in the sanitation department.

I was responsible for cleaning one of the ovens that Tyson used for cooking the meat for packaging. I would start work at midnight and get off at six o'clock in the morning; getting paid for eight hours of work. Then, I would go home, eat breakfast, and go out to work with Danny and Susan, doing whatever was on the farm's agenda that day.

As a result of working at Tyson during the night, and being a farmhand during the day, I had a habit of sleeping until it was absolutely necessary for me to rise up and get to work on time.

If a sanitation employee clocked in late, or clocked out before six in the morning, the eight-hour incentive was withheld, and we would only be paid for the actual time we were on the clock. Thus, I had to be at work by midnight, or take a cut in pay.

One such night, I ran out of the apartment as usual, like a cat with its tail on fire. Upon jumping into my pickup (I had a different pickup by then), and turning the key to start the engine, I was abruptly faced with a dead battery; the pickup would not start.

I had the trip to town down pat. I knew the roadway well enough that I could race to town at speeds up to seventy miles an hour, and be at the clock ready to clock in within five minutes flat (It normally took at least eight to ten minutes to make the drive to town safely). I did not have a minute to spare. Thus, I jumped into Danny's Toyota long-bed farm pickup (one of his favorites), and began the race to work.

The roadway had a sharp left-hand curve in it. I knew the curve very well; I could usually make the curve at the speed of seventy miles an hour, but this particular night, something went drastically wrong. I was at the speed of seventy when I entered the curve. All of a sudden, the pickup began fish tailing out of control; it all happened so fast, giving me no time to react.

Just before I lost control of the pickup, I felt the hands of an angel lay me down in the seat. Then, the pickup hit the ditch, flipped over a barbed-wire fence and rolled about three and a half times before it came to rest on its wheels. At the moment the pickup came to rest, I felt the angel release me and I immediately sat straight up in the seat.

I wore slip-on shoes in order for me to be able to change into my rubber boots when I got to work; they were flung off my feet. I found one shoe inside the pickup, and amazingly, I instinctively reached my arm out the window and found the other shoe.

In the black of night, I climbed out of the pickup through the driver's side busted window. I could see well enough to see that the fence was never touched by the pickup; it flew plum over the fence.

I could see that the pickup was totaled, and all I could think about was how angry Danny would be about his pickup.

Yet another amazing thing was the fact that there was a gate just a stones throw away from the pickup. I walked to the gate, opened it, and walked about a quarter of a mile back to the apartment.

Once back at home, I called Danny on the phone and told him I must talk to him about the pickup. He got out of bed and came outside.

We loaded up into another farm truck and went to get the pickup out of his neighbor's field.

God's hands of grace was all over this miracle, because amazingly again, nobody traveled down the road the whole time the accident was happening.

Once back at the scene of the accident, I opened the gate wide, and Danny drove through the gate into the field; we hooked onto the Toyota, and pulled it home.

I called Tyson and told them what happened; also informing them that I would be there as soon as I could.

I do not remember how I got to work, or how I got home, but when I got home after work that morning, the family was shocked that I made it out of the accident alive. I stood looking at the mangled Toyota shaking my head in disbelief myself. The driver's side rooftop was smashed down to the steering wheel; the back glass was busted out; all four tires were flat.

If not for the hands of God's angel laying me down in the pickup seat that regrettable night, I would be burning in hell now, because at that time, I was not saved by the Blood of Jesus Christ.

This was the second miracle God did for me.

However, I continued down the road of life bound for hell, because I still did not want anything to do with church, the Bible, or prayer.

As I bring this story to a close, I am having a hard time keeping my eyes dry of tears due to the amazement of God's love. I have to ask, "Why God? Why did You spare me and not let the death angel have me?" I am very positive this question will find its answer by the end of this writing.

THE FIRE

As if the Toyota accident was not enough, here is another story of God's unfailing love through grace.

The apartment and laundry mat was built into a big double-door shop building. The apartment was on one side, with the laundry mat in the middle, next to a garage door for easy access of unloading and loading the laundry carts from the cargo van.

Behind the laundry mat, and next to the wall that separated the apartment from the laundry, there sat a big iron wood-burning furnace. During the winter months, a fire could be built in the furnace so that the heat would be tunneled into the apartment, and heat the shop building at the same time. It was the winter season; therefore, one night, I created a fire in the furnace, and then went to bed.

Leaning up against the furnace were several pieces of plywood. Later that evening, I woke up to a smoke-filled bedroom. I jumped out of bed and slid on a pair of coveralls that I had just gotten for Christmas, threw my keys and billfold in my pockets, and ran to tell Danny that the shop building was on fire. Danny ran outside to see for himself, slipping on the thin layer of sleeted-ice, which had fallen that evening. By the time Danny got back into his house to call the fire department, the apartment was engulfed in flames.

What family was in the house came running out to let the pinned-up animals out of the cattle stalls that were in the back of the building.

Danny ran into the shop building to attempt to get the farm tractor out before the fire mangled it to no good use, but the tractor was difficult to start, and he had to abandon the rescue attempt.

Susan got her cargo van out just in the nick of time, but the laundry mat was destroyed; thankfully, she had the laundry mat insured.

I just stood there watching in total disbelief as all my personal property was consumed.

We decided that the plywood which was leaning up against the furnace, caught fire, in turn, catching the apartment on fire.

What shocked me even more about the fire was the fact that everybody's love seemed to grow cold towards me, as if the fire was my fault. It seemed as if all Danny could do was complain about how his shop building was not insured.

For a little while, Danny's wife, along with Susan, treated me as if I was a disease or something.

Danny's youngest son complained at me, telling me how I should have been in the apartment throwing my personal belongings out in the yard in an attempt to save my stuff.

I gave up on my brother allowing me to stay with him and went back out to Danny's house; getting in his face, I scolded him, telling him that the fire was not my fault, and how he should be Christian enough to let me live in his basement with his invalid brother; to which Danny said he would need to discuss the issue with his wife, because after all, he had to be cautious with her safety in allowing me to live in the main house with the family, like I was some kind of creep or something. Finally, I was allowed to move into the basement.

Danny had a very nice home—five-bedrooms; four bathrooms; a lunch bar adjacent to the kitchen; dining room; huge living room; a two and a half car garage; and a full basement. The man was not hurting; the fire never put a dent in his bank account.

THE FALLING AWAY

As previously written, Danny had a way of subtly using people to progress his agenda; usually with little to no compensation for their efforts.

One example was the Chevy fifth-wheel pickup I bought from him. When we needed to move some cattle with a trailer, Danny seemed as if he only wanted to use my pickup instead of his pickup. It felt very wrong to me. I, being the type of person who holds frustration inside myself until it comes to a boiling point, did not confront Danny about his usury for a long time; it just festered and festered inside.

I was equally becoming frustrated with Susan, because she never verbally expressed her feelings she had for me, if she had any feelings for me at that time. It was Danny who was the one to tell me "Susan said this… Susan said that… Susan did this… Susan did that."

There was one particular time when Danny took the family on a vacation to a water-tourist park in Branson, Missouri. We were standing in line, on a stairway, waiting to board a water ride. As we stood there waiting, Susan came and stood next to me on the stairway; I moved up a couple of stairs; Susan came and stood next to me again, but I moved again. This happened one more time before she gave up trying to stand next to me. I was young, shy, and did not know how to handle the romantic moment with her. I suppose it upset Susan because I did not allow her to stand next to me. Later, after we were back home, Danny told me that Susan wanted to sit next to me when we got on the water ride. I felt bad about it, but what could I do? She gave up trying to keep my company. If she would have persisted, I would have given in to her romantic moment. After all, I had only been showing her my affection in helping her with the farm work for the past four or five years.

Then, Danny told me something that blew my mind about Susan when he said, "John. I overheard Susan ask her sister 'What would you think if I got married?'" Of course, I was the obvious groom; the whole family knew I had eyes for Susan. The problem was, I never heard Susan tell me that she had eyes for me; that bothered me something awful.

When I first moved into the apartment, there was another man name Jack, whom had eyes for Susan as well. However, anybody could tell that Susan definitely had no interest in him.

Jack lived about forty miles away, and raised cattle as well.

He had never married at that time.

Jack would come to Danny's house on the weekends for visiting, as well as on special occasions.

Danny and I went to help Jack work some of his cattle one particular day, and I could see why Susan wanted nothing to do with Jack. He lived in a house that looked like it had been abandoned over one-hundred years earlier. I never went into the house, but Danny told me that Jack lived without running water or electricity; my mouth fell wide open in disbelief. I felt sorry for Jack.

Thus, in a sense, I knew Susan had feelings for me; I just could not get her to open up and express her feelings that she had for me, outside of Danny's informative talking.

At times, I felt as if Danny was just telling me things to get me to stay on the farm as a hand.

Then, there was the negative talk from my brother— "Johnny! You will never marry Susan!" According to CJ, Danny was an old pro at hooking suckers with the hope of marrying Susan so he could get them to help him on the farm;

I was torn between taking Danny at his word, and believing my brother.

In the end, I would greatly regret leaving Susan (I still cry).

JOHN SR?!!!

Then, there came negativity from my natural father, John Sr.

One day, unexpectedly, John Sr. showed up at the apartment for a visit. I was completely taken by surprise. He and my mother had gotten together for a rare fling and decided to come visit my brother for the Thanksgiving Holiday.

While my natural father visited, I told him of my excitement in marrying Susan (even though there were no wedding plans between Susan and me at that time). Disappointedly, with more disgust in his voice than what was in my brother's response, John answered, "Boy! You will never marry that girl!"

At this point, I had to wonder if these critics in my family knew something more about my future than I did; and with that, came the break-up.

THE HOUSE

Danny was kind to me, you could even say generous.

After we had an idea that Susan was planning our wedding secretly, he seemed to be thinking the same way as well. Unfortunately, for me, doubt still clouded my mind.

Danny and I formed a plot where I would agree to buy some land from Susan and put a house on the property, making a homestead for Susan and me to settle into and build our family. Thus, I made the land agreement with Susan. Now, whether or not she knew of the plot Danny and I had made with her land, I will never know.

There was a house in town that was encased in rock. The house was to be torn down, or moved. Danny asked me what I thought about buying the house and putting it on my property. I liked the house, agreeing to let him pay the two-thousand dollar purchase price; I would pay him back later.

Then, I went to work getting the house ready for the move. I took all the rock off and hauled it to a storage area.

The house had a fireplace that had been rocked to the ground underneath the house. The moving company required that the rock be removed from underneath before they would attempt to move the house, due to the weight of the rock.

Then, the big day came to move the house out to the property.

I was excited, yet filled with worries at the same time—where would I get the money to pay Danny back; how would I pay Susan for the land; what if Susan would not marry me after I got the house remodeled? At any rate, the house was moved successfully.

I had my work cut out for me.

I shored up under the fireplace in order to keep the fireplace from falling through the floor later on in life.

Then, sadly, I took flight and vanished.

SIN ENTERS IN

This is another part of this book that you should read with discretion, and open mind.

The first murder ever recorded in history was that of a man named Cain. You will find the story recorded in the fourth chapter of the book of Genesis, of the Holy Bible.

The first man and woman, Adam and Eve, had two sons named Cain and Abel, in respective order.

Abel raised animals, while Cain was a produce farmer.

Verse 8 reads in part "...sin is crouching at the door; and its desire is for you, but you must master it." Regardless of whether or not I was to marry Susan, adultery came knocking at my door, but I did not master it in time to save the relationship with Susan.

I turned and went down a bad road in that I decided that Susan was never going to express her emotions she had for me to my face. Therefore, I rented an apartment in town, moving away from Danny and Susan.

I still remember heading to town with my belongings when I met Susan on the roadway as she was coming home; I stopped her and told her I was moving. She seemed shocked that I was moving away from her; but the decision had been made.

After the move to town, I became good friends with another woman, who I have named Delilah, for what should be obvious reasons.

Delilah also worked in the sanitation department for Tyson. Although we worked in different areas, we would sit in the break room together when it was break-time.

During our conversations, Delilah told me that she had an abusive husband. According to her, he would make her go naked in the house so he could have sex with her anytime he felt the desire; he would not let her out of his sight with their two children, a boy and a girl; he would beat her if she disobeyed any of his commands, threatening to kill her; she was also ordered to be home within a certain amount of time after she left work so he would know she was not stalling in coming home.

Of course, all of this pulled at my heartstrings, causing me to fall in sympathy-love with Delilah.

Let me say something here about the devil; he comes as an angel of light, lurking about the earth seeking someone to destroy.

Due to the lack of loving parents during my childhood, I was a sucker for Delilah's love-seeming attention, which made up for the lack thereof with Susan.

The devil came disguised as sympathy, and false compassion because of Delilah's abusive husband (ex-husband now).

I was young, vulnerable, and just plain stupid to get involved with Delilah.

Delilah began coming over to the apartment about an hour before we were due at work; however, before my sinful fall with Delilah, God sent a messenger to my apartment to warn me of the "crouching" sin.

It was the summer season and I did not have an air conditioner to keep me cool. Therefore, I slept with the front door to the apartment open; the doorway had a screen door.

One night, I was awaked by someone's voice inside my apartment; I recognized the voice to be Danny's voice. He told me that he knew of my relationship with Delilah; that she was a married woman, and if I was not careful, her husband would hurt me for messing around with his wife. Then, as fast as he appeared, he disappeared into the black of night. Unfortunately, I did not heed the warning.

As mentioned above, Delilah would come over before work and visit with me. We would sit out on the front porch with her in my arms, and my hand in her panties, rubbing her vagina.

One night, Delilah came for her normal visit; however, she surprised me with coming a bit earlier than usual; catching me naked, yet sound asleep. Delilah undressed herself and climbed into my bed. Once I was awake, it did not take long for me to figure out that Delilah was not wearing anything but her birthday suit; as fast as a lightning strike, Delilah and I had sex. Sin had crouched, but I failed to master it before it mastered me.

At this point in life, I had not had sex with any girl for about five years. Thus, I had no power against the temptation. As well, I was not a born-again Christian at this time, but that does not change the fact that I sinned in committing adultery with Delilah.

After the childhood sexcapade with Marcel, having girlfriends and sex with girls seemed to flee from me.

As a teenager, I only had sex with four girls; and, the number is the same since becoming an adult. For me, that is worthy of a reward, especially considering how many girls I WANTED to have sex with after Marcel, and before my first marriage. Since stepping into adulthood, it has been as if God put a big red X on my forehead that tells girls to "RUN! THIS MAN IS PURE AND SHALL NOT BE DEFILED!"

Of course, I understand how wrong having sex outside of marriage is in the eyes of God now; thus, I will not defile the marriage bed ever again. As well, in the pages that follow, I will explain how strict I was about NOT having sex out of wedlock when I married my third wife, who I am currently separated from now.

Nevertheless, we are all human, and without an absolute devoted life to Jesus Christ, we are all prone to follow our fleshly lusts; those types of Christians are known as carnal Christians.

With that, I have had my fair share of being just that, a carnal Christian.

CHAPTER FIVE: Here Comes Disaster!

"Do not be deceived, God is not mocked; for whatever a man sows, this he will also reap. For the one, who sows to his own flesh, will from the flesh reap corruption…"

(Galatians 6:7-8).

s a result of the fling with Delilah, she divorced her husband and married me.

Delilah had two children with her ex—a boy about nine years old, Anthony, and a girl who was about seven years old name Sheryl.

Delilah gained joint custody of the children in the divorce.

After the divorce and our union, I got a healthy understanding as to what the Bible means when it says, "For the one, who sows to his own flesh, will from the flesh reap corruption…"

After you read this chapter, I pray that you will have a much better understanding of the same.

Delilah and I were married in 1998. We did not have a wedding; we just walked into the justice of the peace and signed the papers.

We lived in town for some time before we decided to move to her parent's home in Grand Junction, Colorado.

One of the things that Delilah's ex restricted her from, while they were married, was allowing her to go to Colorado in order to visit her parents; she had not seen her parents in ten years. Therefore, after our union, we flew from Tulsa, Oklahoma to Denver, Colorado, then, traveled by car rental to her parent's home in Palisade, Colorado so she could visit her parents.

It was my first flight on an airplane, and I was sick as a carsick dog for three days after we landed. Flying was not my thing then.

YOU NEED TO SEE A DOCTOR

I was having trouble with mood swings. One moment I would be happy; the next moment I would be sad; and even the next, I would be angry. Delilah questioned me about the mood swings, to which I had no answer. I never noticed the mood swings before our union.

I talked with my natural father about the mood swings because some of his traits were passed down to me through his DNA. John Sr. told me that he indeed had a similar problem, and for me to have a doctor check my system for a lack of Serotonin, adding that the doctor would prescribe some medicine that will take care of the problem.

Serotonin is an important chemical and neurotransmitter in the human body. It is believed to help regulate mood and social behavior, appetite and digestion, sleep, memory, and sexual desire and function.

Most of the symptoms fit me; thus, the doctor did prescribe the medicine called Serzone. After I began taking the meds, I had no more trouble with my emotions; I was as mellow as a cat napping after feasting on tuna. Keep this in mind, as it will lend to another miracle later in this book.

THE REAPING BEGINS

Danny was correct with the warning of Delilah's ex-husband hurting me for messing around with his wife. He began by starting trouble in filing a complaint with Child Welfare Services that accused me of violating Sheryl. The Child Welfare worker did not think it was a good idea for me to stay there, even though there was no evidence to support the accusation.

That was just the beginning of the trouble.

I was not sure what to do about the accusation with Sheryl, so I took a trip to Seattle, Washington to visit my mother, who temporarily lived there; then I went to live with Delilah's parents and prepared a place for my new ready-made family to come thereafter.

After I saved some money and secured a place for the family to live in, I went back to Arkansas to get the family.

COLORADO! HERE WE COME!

Although Delilah's ex did not catch up with me, he camped out at our house the day we packed the U-Haul truck and waited for an opportune time to confront me.

With fear of what her ex might try to do to us looming, we went to visit Delilah's brother, Joe. While there, we decided it would be best for Delilah and the children to stay at her brother's house while I went back home and finished packing the U-Haul truck.

Sure enough, the ex came to the house and knocked on the door. I told him that I did not want any trouble with him; then, I called the police; He vacated the premises and I finished packing the truck.

I drove the back way out of the trailer park where we were moving from so I could monitor the road behind me, just in case the ex followed me; although he did not follow me out of the park, he saw me in town and began to follow me there; as a result, I drove the U-Haul to the police station and that caused him to leave me be; I then drove to Joe's house and we waited until the next day before heading to Colorado.

We thought we were safe from any more trouble with the ex-husband once we arrived in Colorado; nothing could have been farther from the truth.

WHOA! THE MOUNTAINS!

We settled into the home that I rented previous to their arrival; Delilah and the children seemed to be very happy.

Delilah had two older sons from a previous marriage who also lived in Colorado.

Delilah was ecstatic for some time because she was able to spend time with her family whom she had not seen in many years.

I was thirty-two years old at this time and felt a bit awkward with Delilah's older sons because I was not much older than they were. It seemed as if they were silently laughing about me being their stepfather; not that I was trying to be any sort of authority figure in their lives. I let Delilah deal with the children anyway, because they were just that, her children.

I worked a lot of the time. At first, I landed a job working for Delilah's cousin, who built custom homes. I did not care much for the job because carpentry is not one of my skills, but a job is a job when you have bills to pay.

Eventually, the carpentry job was not providing enough of an income for us to live on, as we desired. Therefore, I got a second job washing dishes for a Red Lobster restaurant. I liked this job; it kept me busy enough that I could forget how tired I was from working so much.

Delilah and I bought a house in a small community town called Clifton. The location was closer to her parents so we were able to visit more often.

I liked my new parents-in-law, Jim and Nancy. Delilah's father was a hoot; never having a dull moment.

He enjoyed sipping hard liquor behind Nancy's back.

Just as Danny taught me one quirky saying, Jim taught me one of his own when he said, "John. If you can't have fun, it's no fun." I thought that was so comical.

Jim was a rock cutter and polisher. They lived on a hilltop where Jim had tons of rock laying around; because of Jim, I fell in love with rocks. Jim gave me several rocks, and even taught me how to bring the natural shine to the surface of a rock with a grinder and diamond sanding pads. Once I saw how pretty the rocks were after being polished, I became a rock hound. I would go out in search of rocks; any type of rocks. I came away from Colorado with some lava rock, petrified wood rock, oil shell rock, and you-name-it-rock. I also came away with some dinosaur bones, some of which Jim gave me, plus a small bone I picked up on a trail we blazed during one of our tourism outings (shhhhh...I was not supposed to take it home). I was fascinated with rocks.

It would not be long before I would be a worshiper of The Rock—Jesus Christ.

The house we bought was in a valley between some of the most beautiful mountains of Colorado.

Jim taught me a lot about the mountains. In the distance, we could behold the beauty of the Rocky Mountains, which stands between travelers on their way between Grand Junction and Denver. On the other side of town, you could see some of the long, stretched out mountains of Utah. Up close, and within reach of hiking, The National Monument and Mount Garfield beautify the skyline.

I loved being able to go outside and see the mountains with the sunrise and the sunset as a backdrop. It was almost as sweet as waking up to the sound of the ocean waves rolling in at sunrise. Oh, how I miss that place. I began a rock collection. I preferred having a rock garden as to a flower garden.

Some people surely think of me as crazy because I collect rocks.

I have a pet rock named Big Boy; he is at least a one-hundred and fifty pound lava rock. Then, there is Pretty Boy; he is a piece of oil shell rock that I dug out of the ground and proudly hauled home. He weighs in at a good one hundred pounds. I had a fun time getting him into the trunk of the car, but I managed. I have moved the rocks from place to place through the years. I have a motto: "When you see my rocks gone, you know I am gone." With that, let's move on.

A HARD BLOW TO SWALLOW

It was time for the children to go spend their time with their father. Although Delilah did not show much concern, I was worried that the children would not come back.

We drove the children back to Arkansas so we could spend some lasting moments with them, knowing we would not see them for the duration of their visit there.

We had some excitement along the way; as in being pulled over by the Highway Patrol for doing eighty miles an hour in the sixty-five mile an hour speed zone. I was racing another car, and winning! The nice officer gave me a warning, which I heeded.

Upon arrival in Arkansas, we met the children's father at the police station for the exchange with him. It was a sad moment when we said our goodbyes; it still is saddening.

We made the exchange and went back home to Colorado in silence.

When it was time for the children to come home, we drove back to Arkansas to pick them up, but her ex-husband never showed up at the police station with the children. Delilah filed a kidnapping report with the police, gave them our phone number, then, we waited in hopes for the phone call that never came.

The consequences for our sin of adultery had dealt a hard blow, a low blow. Where there was once love, there was now hate. It only got worse.

IN THE RED

Our financial situation was way in the red. Eventually, we filed bankrupt and got some relief. By this time, we had bought a new car that we kept from the bankruptcy along with the house.

I acquired a paper route delivering about three-hundred papers on Sunday, and a little less than that on Monday thru Saturday. The paper route was fun for a time, until my arm began to hurt from throwing the papers, and I lost sleep.

Delilah worked for a cold-call company where she called random phone numbers and attempted to sell some sort of product. She was good at her job because she had a lightning fast mind when it came to the gift of gab. She knew exactly what to say, and when to say it. She worked the afternoon/evening shift.

SOMETHING DOES NOT FEEL RIGHT

Delilah developed a drinking problem because she began drinking beer, what seemed like, all the time. On my days off, I noticed that she would begin drinking beer about nine in the morning, and did not stop until late in the evening.

We hosted a cookout at our home, inviting several guests. The older sons were there, and along with Delilah, they were treating me as if I was an outcast.

Delilah went as far as to flirt with one of the male guests, right in front of my face. She seemed to flirt with him to spite me, seemingly trying to make me upset. However, I loved Delilah, and gave her the benefit of the doubt.

Due to the way Delilah and the boys were acting, I decided to "bug" the house by placing a mini tape recorder in a flowerpot, which hung in the corner by the kitchen table. I heard things that were even more upsetting. The boys were saying derogatory things about me while Delilah just laughed along with them.

As well, I bugged the car with the tape recorder so I could hear what might be going on while Delilah was at work. I knew that she took her work breaks in the car, along with a male co-worker, where she could drink a beer or two, along with smoking the nasty cigarettes that she smoked.

She was not being good to me in bed anymore neither and I wanted to know what was going on behind my back. Unfortunately, for me, I "saw" the truth.

Delilah began coming home later and later from work. Therefore, I began watching her from a distance after her shift ended.

I saw that the male co-worker would ride with her.

One night, I followed Delilah and her co-worker; she led me straight to his house, and then, went inside. I waited a few minutes to see if she would come back out in a timely manner, but when she did not, I snuck up to the house to see if I could peek in a window.

The weather was fair that night, with mild temperatures, thus, I found an open window where I could listen to any conversation they were having. To my disgust, this is what I heard; READER'S DISCRETION IS ADVISED.

The co-worker: "I can't get it up."

Delilah: "What do you mean, you can't get it up?"

The co-worker: "Sometimes, I suffer from male dysfunction."

Delilah: "Here, let me see if I can help."

The co-worker: "It's no use. It's not working."

Delilah: (Laughing while saying something sarcastic).

I had heard enough! By this time, I was going through several different emotions—anger, resentment, hatred, sadness, and gloom. My mind was racing. I was thinking, "What can I do to save my marriage?" Everything I tried utterly failed to show Delilah that I loved her.

I NEED SOME "FEEL GOOD" MEDICINE!

America was still ringing in the new millennium about this time.

Most people, including myself, were waiting for the anticipated "Y2K" computer crash. Talk was all around of how the computers would not work properly and so forth. I was not a computer buff, so I did not pay much attention to the scare. At this point in life, if the whole world crashed, what was that to me? My "world" had already crashed!

From 1993 to this point, God continued keeping me as a "dry drug addict"; I just could not find anybody who would sell marijuana to me so I could smoke it and relieve the tensions of life. God only delivered me from alcohol in 1993, but left me with a desire to smoke pot.

That was until I began working for a company that installed fiberglass insulation

inside newly built homes. This company also installed insulation along the inside of the underpinning, which incased the bottom side of mobile homes.

I worked as the warehouse manager for some time, loading the company vehicles with the needed insulation that each job called for on the following workday. Along with stocking and cleaning the warehouse, I was responsible for loading the trucks each afternoon as the crews returned from their workday.

Along about the first of February in 2000, I discovered how I could make more money installing the insulation with a work crew, than I was making with keeping the warehouse.

By that time, I had been with the company for six months or more, and began bucking my manager for another buck or two in pay (Laughing out loud. Pun intended). The manager told me that there were no opportunities for a raise in the warehouse position, and if I wanted more money, I must transfer to a work crew and hang insulation. On top of the hourly wage that came with hanging insulation, a worker could make more per hour with doing piecework; the faster a worker hung the insulation with quality, the more the worker earned per piece of insulation hung.

The job was itchy, cold, and hot. Day after day, I went home with fiberglass pieces stuck to my body, with almost no relief.

After leaving the warehouse, I began working with a crew, where just about every crewmember smoked marijuana on the way to the jobsite.

I resisted the temptation to smoke with them for a month or so, only inquiring as to why they smoked in the company vehicle every day. Were they not concerned about getting into trouble with the company?—even more than that, with the law? (How ironic it is to me now; Colorado was the first state of the United States to legalize the use of marijuana for recreational purposes).

Thus, day after day, I climbed into the cab of the truck, knowing that I would be forced to smell that sweet smelling aroma of the drug I resisted. Then, came that fateful day when I gave in and began smoking marijuana again. Ahhh! Finally! Relief from the problems of life!—but, only for a moment.

When I went back to smoking the drug, it may have relieved the tensions of life, but it in no wise way changed the problems I was having with Delilah and her boys. The turmoil continued, and her attitude towards me got worse.

As well, and ironically, one of the boys smoked marijuana as well, making it easy for me to get more of the drug after I resigned from the insulation company.

I went to work for a huge concrete outfit; employing upwards to a hundred workers.

As I wrote in a previous chapter, I never did mind doing hard work; it made me feel good about myself at the end of the day. Along with that, marijuana helped ease the body pain that came with pushing and pulling the concrete day after day.

I was happy though, for a while.

I continued throwing the newspaper route, but had previously given up the job at Red Lobster; it was just too much to handle.

A DOG RETURNS TO ITS VOMIT

In a few pages, I will be sharing how God worked the miracle of salvation in me.

Before that though, this part of your reading should show you how merciful and loving God really is to us.

When you hear a voice say to you, "You are too far gone for God to save you.", or, "You have committed far too great a sin for God to save you." I am here to testify that it is a lie from the lying devil's mouth. Every human being is already saved from the pit of hell because of what Jesus Christ did on the Cross. All you must do to be saved is to believe what the Bible says, repent of your sins, and confess with your mouth that Jesus Christ IS LORD of your life; then, keep Him as LORD of your life.

Everything that I write from this portion of the book forward is the honest to God's truth; it all happened just as I say. It is up to you as to whether or not you believe it.

I became strung out on the marijuana.

One thing about drugs is this, there comes a point in your use of drugs, where they just do not help you cope anymore; you need more and more.

That is what happened with me—marijuana just was not giving me the needed relief I needed anymore. Therefore, one day, I longed for something more. I looked into the refrigerator for something that would bring me more comfort. For some people, that "more" is food; but food was never one of my comforters, alcohol was. The devil lied to me that day and said, "There is some beer. Delilah is doing it. You should drink some of her beer out of spite to her." That was all it took for me to get past the temptation and pop a top on the first beer can; and with that, I was hooked on alcohol once again. The previous seven years of enjoyed freedom from alcohol just went down the windpipe; it did not change a thing.

CHAPTER SIX: The Real Supernatural Power!

"For I am confident of this very thing, that He who began a good work in you, will perfect it until the day of Christ Jesus."(Philippians 1:6).

If you are recovering from alcohol, you cannot afford to drink one beer. The moment you drink it, there is no stopping the second, third, fourth, and beyond. It serves you a disastrous lifestyle thereafter.

It would not be until later in my walk with Jesus Christ that I would read the following verse of Scripture, and even longer before I actually applied it to my life: "Like a dog that returns to its vomit, is a fool who repeats his folly." (Proverbs 26:11). I have been a fool so many times. However, if it were not for God…

As well, maybe you are bound by alcohol and think that there is no hope in sight; keep reading. I am here to tell you, and show you by example, that there is nothing, and I mean NOTHING, that will ever separate you from the love of God, which is in Christ Jesus. NOTHING!

YOU ARE GOING TO ATTEND THIS CHURCH

I continued working for the concrete company. I was proving to the company how I was a good, faithful worker.

The company put me working with the "curb and gutter" crew—the crew responsible for forming and pouring the concrete curb and gutters that channel the rainwater to the storm drains of parking lots.

We were working for a huge church that was nearing completion.

The curb and gutter crews must be sent in to get their work completed before the pavement can be laid in the parking lot. When you see the curb and gutter crew show up, you know that the job is nearing completion.

The pastor came out to the jobsite with a few volunteers; they cooked hamburgers and hotdogs for the crewmen.

When lunchtime was drawing near, the pastor began to walk around and inform the workers of the pending feast. While he made his rounds, he was saying a few words of encouragement to the workers. When he made it to my area of work, I was standing with four or five other crewmembers, listening to him talk, when suddenly, I heard a voice inside me say, "You are going to attend this church." Laughing it off, I said, "Oh no, I'm not! I don't attend church!", then, I went back to listening to the pastor talk.

GOD JUST TOUCHED ME!

About two weeks passed.

For approximately the past three months, I had been indulging in marijuana and alcohol, which was no longer working for me.

The marriage with Delilah was still on the rocks.

I was growing increasingly tired of working so many hours between the newspaper route and the concrete job.

I needed a way out of the sickening problems I was facing, but I just could not find any relief.

I did my smoking out in the garage area.

We built a petition wall in the middle of the garage in order to make two rooms. One room was for a lounging area with a couch, loveseat, and a television. The other half of the garage became the area where I rolled the newspapers in preparation for the morning's dreaded throw.

Wednesday, June 28th of 2000, I was making my way through the kitchen to step out into the garage and get high on some marijuana. The kitchen was a narrow walkway with the cook stove, refrigerator, and counter space on one side, while the other side contained more counter space and the kitchen sink. The petition wall along the sink area had an open window that looked into the dining room area.

I got as far as the kitchen sink when this thought rolled through my mind, "Somehow, someway, I am going to fix this." I was thinking about the rocky marriage, the tireless days of working, and the dreadful habits I had encountered.

At that precise moment in time, I felt a poke in my chest, along the heart area. It felt as if someone took a sewing needle and pricked my skin with the point.

At the same moment, the desire for alcohol, marijuana, disgust with the marriage, and dreaded work schedule just disappeared.

I felt a soothing feeling of something like warm oil begin on the top of my head and continue down my chest until the feeling was at my abdomen area.

My heart was filled with joy as I exclaimed aloud, "God just touched me! I've got to go to church and praise Him!"

God had set my soul on Fire!

I decided to go to church the following Sunday, which was July 2nd.

The voice I heard just two weeks earlier was correct.

The new church building was not completed at that time. Therefore, I looked in the phone book to find where the church was holding their meetings.

When I showed up at the church, I busted through the doorway with the biggest smile of my life on my face!

As I shook the first usher's hand that I saw, I said, "I am here to serve God! Where do I start?!" The usher giggled as he said, "Whoa, whoa, whoa. Settle down. We have a process here. Let me show you to your seat." The usher, named Ted, ushered me to my seat.

I sat down with anticipation in my heart, waiting for the service to start.

At the end of the service, I went forward when the pastor called for sinners to come home. I got down on my knees and reached for the sky as if someone was pointing a gun at my back. Right there, in front of God and everybody, I asked Jesus Christ to come into my heart and be my LORD, forever.

It was the best feeling in the world to know that I was saved; there is no doubt.

SHE'S GONE

The notable miracle of salvation had occurred by the hands of Jesus Christ Himself.

Let me note here that I did not ask Jesus Christ to touch me on that awesome day. It was His choosing to set me free of alcohol, marijuana, and all the negative emotions that plagued me. I was not seeking His deliverance.

As previously written, when the voice (I now know that it was the Holy Spirit) told me I was going to attend that particular church, I laughed, telling Him that I did not attend church.

However, Almighty God is sovereign. When He wants to do something, there is nothing that can stop Him, not even you. I will prove what I am saying in the coming pages as I tell of another notable miracle that is unexplainable, except to say, "God did it."

I have found that God has a way of squeezing you enough in order to get you to submit to His will. I have seen it in my own life, time after time, after time. When He wants something accomplished, He is relentless in pursuit.

Take now for an example. This book has been in the making for about seventeen years now. I began the first attempt to write this masterpiece in 2003 or so, but shelved the idea due to not being able to get the words on paper. Then, another attempt was made in 2015 or so, but I shelved it again due to lack of confidence in my writing skills. This time (January of 2020) is the real deal. However, God has been hounding me for the past several months saying, "Just write son!" I have resisted, and resisted, and resisted, with vehemence tears, because I just was not confident in the fact that I can write this book.

How did God handle it? Through some unforeseen circumstances, which I will write about at a later time, God has narrowed my life down to the point to where I have no choice to write, or shelve the book forever. I cannot live with my conscience like that.

I went home from church that day a changed man.

I witnessed to EVERYBODY about Jesus Christ, beginning with my now-ex-wife. I told her of how God touched me that awesome day, and how she needed to turn her life over to Jesus and accept Him as her savior. My last words to her about the matter were, "I like this Jesus thing, and I am going to pursue it." I had no idea what I was saying; neither did I care.

Delilah had no words to say in response to my newfound excitement.

The Fourth of July was a couple of days away, and we had some sort of cookout for the holiday.

The morning of July 5th meant that it was time to go back to work. I got ready for work as usual and told Delilah goodbye for the day. She was jotting down some things that we needed from the grocery store and asked me if there was anything I thought we needed. I may have mentioned something or the other and then walked out to go to work.

I had an uneasy feeling about Delilah all day; I just knew something was not right. I left work early due to the uneasiness in my soul. Sure enough, when I walked into the house, it was just about empty; Delilah had taken all the furnishings except for the bedroom suit and a mirrored jewelry case that I had bought for her.

Emotions flooded my soul—anger, resentment, bitterness, sadness, guilt, and a whole lot of tears flowed from my eyes. I moped around the house in depression for about a month.

Delilah asked me to go with her to the courthouse and sign the divorce papers with her. Although I pleaded with her to give me another chance, she insisted in getting the divorce.

Thus, she let me have the new car and the house. Later, after I moved back to Arkansas, I gave the car back to her and signed the house over to her and her sons with a quick claim deed.

I called my mother and told her of the miracle I had received from Jesus Christ, but she said, "Oh Johnny! Surely you don't believe that nonsense!" I was very hurt because I thought my mother would be happy for me; I was sadly mistaken.

Jesus Christ had set a fire ablaze in my soul. Everywhere I went, it was Jesus, Jesus, Jesus, and more Jesus. I was so excited about my new way of life. I would play praise and worship music for a couple of hours each day while I danced, sang, and shouted praises to the Lord Jesus. I also delved into the Bible hard and heavy. I began reading in the book of John first. I read chapter after chapter.

I got to chapter 9 and read how Jesus healed the blind man's eyes, and a new fire was set in my soul for Jesus Christ to heal my eyes just as he did for that blind man. I jerked the eyeglasses off my face and proclaimed, "Hey Jesus! Heal my eyes too!" The eyesight did not come clear at that moment. In fact, in a later chapter, I write about a challenge I went through with the eyesight in 2007-09.

It was about this time that God began to speak to my spirit by His Spirit. Just about the first thing He said was, "You are going to be like a John the Baptist. You will go before my Son, Jesus Christ, and His return." I just finished reading about John, and how his head was chopped off for telling King Herod the truth; the king was breaking the law by marrying his brother's wife. When God spoke that to me, I explicitly remember grabbing my neck and shouting aloud, "You mean I am going to lose my head?!" However, at the time, I did not care what happened to me, as long as I could be with Jesus.

I was walking through the house reading the Bible when I heard God say, "I have chosen you to be a prophet to the nations. You shall go to whomever I send you, and you shall speak whatever I tell you to speak. Do not be afraid of their faces, for I am with you." I had no idea what that entailed, until later when I knew God wanted me to give someone a message, then, with knees knocking, I had to tell them. Sometimes I failed in never giving the message; other times I gave the message, took their scolding of how I had not heard from God, and then felt relieved that I had accomplished what God wanted me to do.

FOOTBALL?!

Ted, the first usher I shook hands with, became a good friend of mine.

He and several other men were heavily involved with having football parties. The guys would rotate between each other's homes and watch the weekly NFL football games.

My home was placed on the list, and the guys gathered in my home for a couple of football games as well.

The first game I was invited to was at Fred's house; I believe the Giants were playing (Fred's favorite team). During the halftime show, Fred played some Pink Floyd music. I remember being amazed that God would allow Christians to listen to rock-n-roll music. I specifically asked Fred, "You mean God allows you to listen to that music?" He responded with, "Sure He does. God is a good God." I was not so sure about the Lord allowing us to listen to that type of music, and have since discovered that it is not good for me to listen to such music because it takes me away from my devotion to Jesus Christ. However, at that moment in time, I was a baby Christian, not knowing any better.

NO. I WILL NOT GO.

About the first of September, of 2000, God spoke to me saying, "I want you to move back to Arkansas." I resisted and rebelled back with, "No. I like it here. I love the mountains."

God was patient with me and gave me about a month to continue having fun with my newfound brothers before came back insisting, "I want you to move back to Arkansas." I gave in a little inquiring, "I don't want to go back there. Why do you want me to go back to Arkansas?" He answered with one name, "Susan", placing her face in my mind. Nonetheless, I continued to resist. Susan was not enough to pull me away from the fun I was having, and the mountains. Besides, I had met another girl who I wanted to be with more than Susan.

God patiently waited about another month before He gave me one more chance to obey. This time, I gave in to His gentle command.

BREAKING OF BAD NEWS

Over the previous few months, I made several friends at church.

When my 33rd birthday came into play that November 25th, Ted made secret plans for a surprise party, disguising the party as dinner at a Mexican restaurant.

There must have been twenty or more of my new church family at the restaurant. I was having a good time with everybody.

They told the wait staff that it was my birthday, and the staff put a sombrero on my head and sang a birthday song.

I knew I needed to tell the family of what God was asking me to do in moving back to Arkansas, but I dreaded every minute of it. By the end of the party, I announced that I would be moving away. It was a sad moment, and still is disheartening.

Maybe you are thinking, "How can he say that now, after all these years." I say that because I have had a lot of turmoil in my walk with Jesus over the past twenty years.

THE DREADED MOVE

Somewhere around December 1st, I began making the dreaded, but necessary plans, for the move back to Arkansas.

The newspaper company preferred that I have someone in place to take over the paper route before I resigned the position. Once that was accomplished, there was nothing left to do except get to pack-n-it.

One thing about God is this—when He wants you to do something, He wants you "moving" in the direction that He is leading you to go.

The Bible teaches that there is a time and a season for everything under the sun (Ecclesiastes 3).

I packed a mid-size U-Haul for a one-way trip, loaded the car onto a car dolly, and made sure I had the most important things—the rocks, then, I sadly drove away.

One thing that was very sad about leaving was that I just got acquainted with the next door neighbor, who had bins and bins of rocks in his back yard. He told me to take all the rocks I wanted. I had to inform him of how I was moving away and just could not take the rocks with me. If I could have stayed, I would have mountains of rocks in my back yard now!

I drove as far as Missouri before I got too sleepy to continue, then, I stopped for a nap.

When I awoke, I drove on in and finished the trip at my brother's house.

I unloaded the U-Haul of belongings, and rocks, into an open shed, then, threw a tarp over the mess.

I was not concerned with rushing to see if Susan still liked me or not, I needed a job, and fast. I was rather concerned that Susan would not like me anymore. I mean, after all, I did run off and commit adultery, leaving her holding the bag of work and unfinished house. What woman is there that would even think about allowing a loser like me back into their life? Did not God tell me that Susan was the reason He asked me to move back?

There is one thing about having a big food processing plant in a small town, a job is usually easy to secure. Thus, I went back to work for Tyson Foods. Amazingly enough, Tyson gave me a chance to catch chickens once again, but after I went back into a chicken house and began catching the nasty beasts, I decided that working inside the plant would be the better idea; and that is exactly what I did.

CJ was kind enough to let me stay with him for a little while, until...

WHAT ARE YOU DOING HERE?!

I moved back to Arkansas somewhere around December 15th, of 2000. Thus, it was just days before Christmas.

About midnight, I decided to go out to the local Wal-Mart and get a few items, besides, I just wanted to get out of the house and walk around. I was afraid to go out in public during the day, because I did not want to take a chance and see Danny or any of his family in town, especially Susan; I was embarrassed of the adultery. There I was, walking around Wal-Mart at a time of night when most people, like Danny, should be at home in bed fast asleep. However, just take a huge guess of WHO I saw walk into Wal-Mart. Yeah, Danny and his whole family! I hoped that none of them saw me, or recognized me, until I saw Danny coming towards me! I told Danny that he was the last person I thought I would see in Wal-Mart that late at night. He told me that it was Christmas time, and he was out with the family doing some gift shopping.

I questioned him as to whether or not Susan saw me; to that, he answered that he did not know. I expressed how I was pretty sure she would not want to see me anyway. He told me how she was hurt after I abruptly took off, but that he did not think she hated me.

Danny devised a plan in that I would slowly begin to come out to his house and help him with the farm work again, saying that Susan might warm up to me once again. I agreed to do as he suggested.

Danny usually had some good ideas that made sense. After all, he was a millionaire two or three times over.

A DUMP, BUT A DOOR

As mentioned, Danny had several acres of land; included with that land was a rental property or two. There just happened to be one such rental that Danny allowed me to move into and begin my stay, as well as another attempt at winning back Susan's heart.

The property sported a trailer house, and was no more than a quarter of a mile from Danny's house. The trailer house was a drafty dump of a dwelling that should have been used for a fire department drill. Some of the living room floor needed replaced; some of the windows were missing, or boarded up. The bathroom tub was caked with soap scum, and the shower was not any better. I wondered if the kitchen floor would even support a refrigerator. I could not even begin to tell you what was wrong with the plumbing of the run-down heap. However, it was an open door back to where God wanted me to be.

HALLELUJAH! I'M HEALED!

Are you ready to read about another supernatural miracle? Surely, you remember the story I told you about the medicine I was taking for the lack of serotonin being made in my brain? At this point, I had been taking the medication for about three years, with success; but a greater "success" was waiting for me.

I was to a point where I could not afford more of the medication, and I only had a few doses left of what I did have.

Since I made Jesus Christ the Lord of my life, I did my best to do what the verses of Scripture in the book of Proverbs teaches—"Trust in the LORD with all your heart, and lean not on your own understanding. In all your ways acknowledge Him, and He will make your paths straight." (Verses 5-6).

Therefore, I sat down in my living room recliner and simply said, "God. I am almost out of medication. I don't have money to buy more. What do you want me to do?" He softly responded, "Stop taking the medicine." I wanted to be sure of what I heard, so I asked, "Are You sure?" He gently said, "Yes." I pardoned His guidance once again with, "What should I do with the rest of the medicine I have?" He quickly responded again with, "Stop taking it. You are healed." Thus, I tossed the rest of the medication in the trash and did not look back. I have not needed any of the medication since that time.

MY NAME WAS IN THE TRASH?!

In 2001, I began looking for a better job. It seemed as if God was moving me into more of an area of expertise than just being a blue-collar worker at Tyson Foods. I spoke with an electrician as his helper, giving him an application by "word of mouth", which consisted of my name, past experience, and a telephone number. The electrician could not use me at that time, but took the information anyway.

About two weeks later, a plumber, whom I shall name Nick, (He had a last name of "Plumb") called me, saying that he needed a helper immediately. I began meeting Nick in the mornings in order to ride with him to wherever it was we needed to work that day. I thought Nick was a great guy; he seemed to be very smart about plumbing.

I had not talked with Nick about working for him, so I was curious as to how he was able to get my phone number. He told me that the electrician, who I gave my name and number to, was a friend of his, and that he was over at his friend's house telling him of how bad he needed a helper due to all of the plumbing business he had on the books. The electrician told Nick about me, and how I had applied for a job with him, but that he did not need a helper at that time. Nick asked his friend if he still had my number, to which the friend told him that he threw my number in the trash; Nick told me that he dug my number out of the trash, and that was how he got my number. I was shocked that he would go through a man's trash just to get my phone number. Nick said he did not like digging in other people's trash, but he needed a helper in a bad way. He was right about that.

Nick was a very nice man, a Christian man.

Nick started me out at $10 per hour, then, a week later, he saw how good a worker I was and raised me to $11 per hour. I was blessed.

NO! NOT THAT WAY!

I did not know the first thing about plumbing. I knew that you turned the faucet on and water came out; I also knew that you flushed the toilet, and the waste went away. Neil found that out the hard way. We were plumbing a home that was being newly built.

Nick told me to "cut a hole in the floor of the bathroom for the stool." I had no idea what he wanted me to do. Therefore, I got a saw-zall and went to work. After connection the power source to the saw, I began cutting a hole in the floor for the toilet. The only problem was, I was cutting the hole for the whole toilet, which was too big. Nick came in to check on my progress and saw how I was cutting a hole actually big enough for the toilet to fit through, not the toilet flange that the toilet sits on. He exclaimed, "No! Not like that! What are you doing?!" Feeling about as big as an ant at the moment, I shrieked, "I am cutting a hole in the floor for the toilet like you said!" He told me to move so he could fix my mistake. I learned a valuable lesson that day.

Later, I discovered that I have a knack for plumbing.

THIS IS STILL NOT WORKING OUT!

I continued living in the trailer house outside of town that Danny allowed me to live in for the moment.

When I came back from Colorado, I saw that Susan continued to let her hair grow long as I had requested. Susan even finished the construction on the house I set on her property, completing the task with her own money; she even moved some of her clothes into the home. When Danny gave me a tour of the home, he said she just could not live there alone. Susan put the house up for sale. That was all well and good, but still, I could not help feeling as if I was being used by Danny and Susan for my farm labor, and that I would be trapped, and not able to live for Jesus Christ as He created me to live.

Susan seemed to be very overly friendly with Danny, all the time. At times, I felt as if Danny's wife was upset with jealousy at the closeness of the two. I felt sorry for his wife.

As a result, I decided to move back to town.

I met another man name Kevin, in the church that I began attending when I came back from Colorado. Kevin was also single. He agreed to allow me to be his roommate.

I tried to move to town under the radar, but Susan saw the U-Haul at the trailer house and stopped to see what I was doing. I point-blank asked her at that time if she could ever fall in love with me and leave Danny behind. I knew my answer when I she got a bewildered look in her eyes while shaking her head from left to right in a manner that said "No." It was a sad moment, but a sober moment. If I ever had a chance at winning Susan's love, that chance just got packed into a steel vault.

CHAPTER SEVEN: A Jesus Freak

"...he continued kneeling on his knees three times a day, praying and giving thanks before his God..."(Daniel 6:10).

I was still hot on the heels of Jesus Christ as one of His disciples.

Kevin, my new roommate, was a very devoted Christian as well. I was very thankful for Kevin. He had a sharp mind when it came to knowing what the Bible teaches, and he seemed like he did not have a care in the world. He was always mellow, wise, and had a determined faith. He had an ability to teach the Bible in a calm, peaceful manner.

Kevin was a musician. He played the guitar and sang; as well, he led the worship service in church.

Kevin was the assistant pastor of the church. This helped me stay focused on the spiritual side of life, and it gave me someone to be accountable with in my faith walk.

I began attending the same church that Kevin attended. I was in church every time the doors were open.

As well, I listened to several different pastors on the radio. Each pastor would teach the Bible for fifteen-minute intervals each.

One particular pastor that I listened to, named Billy Joe, taught me that we should read God's Word and make personal confessions from the verses we read. I began writing Scripture references on index cards, making God's Word personal to me.

However, for some reason, I was spiritually anxious. As a child of God, it seemed that I was a spoiled brat. I can only attest it to the fact that I had seen the raw, supernatural power of God work in my life; I wanted what I wanted, when I wanted it, and I expected God to give it to me, immediately. Thus, God did give me what "I" wanted, for a while, but, in the end, it only resulted in heartache, turmoil, and even death.

OKAY! YOU CAN HAVE THAT!

I was given the opportunity to work within the famous outdoor stage production called the Great Passion Play. The play is a live performance of the last week that Jesus Christ lived on the earth, just before His ascension to Heaven. I played a Roman temple guard, as well as, I was a part of the crowd that shouted "Crucify Him! Crucify Him!" at the trial and conviction of Jesus Christ, just before He was forced to carry His Cross to His crucifixion. Although I was paid a little money, the money had nothing to do with my part in the play; I was not an actor, and I knew it. Being in the play was more about being a part of something bigger than I was; being with other people who believed in Jesus Christ as I did.

One thing I remember about being in the play was that it was a bit chilly at night. Thus, at the suggestion of a co-player, I wore panty hose under the Roman guard skirt that I wore. Although it felt weird to be wearing the panty hose, they kept me warm.

It was about this time (mid to end of summer, 2001) when I became frustrated with God. Yes, He brought me back from Colorado with Susan on my mind, but after I was back with Susan, it just did not feel right. Therefore, I vacated the idea of ever marrying Susan because it felt like a trap.

One day, as I drove home from work, I was thinking about all that had transpired since God supernaturally saved me on June 28th of 2000.

When I went to church, I saw how happy the married couples seemed to be; how loving they were to their children.

I could not help think about how I wanted a wife and children just as the other men had. It made me feel insecure, as if there was something wrong with me. Thus, in my frustration that day, I screamed at God with a vehement anger, "Why can't I have a wife and children like everybody else?!" After shedding a few tears, I forgot all about it.

GOD, ARE YOU SURE ABOUT THIS?!

It was about a month later and the seasons were about to change from summer to fall.

The cast of the Passion Play were practicing for some special event that would be happening near the end of the play. There were extra cast members there, who were brought in from area churches, practicing for the special event along with us. I was sitting on the side bench waiting for my part to come up for practice when, suddenly, a young woman plopped down on the bench to my left. I was shocked and almost appalled at how this woman, name Mary, just sat down next to me, when there was not really enough room for her to sit. There was another young woman sitting on my left, but she was keeping her distance from me, as a good Christian girl should.

This young woman was just that, young, twenty years young, soon to turn twenty-one.

At this time, I was thirty-three going on thirty-four years young.

With the bluntness of Mary batting her eyes at me, we began talking. I kept thinking to myself, "Who is this girl?!"

I asked Mary if she I could take her to eat something after the practice. She told me that I would need to take her family as well, so I agreed. The dinner out with Mary and her family cost me a whopping $70 that day, but I kept my face in check as I opened my wallet and paid the food bill.

Mary was one of the "extras" I mentioned above.

It was actually her pastor (or Rabbi as they called him) who was heading up the special event.

I discovered that Mary lived over an hour away from me in the state of Missouri. Mary gave me her phone number, and I agreed to call her each day so we could talk.

I did call her every day to talk with her, finding out things as our birthdays were in the same month, only days apart; she had yet to marry or have children; she lived with her family who were a part of the Messianic Jewish religion, and that was why they referred to their pastor as Rabbi Jordan.

I was the type of person who did not like making mistakes. I was constantly checking myself to make sure I was doing the right thing.

As a follower of Jesus Christ, this type of mindset, can hinder a child of God because people who think like that have a tendency to walk in fear more than they walk in faith, and it takes faith to please God.

Thus, I prayed to God every day for two weeks straight, asking Him if he wanted me to marry this woman. His answer was "Yes" every day.

I made up my mind and asked Mary to marry me, to which she said yes. We agreed to be married on her grandmother's birthday—December 28th of 2001.

At the guidance of Mary's friend, we partook of some marriage counseling. The counselor asked us if we were sure we wanted to get married, and with googly eyes, we both said "Yes."

Before it was all said and done, I would regret the day I screamed at God in disrespect—"Why can't I have a wife and children like everybody else?!". I had heard before, "Be careful what you ask God for, you might just get it." I had to change that saying to "Be careful what you scream at God, He may just give it to you." This was the second time I screamed at God, next to the time in 1992 when He supernaturally set me free from alcohol.

One thing worth mentioning here is that the night I took Mary and her family out for dinner, I came home and began telling Kevin about the day, and how I met this girl, but before I told him my new girlfriend's name, he blurted her name out. I was shocked that he knew her name before I told him. I have no idea how he knew because he was not with me at the practice when I met Mary.

On the weekends, I traveled back and forth to Mary's house so we could visit. We talked and prayed together.

I would attend Messianic church services with her and her family. I thoroughly enjoyed being in the services because Rabbi Jordan carried an anointing on him from the Lord.

During one particular service, myself, along with several other members of the congregation, heard a heavenly sound coming from the band. It was such a brief miracle, that one would have missed it if they were not "in tune" with the Spirit of God. As Rabbi Jordan led the worship that day, we heard angels toot their trumpets in the background while the band played music. We knew it was angels because there were not any trumpets in the band.

A PROPHETIC ANOINTING

It was during this time that God allowed me to prophecy the birth of our first two children. Mary and I were sitting in my vehicle when the Spirit impressed upon me to speak saying, "You (I was talking to Mary) will be pregnant very close to the first night of the honeymoon. You will be pregnant with a girl first, then a boy second. The girl's name shall be Angel, and the boy's name shall be Alexander." It happened exactly as I prophesied; we were married the last of December of 2001, and Angel was born ten months later in October of 2002.

Mary's mother was a pest about Angel being born first. It seemed as if every time I saw her mother, she would say, "John. I believe the baby will be a boy." I held my ground telling her, "No. It is a girl first, then the boy." I could not understand why she kept trying to argue with me about the gender of our first firstborn child. I grew tired of her attempts to change my mind and blew up in her face, telling her that I was tired of her saying that the baby would be a boy first. I upset everybody in the house.

THE WEDDING

We went all out on this wedding. Mary's father bought her a wedding gown, and I rented a tuxedo. The wedding was scheduled to be performed by Rabbi Jordan at the church I attended with Kevin. There was lots of food and most people brought gifts. Amazingly, Danny came to the wedding, but understandingly, I did not see Susan there with Danny.

We had a professional photographer shoot the photos.

We even incorporated some Jewish wedding traditions into the ceremony. I do not remember exactly what traditions we partook of, except the light bulb tradition where a light bulb is wrapped in a hand towel, or equivalent, and placed on the floor in a dish, then, the man steps on the light bulb and breaks it with his foot.

There seems to be several reasons for this tradition. One reason is to remember that where there is joy, there is pain. Also, as glass is fragile, so is the marriage. In continuance, being married is a covenant, and in Judaism, a covenant is signed by both parties with the breaking or cutting of something; thus is the tradition of the breaking of the light bulb. Finally, the breaking of the light bulb also symbolizes the breaking of the bride's hymen during the first night of the honeymoon.

AMERICA IS UNDER ATTACK!

I progressed in plumbing experience as I continued working for Nick.

By this time, I had so many index cards of written confessions with God's Word on them that I had to take them to work and make my confessions while I waited for Nick to work out the day's schedule.

Our usual day began with going to the plumbing supply store in order to get the necessary parts we needed for the job or jobs we had to do that day. If Nick did not need my help with carrying out the supplies, I would sit in the truck and finish saying the confession cards while I waited for Nick.

He usually left the radio playing while he was inside. One particular day, September 11th of 2001 to be exact, I was doing just that, sitting in the cab of the truck waiting for

Nick, when suddenly, I heard the DJ announce, "A plane has just hit one of the Twin Towers of the World Trade Center. We are not sure if this is an accident or what is going on, but I repeat, an airplane has just hit one of the Twin Towers of the World Trade Center." Panic filled my mind as I continued to listen to the radio.

At that time, I knew very little about New York and the World Trade Center; in fact, I had barely even heard of the Twin Towers.

When Nick returned to the truck and climbed in, I told him what I just heard on the radio. He became alarmed as well. Nick wasn't for sure what it all meant at the time, but he decided that it might be a good idea if he filled his pickup up with fuel in case this catastrophe caused a shortage.

It did not come to that extreme over the next few days, but what did come of the attack in the aftermath was sad and horrendous. As in the bombing of Pearl Harbor,

America was taken by surprise once again.

George Bush was America's president at this time. A year or so later, I felt led by the Spirit of God to encourage Mr. Bush in sending him a letter and telling him to "...keep going Mr. President; keep fighting; you are doing a great job for America..." I was totally taken aback when I received a letter from the office of the President a month or so after that thanking me for the letter, and encouraging me just the same.

I would like to add my condolences to the families who lost loved ones in this senseless, brutal attack of 9/11. I assure you, the terrorists who carried out the attack have met their Maker, God Almighty, and justice has served them their doom in the lake of fire.

HONEY, GOD SAID MOVE

Prior to the time Mary and I were married, I moved from Kevin's house to an apartment.

It was in this apartment where Mary and I began our honeymoon, and where Angel was conceived. Although this was my third marriage, I was still young and had a lot to learn about love, compassion, mercy, and God.

I continued confessing the Scriptures from the index cards, as well as religiously listening to the fifteen-minute preachers on the radio.

I am sure you have heard of these preachers: Joyce Meyer, Kenneth Hagin, Andrew Wammack, Kenneth and his wife Gloria Copeland, Creflo Dollar, John Bevere, John Hagee, Billie Brim, Oral and his son Richard Roberts, and Billy Joe and his wife Sharon Daughtery.

I listened to most of these preachers on the radio, but it was Billy Joe Daughtery and Joyce Meyer who God used to help shape my faith at that time.

I was especially drawn to Billy Joe; he and his wife Sharon, pastored Victory Christian Center, now known as Victory Church, one of the biggest churches in Tulsa, Oklahoma.

Billy Joe has since passed on to be with the Lord, and his son Paul, has since taken over his father's role as senior pastor.

I listened to Billy Joe just about every day. In January of 2002, God spoke to me and told us to move to Tulsa, Oklahoma, and attend Victory Christian Center.

I did not argue with God this time because there was nothing in that little town to keep me held down. If anything, I had more embarrassing moments to get away from than joy-filled ones. As well, there were more chances for opportunities in Tulsa because it is a town almost seventy-five times bigger than the little town of Berryville where we were living. I was excited about the move because I was a God chaser then; anything God wanted me to do, that is what I did, and with full steam ahead. If I heard God speak to me and tell me to do something, I did it. My legs might be shaking from fear, and my voice cracking, but I did whatever I believed God told me to do; and it did not matter whom I had to go through to get it done, no matter what it cost me. That is still the case today.

I have learned since then that God will lead His children into situations to prove to their selves what is in their hearts. God already knows what we will do before we get to any situation. However, it is WE who do not know how we will react until we get to that situation. Some of those situations are also meant to teach us how to walk in faith or to show us what God is requiring us to change in our own hearts. Some of those situations deal with mindsets we acquire throughout our childhood and into adulthood.

In the book of Romans, chapter twelve, and verse two of the Holy Bible, the Apostle Paul wrote—"And do not be conformed to this world, but be transformed by the renewing of your mind, so that you may prove what the will of God is…"

We also must be tested to see WHO or WHAT we will serve—Jesus Christ or the world.

One example from my life is in the fact that I grew up not learning what true love is; true love according to God's love.

The love my natural father showed me was in the form of abandonment, as well, the love my mother showed me was scorn, frustration, non-patience, and disgust.

That is not the way God loves us. God's love is described in chapter thirteen of First Corinthians, in the Holy Bible. I will write about some of the "life lessons" I went through, and what they taught me about "how" to love people as Jesus Christ loves people.

As Christians, we have two natures battling within us—the spirit and the flesh. The flesh nature is selfish, and always wants revenge for the wrongs it thinks it has suffered.

However, the spirit is giving, and suffers to its own hurt, if necessary; always forgiving, always humble.

God will also lead you into situations to teach you "how" to forgive those who hurt you. The world's forgiveness is this: "I will forgive, but I will never forget." If one can't forget a wrong done to them, the "wrong" continues to fester inside their heart, causing that person to hold hard feelings toward those who hurt them. That is not God's way of forgiving. God's way of forgiving is that He forgives us, then, He removes the wrong we committed from us; as far as the east is from the west is how far God removes our wrongs (Psalm 103:12). To me, that is God "forgetting" what I did wrong. Thank you Father.

WEST BOUND, LOADED UP AND MOVING

I had a little Mazda B2200 pickup that we loaded with most of my belongings, along with a small U-Haul trailer we packed to the gills with many of Mary's furnishings. Then, we said our goodbyes and left Berryville, headed for Tulsa.

Mary had $6,000 dollars saved when we got married, so we had no worries about how we would rent a place to live when we got there.

When we got to Tulsa, we stopped at a convenient store in order to decide our next move. I was exceptionally concerned with being victims of a crime or something of that nature due to the size of Tulsa. However, after getting to Tulsa and meeting a few people, my fears subsided.

We began with finding Victory Christian Center so we could see the church we would be attending. From the looks of the church building, it did not look like one of the biggest churches in Tulsa, but after we attended our first service, we knew better.

Then, we got a newspaper so we could look for a place to live.

We wanted to live relatively close to the church so we did not have far to drive or much traffic to maneuver. We quickly found that we could not just drive into a big city and expect to rent a place to live immediately, there were applications to fill out, along with background checks and all that goes with that process. There were some apartments within five minutes of the church, but they were a bit out of our price range. We finally found an apartment complex about fifteen minutes away that had a two-bedroom apartment for rent. We rented an apartment there and settled in.

We then went shopping for the rest of the necessary furnishings that our lives required. I needed a shelving unit so I could display my mini rock collection. I am sure the neighbors thought I was crazy when I drug Big Boy (the 150 lb. volcanic rock mentioned earlier) up the staircase in a blanket to the second floor where the apartment was located. Thankfully, back then, I had a back that was able to carry Pretty Boy (the other 100 lb. oil-shell rock) up the stairs. Now, when I move the rocks, I use a utility dolly to load and unload them from the truck, then, I roll them to where I want them to sit, instead of carrying them.

We also bought a desk with desktop computer. That is where I began the first writing of this book before I shelved it due to lack of confidence in my writing skills; I just could not get the words typed out properly.

LET THE SERVICE BEGIN

After we were settled into the apartment, we were eager to get to church and get started meeting the people and serving where we were allowed to fit in. We were quickly plugged in; Mary was placed in the nursery helping with the children, and I found my place on the usher team. That is the place of service I wanted to be in when I first walked into that church in Colorado; I had found my niche.

There was not much to being an usher—greet at the door before service, keep an eye on the crowd during the service, pass the offering buckets when the pastor called for the ushers to do so, be available to catch people if they fell under the power of the Spirit during the altar call, and clean up after service.

I especially liked the head usher at Victory because he was well organized with how the ushering should be carried out. In the past twenty years, it is the best ushering system I have seen at any church I have attended. Most churches that I have attended over the years do not even have an ushering system. Many times, I wanted to implement an ushering system at several churches where I attended, but nobody was interested in it.

Anytime the doors were open, we served in our respected duties.

As well, Victory held services in the Oral Roberts Mabee Center on Sundays, which was across the street from the Victory church building that housed the rollaway sanctuary-slash-Victory School.

It was at our first Mabee Center service that we saw just how big Victory Church was (and still is).

Then, we found out that Victory also had a Victory Bible Institute (a Bible college) about a block away from where we lived.

On top of that, Victory established what they call the Dream Center in North Tulsa; a place that Victory established to help the poverty-stricken area of Tulsa.

I acquired a class B CDL endorsement on my driver's license and began bussing the homeless people from the shelters of downtown Tulsa out to the Dream Center for services.

As well, I bussed children from the low-income housing parts of town to the Saturday afternoon services held at the Bible College. Seeing those children come from the run-down homes and get on the bus with excitement made my day. It was such a blessing to see the children have brief moments of joy. Victory would order pizza from a local pizzeria and hand out slices of pizza to the children as they exited the bus at their homes. It was sad to know that the pizza may just have been the only meal the children had that day. Life was good.

TIME TO GO TO WORK

Mary's savings did not last forever, and it became time for me to find a job. I went to work for a large plumbing outfit called All American Plumbing. The owner did not look like a businessman; he looked like a biker-dude with his long grey hair and beard. He looked more like an owner of a beer joint, rather than a thriving plumbing company. The job was a good job though.

I worked out in the field as a helper for some time until the supervisor saw that I was a man of detail. I advanced to the position of warehouse manager. I would go to the various jobsites and get a parts list from the crew foremen; then, I would fill the orders.

On top of that, I kept the warehouse clean and organized, while once a week, I would wash and detail the five company crew trucks that the men used to travel to and from the jobsites.

I enjoyed working for this company until they went against their word and terminated me.

THE HOLY SPIRIT ALARM CLOCK

During prayer one morning, the Holy Spirit said, "Let Me be your alarm clock." I was afraid at first because I did not want to wake up too late, thus, making me late for work. At the time, I had no idea that the Holy Spirit was training me to trust Him. I agreed to let Him be my alarm clock and He never let me down; He is always faithful.

GOD AS MY REAL FATHER?!

From my study of God's Holy Word, I learned that God was "our" Father. I could understand that. Jesus Christ talked a lot about God being His Father, which God was His real Father, but when it came to me believing that God wanted to be my "real" Father, that was a different story. I was stunned for a time. My mind just could not fathom how this great big God wanted to be my personal Father.

Some Scriptures about God being our Father, that I studied, come to mind from the Holy Bible—Romans 8:14-17, "For all who are being led by the Spirit of God, these are sons of God. For you have not received a spirit of slavery leading to fear again, but you have received a spirit of adoption as sons by which we cry out, 'Abba! Father!' The Spirit

Himself testifies with our spirit that we are children of God, and if children, heirs also, heirs of God and fellow heirs with Christ..." Then, God blew my mind with this verse of Scripture, "A father of the fatherless...is God in His holy habitation." (Psalm 68:5). When I saw that verse, my chin dropped so far to the floor, you could have crammed an elephant in it! I had been a "fatherless child" because my natural father abandoned me before I was born!

Thus, I began referring to the man who conceived me as "my natural father", and of God as, "my real Father."

Although I saw this truth, it would be a few years before I actually believed that the Almighty God was my real Father, as well, a few more years past that before I believed that this same Almighty God actually loved me as His "real son."

Now, I refer to God as just "my Father." Plus, I really don't care what people think about it because it is the truth.

NO DOCTORS!

While I worked for All American Plumbing, I experienced a health problem that brought severe pain to my body. When the problem first began, I had no idea what was going on, all I knew was that the pain made me double over and roll on the floor or bed crying out in agony.

I had the same problem back when I worked for Tyson Foods. After I transferred inside the chicken plant, I had the same double-over pain, which sent me to the infirmary. I rolled and rolled in the floor crying out for the nurse to give me something for the pain, but the nurse had no idea what to do for me.

This time, I did not know why I was having the pain again. I prayed and prayed to God, asking Him what He wanted me to do about the pain. His answer was that He wanted me to depend only on Him for my physical healings. However, the pain became so severe, that I disobeyed God and drove myself to the emergency room. Once inside the ER, the nurse put me on a stretcher in a room by myself. I was in so much pain that I just hollered at the nurse saying, "Can you not see that I am in pain! Aren't you going to give me anything for this pain?!" They simply replied, "We will be with you when we can Mr. Jackson."

I did not receive anything for the pain that night, but a big fat hospital bill worth about $1,800+! I remember going to God in prayer about the hospital bill, and I can still hear Him say, "Son, are you going to trust the stripes of Jesus Christ for your healings now, or the doctors?" Right then and there, I made up my mind to trust God for my physical healings. I have been tested time and time again.

After I passed the kidney stone that was lodged in my urinary track, the pain subsided.

Then, over the course of the next few months, God tested me with three more kidney stones. The symptoms became apparent and I knew when a bout with a stone was happening.

When the second fight came, I had a little trouble overcoming the stone, but I eventually passed that test.

The third fight with a kidney stone came while Mary and I were sitting in a restaurant having breakfast with her parents. I excused myself to the restroom and told the devil that I was in no wise way giving into his attack.

The fourth and final stone of that series of battles came one day while I was at work.

The supervisor and I were sitting in the company pickup waiting to meet with some businessmen when I felt the symptoms coming on. I had nowhere to go in order to command it to leave me alone, so, I sat there in the pickup speaking under my breath to the stone, telling it to leave me alone. The stone obeyed my command and I did not have another problem with another stone until 2015.

HOW GOD SHAPED MY FAITH

The Holy Bible teaches this, "So, faith comes from hearing, and hearing by the word of Christ." (Romans 10:17). Thus, if you want to increase your faith, read the Holy Bible.

On top of that, you can study the lives of great men and women of the faith who have passed before you and proven the "words of Christ."

For me, the Holy Spirit led me to study great men and women of the faith as John G. Lake, Smith Wigglesworth, John Dowie, Aimee Semple McPherson, Maria Woodworth-Etter, Kathryn Kuhlman, and Benny Hinn. All of these that I have mentioned were (At the time of this writing, Benny is still a healing evangelist) great men and women of God who walked in God's power to heal. In the beginning, I was not sure why I became mesmerized with these faith healers.

I was especially fascinated with John G. Lake and what God did through his ministry. John opened what was called "healing rooms" In Washington State. At one time, more people were going to John's healing rooms than were going to the local hospitals. Spokane, Washington was known as the healthiest city in America, and maybe the world.

One of my favorite stories about John G. Lake, my second earthly hero, next to Jesus Christ, is when he was ministering in South Africa and the Bubonic Plague broke out.

Britain sent doctors with supplies to the area where John was helping take care of the sick.

The doctors asked Mr. Lake how he was protecting himself from the plague. I love the answer John gave when he said, "I believe 'the law of the Spirit of life has set me free from the law of sin and death (Rom.8:2).' As long as I walk in the light of that law [of the Spirit of life], no germ will attach itself to me."

Everything about God is by faith. John G. Lake was exerting his faith against an evil force that was killing people. Even though Mr. Lake explained the Gospel to the doctors, they were not convinced. In turn, John told them to observe some cells of the Bubonic Plague under a microscope and they would see the germ staying alive (No pun intended John Travolta). However, John instructed the doctors to take the same germ, put it on his hand, and then observe the miracle under the microscope of the germ dying on his hand. When I read that about Mr. Lake, it seemed as if his faith just leaped off the page and into my heart. I felt that if a man, as in John G. Lake, could believe God's Word and see results like that, I could believe the same Word and see results like that.

I feel it appropriate to talk about just that very thing here, called COVID-19 (Coronavirus). If you just read that statement, you will have heard about this deadly disease by now.

The virus began in Wuhan, Hubei Province, China where the experts believe a bat infected a reservoir of seafood/live-animal market, giving way to animal-to-person spread. The disease has infected some 144,500 people across the world from China to America, claiming some 5000 lives across the same. They are calling the virus a pandemic.

The virus spreads through a person's cough spit. The disease can cling to a surface for a couple of days. When a person touches the infected area, in turn touching their mouth, face or eyes, they contract the Coronavirus and spread it further.

As of today, March 15, 2020, businesses are shutting down across America. People are being quarantined in mass numbers. Many businesses are asking employees to work from home, and if a worker feels sick, to go to the doctor and take a test for COVID-19; if they are infected, stay home.

Considering how I believe as John G. Lake believed, in Jesus Christ and His power, I have already taken spiritual measures and prayed against the Coronavirus attaching itself to me or any place I walk into. As well, the virus will not attach itself to any of my family. In the Name of Jesus Christ. Amen.

President Donald Trump set March 15, 2020 as a national day for prayer.

I love our President. President Trump is a straightforward type of guy. The way he sees it, is the way he calls it.

One thing I love about our president is the fact that he walks by faith.

Did I mention that Mr. President Trump is a billionaire of the United States? Yeah. He is a billionaire. That perked my interest towards him when he signed up to run for the next president. He knows a thing or two about money; just what America needed. His money skills have spoken for himself as well. The national unemployment rate dropped into the 3.6 category, the lowest it has been in fifty years. We love you Mr. President.

Smith Wigglesworth is another one of my favorites because his life and ministry brings me hope in that God is not finished with me. Mr. Wigglesworth was 48 years old before God baptized him with His Holy Spirit fire and he began to preach and heal in the name of Jesus.

Smith's wife preached before he did because he had a speech impediment and would not take the stage.

He was also a plumber until God began to use him to heal the sick.

As well, Mr. Wigglesworth brought the dead back to life on a number of occasions.

These men and women's anointing resonated with the anointing that God has placed inside of my spirit. Through my study of these men and women, I discovered that my passion is to see the sick healed by God's supernatural power. When I see or hear of someone sick, crippled, blind, deaf, maim, or have just died, everything in my being screams, "Be healed in the Name of Jesus Christ!" Or "Your dead can be raised to life again! Do you not know this?!" My problem is that I get anxious and want to jump out of the fire God has me in and make my calling happen before God's timing.

Christian, search within yourself, what are you passionate about? Follow the Spirit.

ANGEL WENT BREACH?!

After Mary and I got moved to Tulsa and settled into our routine lives, besides working every day for the plumber, I focused on prayer and the study of the Holy Bible; specifically the Gospels of the New Testament. I had heard the text of Matthew 26:40 preached enough that I felt it very important for me to pray at least one hour each day. As well, in giving my best attempt to follow the teachings of Jesus Christ to the T, I spent at least an hour of every morning in my "inner room" (Some teach "prayer closet") of our bedroom as Jesus instructed according to Matthew 6:6.

I also studied fasting, and as a result, felt led by God's Spirit to complete a series of fasts (When a person abstains from food or a daily habit). The Spirit instructed me to complete a three-day fast, a seven-day fast, a fourteen-day fast, a twenty-one day fast, and a forty-day fast.

Through the instructions of a Christian friend, I learned that when fasting, one must begin slow and condition the body before jumping into the forty-day fast; as well, when coming out of a fast, it was wise to eat a soft, light meal for the first meal, and continue eating soft foods until the body is back to normal.

Thus, I completed all the fasting, including the forty-day fast.

Little did I know, this was teaching and training me for an important fast, a very important twenty-one day fast.

The doctor set an expected due date for Angel on or about October 28th of 2002.

I knew the truth about Halloween and I despise this day that the world considers a holiday. There is nothing good about Halloween.

I believed by faith that I should fast twenty-one days during the time that Angel was to be born. I did not want Angel born anywhere near the devil's day. I felt very strong about Angel's birthday being a couple of weeks before or after Halloween, but not close nor on that date.

Therefore, I started the fast about two weeks before October 31st of 2002, and looked to end a couple of weeks after Angel's birth, causing her to be born a couple of weeks after Halloween.

At some point during the twenty-one day fast, a couple of church friends invited us to their home for a baby shower to celebrate the anticipated birth of Angel. All was well until they brought out the cake they had prepared.

I learned from Jesus not to tell people when we are fasting, but to wash our faces and anoint our heads so we do not appear to be fasting to other people, thus, I did not want to tell our friends that I was fasting.

At the same time, I did not want to hurt their feelings by not eating any cake. Yeah. You probably guessed it by now; I ate a piece of cake and broke the fast. With the first bite of cake, I knew that the devil got the best of me and that I did something very bad by breaking the fast.

Jesus Christ teaches, "Keep watching and praying that you may not enter into temptation; the spirit is willing, but the flesh is weak." (Matthew 26:41). I believed by faith that I was on the right track; my spirit was willing and able to carry out the fast. However, my flesh was weak, and when temptation came, I failed because I did not watch and pray.

I had no idea what the full repercussion of my mistake was until Mary's water broke about 11 PM on the evening of October 30th, 2002.

We rushed to the hospital and the nurses on staff checked to see how much Mary was dilated.

The next thing I knew, one nurse said, "She is breach! She needs an emergency C-section!"

Then, in horror, I watched them roll Mary down a hallway with me following. When they got to the end of the hallway just before the elevator, one nurse said, "Sir! I need you to wait in the waiting room!" I replied, "But I want to be with my wife!" To which she exerted "Sir! You can't be in the operating room with your wife! Please wait in the waiting room! We will come get you when everything is okay." As Mary was being rolled away, I looked into her face and saw a fear as I have never seen, nor want to see again.

By then, the time was closing in on Midnight and the clock was about to strike the hour of Halloween.

Unfortunately, for me, I became vehemently angry with God. Somehow, I thought it was God's fault, when it was really my fault.

I did not want to be in the presence of any people, so I went into a dark empty patient room and sat down in a dark place. As soon as I sat down, the tears began to flow uncontrollably.

I do my best to forget about that moment, because, at times, the tears still flow uncontrollably (As they are right now). At that moment, I told God, "I don't know if I will ever get over this, or if I can ever forgive You."

The hospital recorded Angel's birth at 1:55 AM, on October 31st, 2002.

Don't get me wrong, when the nurse brought Angel out and called my name, then laid Angel in my arms, I looked at my new baby girl and thought, "Oh my God! What do I do with this baby?!"

A love came into my heart for Angel, and I brought her to my chest and cradled her, until she was ripped from my arms three years later.

The Holy Bible teaches: "And we know that God causes all things to work together for good to those who love God, to those who are called according to His purpose." (Romans 8:28). I felt as if the fast leading up to Angel's birth turned out for my bad, and I could not see any good coming out of it in the end.

TRAIN YOUR CHILD UP IN THE WAY THEY SHOULD GO

I loved Angel more than anything else in the world, and Jesus for that matter. I was very protective of her; she was like gold to me. That was bad in a way because I had read in the Holy Bible where Jesus said, "If anyone comes to Me and does not hate his own father and mother and wife and children and brothers and sisters, yes, and even his own life, he cannot be My disciple…So then, none of you can be My disciple who does not give up all his own possessions." (Luke 14:26, 33). I did not realize that I loved Angel more than I loved Jesus Christ.

At church, I would not allow Angel to watch any of the silly cartoons as in Veggie Tales; I would go get her when they began showing the nonsense and set her out in the auditorium with me while I finished with the usher's clean-up duties.

I was very stern with Angel about being obedient as well. In my studies of the book of Proverbs of the Holy Bible, I understood that a child is to be disciplined and kept under control; therefore, I was overbearing at times in my attempt to keep Angel "in line."

As I wrote earlier, I had a lot to learn about love, and the way God loves us. I had yet to fully understand what the Holy Spirit of God meant when He inspired the writer to pen, "There is no fear in love; but perfect love casts out fear..." (First John 4:18). The way I "loved" was coming from a spirit of fear. I was afraid to release Angel to the care of God because I was not familiar with God's way of love. Thus, as Angel sat out in the auditorium waiting for me to finish my work, I had to check on her every three minutes because I was afraid she would disobey me. As I look back on it now, I was very immature. At all cost, "I" had to make sure Angel obeyed me, or else. I laugh now thinking, "Or else what?"

I realize now that I was a cruel father to Angel, even if Jesus Christ wanted me to forsake all and follow Him.

At home, I did my best to keep Angel's heart pure, guarding her from nonsense television. The rule of the house was that Angel could not watch anything on TV but spiritual programming. She loved watching the Christian program called The Hour of Healing with Richard Roberts. Angel would stand five feet away from the television in anticipation to watch the show. I took too much pride in my ability to control what she could watch.

I went as far as not allowing any toys in the house with the word "magic" on them; nor did I allow Angel to view The Chronicles of Narnia or anything of the sort.

JESUS CHRIST WANTS YOU!

All American Plumbing Company gave me paternity leave when Angel was born, then, about three weeks into the leave from work, the supervisor came to the apartment and informed me that they changed their minds and hired someone else to replace me; demanding the keys to the company vehicle I was allowed to drive to and from work.

This was one of those situations where I had to implement God's concept of forgiveness.

I was hurt for a little bit before picking myself back up and finding another place of employment.

That is one thing I liked about the big city, if you lose one job, you can most likely find another job by the end of the day, or week at the most.

I went to work for another smalltime plumber. His business, Patrick Plumbing, was not anywhere near as big as All American Plumbing. I lasted about three months with Patrick Plumbing before he termed me for bragging about applying for a better job, which never panned out. What I thought was "faith" talk, turned out to be arrogant pride.

I found yet another plumber's helper position with another smalltime company in a nearby town.

The drive to and from work was about a thirty-minute drive in congested traffic, but it was an income that provided a living for my wife and new baby girl.

I enjoyed working for this company. The work was easy. The business owner had a large contract to plumb new houses as they were constructed within a good size housing addition. The contract called for him to plumb the houses from start to finish, which afforded him work from months to a couple of years. I was set with long-term income except for one thing, I was a disciple of Jesus Christ, and I felt as if I should be a witness to the job foreman.

Andy was a youngster. Don't get me wrong, he was a very nice young man who taught me a lot about plumbing. I felt as if he needed to accept Jesus Christ as his personal Savior, and I set my heart on getting him saved, every day. I was constantly in his face with "Jesus loves you! He wants you to be saved! Jesus wants you to serve Him now!" In being a young snot-nose son of God myself, I did not realize how irritating I must have been to him.

In the end, he invited me to his house for "some fun and food." I had an uneasy feeling about accepting the invitation; something just did not feel right, so I turned down his invitation. It was not long until I was termed from that job also.

WHOA! THAT'S A MIRACLE!

Before I was termed from that job, God had a surprise for the foreman whom I was hounding with the Gospel; for that matter, it was a total surprise for me as well. This was the first raw supernatural miracle (without human involvement or persuasion) I witnessed

God perform up to this date.

We were meeting at a co-worker's house and riding together in the company pickup to the jobsite. One particular day, after we finished the day's work, the foreman dropped me off at the co-worker's house, then, for security reasons, he and the co-worker took the tool trailer to the owner's house so they could leave the trailer there.

I was tired and ready to get home to see my baby girl.

However, when I climbed into my B2200 Mazda and twisted the key to start the engine, nothing happened. I thought to myself, "Aw man! What now?!" I had never had a problem with the pickup up to that moment and had no idea what could be the problem. I twisted the key a few more times with no results.

The headlight switch caught my eye, and I realized that I forgot to turn the headlights off when I arrived at the co-worker's house that morning; the battery was dead.

My mind raced with thoughts of how I was going to get home to my wife and new baby.

The street I parked on had a slight downhill incline to it, so I decided to push the pickup backwards in order to use the clutch to start the engine. I pushed and pushed, then jumped inside the cab and popped the clutch, but I could not get the engine to start.

The street ended and I found myself sitting in the cab of the pickup wondering what to do next.

I had noticed a young teenager, about twelve years old, watching me push the pickup.

When I wound up stranded in front of his house with nowhere to go except back up the inclined street, I asked the boy if he would help me push the pickup. Together, we could not get it moving fast enough for me to clutch start the engine. I thanked the boy, telling him that it was no use pushing any more.

I was at my wits end when I saw the foreman dropping the co-worker off at his house. I frantically waived at him to come down to where I was stranded. He sped down and asked me if he could help me. I told him that I left the headlights on and it drained the battery. He was eager to help and jumped out of his pickup to get the jumper cables for me. After he raised the hood on his pickup, he got back into the cab of his truck. I hooked the black cable clamp to the negative post of his battery, then, hooked the positive cable clamp to the positive post of the same battery.

I then focused my attention on my battery, clamping the negative clamp to the negative post first, then, taking the positive clamp in my hand, I attempted to clamp it to the positive post of my battery. I never got that far, because when I got the clamp within about one inch of the battery, THE PICKUP ENGINE STARTED ON ITS OWN! I never touched the positive side of my battery with the positive cable clamp! There was nobody in the cab of my pickup! (Unless you acknowledge the angel, who no doubt, had to be the one who started the engine!).

I was surprised, yet filled with joy, because I knew that it was God who started the engine of my pickup!

Grinning from ear to ear, I looked over at the foreman and his eyes were as big as silver dollars! I had a smile as big as Tulsa on my face and laughed when he exclaimed, "There is Somebody with you!"

I put his jumper cables into the back of his pickup bed and closed the hood to his engine compartment. I barely got the hood closed before he burned rubber out of there!

I laughed and praised God all the way home!

The story you just read is the truth. I believe God wanted to prove Himself, not only to me, but to the foreman as well. God showed up and showed out to show Who He is. Jesus Christ is the same, yesterday, today, and forever. (Hebrews 13:8). I believe that God performed the miracle of starting the engine to show us that it was the One True God who was with me that day. As well, the foreman's exclamation of "There is Someone with you!" further proved it.

This miracle reminds me of some of the miracles God performed through the hands of his servant Moses when he stood in front of the Pharaoh of that day telling him to "…let My people go." (Exodus 8:1).

This miracle attests to the fact that the Lord Jesus Christ is still alive in our day; and that is why I continue to serve Him to this day.

BAPTIZED IN THE SPIRIT

It was along about this same time in 2003 that I was baptized in the Spirit with the evidence of the prayer language in tongues.

Now, I understand that this subject is highly controversial among the different Christian religions. Some do not believe in the baptism of the Spirit, and even others believe it to be of the devil. I am here to testify to you that it is real; I pray in the Spirit with tongues every day. I will not go into depth here to prove it to you Biblically because that is not the purpose of this book.

Mary and I went to a lady-friend's house so I could do some work on her bathroom plumbing.

After I finished my work, the three of us made a circle so we could pray. Our friend asked me if I was baptized in the

Spirit with the evidence of speaking in tongues. I told her that I had never heard of it. She explained a little to me telling me that I only needed to ask for the baptism and God would give it to me. She led me in a prayer asking for the baptism. Then, she said, "just let it roll out of your spirit." I closed my eyes and waited but no tongues rolled out at that moment. She went on to say, "It will come", and to keep believing. We finished praying and went home.

Three days later, I was sitting in my prayer closet praying as usual when all of a sudden, the tongues began rolling out of my spirit! It was like a wellspring of fresh water springing up out of my spirit! I was at a new level of spirituality! Finally, I felt as if I was in the big-boy spiritual league!

Since then, every time I quit praying in tongues on a daily basis, life goes sour. On the other hand, when I am diligent to pray in tongues, the devil's strongholds are broken, and God's power takes their place.

A prayer-less Christian is a weak, defeated Christian. I have heard it said, "Nothing happens until someone prays." In today's society, I find it difficult to find Christians who really want to pray. What many Christians do not understand is the fact that you are not going to just waltz into the power of God without some diligent praise and prayer.

Anytime I have walked in the power of God to heal, I spent hours in the presence of God, praying in tongues, worshipping Jesus Christ with music, and reading the Holy Bible out loud for hours. I did not jump out of bed and holler "Good morning Daddy!" on the way out the front door, and then command healings in the Name of Jesus Christ. It takes faith, prayer, and a hunger for God to change things.

Later, I will be telling of two times when Jesus Christ appeared to me. The first time, I was travailing with tears, deep in prayer.

The second time, I was deep in worship and prayer.

An old-time preacher said it this way, "No man is greater than his prayer life…Let me live with a man a while and share his prayer life and I'll tell you how tall I think he is, or how majestic he is in God."—Leonard Ravenhill

GOD OPENED HER WOMB!

Let's chalk another miracle up for the Lord Jesus Christ, shall we?!

One night, another lady-friend of ours was at the apartment visiting. Our friend mentioned that she could not give birth to children. Mary and I smiled at each other because we knew a God who could open her womb and give her a child. As our custom was, we prayed with our friend when she was ready to leave that night. We asked God to open her womb.

To God's glory, about a month later our friend announced that she was pregnant!

Praise God!

END TIME PROPHECY

One night, along about this time, Angel and I were watching our favorite show, "The Hour of Healing with Richard Roberts." I usually sat in the living room studying the Holy Bible while watching TV with Angel.

Suddenly, this prophecy came to me—"There is a huge revival coming! This revival is the last great revival before Jesus Christ comes back for His people. There will be miracles after miracles after miracles happening. The power of God will be so strong in the meetings that you will see missing limbs growing back right before your very eyes!" I had not heard that said anywhere else until the Lord spoke it to me that night. Mary was sitting on the couch, so I looked at her and told her what I just heard God say.

Later, as we watched more spiritual programming, Billie Brim confirmed what I had heard about the end time revival from the Lord.

In later years, I read a prophecy that Smith Wigglesworth gave in 1937 saying, "You will have the privilege to see and to participate in the most glorious and mightiest sweeping revival that has ever been known in Christian history!" — Smith Wigglesworth

This revival will start very small and then spread like a wildfire, and will surpass any revival before it.

PRISON MINISTRY

I began ministering with a man name Charlie, who was head of the prison ministry in Victory Church.

Charlie has since gone home to be with the Lord Jesus.

I admired Charlie because it seemed as if the only thing Charlie thought about was ministering to the men inside the prison system (and his beautiful wife). He was always eager to get to the prison and see the guys.

We traveled about an hour and a half south to a prison known as Boley Prison.

The men in the prison were always happy to see Charlie, and anybody who came with him for that matter.

As a criminal, I spent two weeks inside a prison before they shipped me out to a work release security house; my sentence was only for ninety days, which was not enough of a prison sentence for me to spend in actual prison. I was scared to death for that two weeks; I only came out of my cell for food and medical check-ups. Thus, this was my first real encounter with the inside of a prison as a "free" man. I will not lie, I was a little uneasy at first, but being inside with Charlie, and seeing how nice and on fire for Jesus Christ the inmates were, my fears were calmed rather quickly.

I went inside the prison with Charlie for several months until a time came when he asked me to speak to the men in his place. I remember standing behind the pulpit being very nervous because I did not have any real speaking experience to speak of in my life resume. As well, it did not help matters much with Charlie sitting in the audience.

My sermon started out smooth, but before the end, my mind got cloudy, my mouth grew dry from being so nervous, and I began stammering with words. I can still see Charlie rolling his eyes at me when I was stuck on one phrase; I kept saying the same thing over and over, just in different ways. I was never so happy to finally sit down and let him take over.

Then, there the real test came. Charlie asked me if I would go to the prison and minister in his absence. I told him that I did not mind going. I felt no fear that day.

I made the hour and a half trip to the prison, walked through the checkpoint with no problems, and greeted the joy-filled men awaiting me on the other side of the fence.

Everything went well. The anointing of the Holy Spirit was on me, in me, and flowing through me. I spoke with power and authority as a representative of Jesus Christ.

We had a powerful time of prayer at the end of the service with the men running to the front for prayer.

It felt like an outer-body experience where I was in the background watching God work. The John Jackson as I knew him was dead, and the Holy Spirit was in his stead.

Charlie needed to be absent again and asked me if I would go conduct the meeting again. I felt confident that I could "make it happen again." Except this time was different. I became worried. I was nervous going through the checkpoint. Greeting the men was cold. It seemed as if all I could think about was getting into the flow of the Spirit like the previous time, but it never happened. My mind was too involved and wanting to control the meeting.

I remember being very angry with God as I drove out of the parking lot that day. I also remember telling God, "I will never preach without Your anointing again!" I meant every word I spoke to God that day. Since then, I have spoken a scripted speech to men in a prison, but I have not preached a sermon.

GOD HAS SET YOU FREE

As I have previously written, the devil puts strongholds on us when we are children.

Although all our days are written in God's big book of life before we are born, God uses these "strongholds" to make us stronger—in faith, in love, and in trusting Him with our lives. Thus, the devil's stronghold of sexual lust continued to plague me, even as a Christian.

The sexual lust problem was not in the form of masturbation at this point because I was married, the problem was in looking at pretty women. I struggled and fought the devil in this area on a constant basis, and for many years.

Victory Christian recorded a live worship CD in the Mabe Center with the congregation involved. I was responsible for ushering from the front row of the congregation, thus I was in the front row during a practice session.

When practice was complete, a lady from the choir came to me from the stage and said, "God has delivered you from that. You should not go back." Of course, I knew exactly what she was talking about.

I wish I could say that I did not go back, but I did. It would be several years, and more trouble than wanted, before I finally became fed up and stomped the devil's head.

GOD SPEAKS AUDIBLY

It was May 6th of 2004, and life was going as usual. Church, work, home, prison ministry, and driving the bus, were our normal routines. I spent a great deal of time in prayer, and we spent a great deal of time in service in the church.

As most people my age did, I grew up saying the pledge of allegiance in school.

However, after I became a Christian, I made the decision to refuse saying the pledge of allegiance to a flag, but pledge my allegiance to Jesus Christ only.

As the National Day of Prayer played out that first Thursday of May in 2004, my mind was still firm in my stance only to honor Jesus Christ and His Kingdom, not a flag.

In the early morning hours of May 6th, Victory Christian Center hosted a time of prayer inside the Mabe Center to honor of the National Day of Prayer.

Along with the pastor of Victory, there were other dignitaries present, as well as the mayor of Tulsa himself.

I took part in the prayer time and then made my way up the flight of stairs to the second floor landing that is just below the balcony seating. I stood at the top of the stairs for a few minutes before my planned exit to start my workday.

As the dignitaries led the crowd in the pledge of allegiance to the American flag, this thought went through my mind, "Where is the honor for Jesus Christ?" At the precise moment of time that the thought went through my mind, I heard an audible voice behind me say, "I have called you to preach." I knew Whose voice it was, and without turning or hesitation, I replied with a simple "No." With a little more sternness in His audible voice, God came right back with, "I have called you to preach!" With about the same sternness in my voice, I stated again, "No!" With more sternness, God audibly said, "I have called you to preach!" With contempt in my voice, I whirled around and glared into the dark balcony. Speaking with no fear, I said, "I said no! I will not preach without Your anointing!" In a soft audible voice, God said, "Just say yes." I was dumbfounded at His reply, so I asked, "What?" He softly spoke again, "Just say yes." My fierce emotions subsided and I simply obeyed with a simple, "Yes."

I walked out of that place with determination to preach; but I will not preach without the anointing of the Holy One, Jesus Christ, or His timing.

Think what you will, but I know what I heard that day, I heard the audible voice of God. His voice filled that dark balcony, but when I looked into the balcony, it was as if He was sitting there in one spot. I still have a vision of Him sitting there relaxed with His hands clasped together as if he was watching a play down on the stage.

GOD ALSO HEALS DOGS!

During this time, I got a phone call from my mother while she was visiting family. She was in tears as she told me of how her precious little Lhasa Apso dog, Missy, was on her deathbed at the vets because my mother tied her leash onto the back bumper of a pickup to allow Missy time to use the bathroom, and give her some fresh air. A man got into the pickup and drove off, not knowing that Missy was tied to the bumper.

It still brings tears to my eyes just thinking about how upset my mother was on the phone. I knew how much my mother loved her little dog.

I prayed for Missy to be healed with my mother on the phone. I can still hear the relief in my mother's voice as she hung up with "Thank you."

You know what?! God healed Missy! Other than scarring, you could not tell that Missy was that close to death. God performed miracle dog surgery on Missy!

WE ARE PREGNANT AGAIN!

In that same month of May, and a short time after the National Day of Prayer, Mary became pregnant with our second child, Alexander.

The doctor projected his due date for February or 2005. I had no problem with the projected due date; besides, I had enough of a hard time with Angel's birth that I did not want to rock the boat with Alexander's birth.

Alexander was born on January 9th of 2005.

Angel had complications due to my frailty but Alexander had his own complications.

Somehow, he got his head stuck in his mother's rib cage and came out with a red birthmark in the middle of his forehead; I had nothing to do with that blemish.

Other than that, Alexander was born as healthy as any bouncing baby boy could be.

For some reason, I was not as excited about the birth of Alexander, as I was about Angel's birth. I suppose the "Wow! A new baby!" syndrome had passed by the time he was born. Don't get me wrong, I was happy about his birth.

As well, we were breast- feeding parents. So much so, that with Angel, we had to get a breast pump for Mary so she could save and freeze the breast milk. The breast milk supply took a drastic downturn with Alexander when he was about six months old.

"WE WILL CALL DHS"

Alexander began losing weight. Mary, nor I, knew what was wrong with him; we just knew that there was something wrong with his health. I prayed and prayed for God's direction with our ailing child.

As previously written, I am the type who does exactly what I believe God is asking me to do in any situation, in spite of anybody's opinion. If I believe God told me to do something, I will fight every nation's army put together to do what God told me to do.

Thus, I told Mary that God did not want me to take our son to the doctor, but to trust Him alone.

I plainly asked Mary if she was with me or against me; she said she was with me one-hundred percent.

Mary and I did not try to hide our son's health issue, but continued our service in the church. This meant we continued taking Alexander to the church nursery while we performed our normal duties within the church.

After Mary agreed to be with me all the way in what God wanted us to do concerning Alexander, I thought no more about the situation, but gave it over to God in trust that He would take care of the situation, and our son.

One day, the nursery supervisor called Mary and me into her office. She expressed her concerns about the weight that Alexander was losing, and the rate he was losing it. I explained that we were praying about it and trusting God to do what He wills about the situation. She suggested that we take our son to a doctor to have his health checked. I expressed my gratitude to her for her thoughtfulness, and in turn, informed her that we would not be taking Alexander to the doctor. I was dead set on my decision.

My mother expressed her concerns to me as well, stating, "Johnny! You need to take him to the doctor!" After much arguing, she saw how set I was on obeying what I believed God wanted me to do. My mother shrieked with, "Johnny! You mean you will sit there and let your son die?!" I told her, "If that is what God wants, then YES!"

My mother and I did not speak for a long time after that.

Mary and I were part of a small group that met within the home of one of the associate pastor's house.

This pastor came to me and talked with me about taking our son to the doctor. However, my faith was in God's Holy Bible at this point and I began quoting Scriptures to this man. One of the Scriptures I quoted him is from Isaiah 53:5, "…and by His scourging, we are healed." Our conversation became heated at that point, and he raised his voice at me saying, "John! Stop quoting Scripture to me!" He then turned and walked away.

I would be lying if I said I was not worried at this point. I continued praying to God with tears. I heard God say, "Son. I want you to crucify your son to Me just as My Son was crucified for you." I gasped at His answer, balling with tears at such a thought.

The last nail in the coffin was when the assistant pastor under Billy Joe came to me and told me one last time, "John. Take your son to the doctor or I will call DHS (Department of Human Services)." I kept my stance telling him, "You will just have to call DHS because I can't take my son to the doctor."

And that was the end of that fight; we were on to the next battle, in a court of law.

After it was all said and done, I bumped into a former friend from Victory. We discussed my stance on the reasoning of why I would not take my son to the doctor. He expressed his opinion and I thanked him. He had one final question: "John. If you had it to do over again, would you take your child to the doctor?" I simply replied, "I would pray and ask God what He wanted me to do, then, I would do what He said."

THE COURT BATTLE

One night, there came a knock on the door of the apartment. When I opened the door, I was faced with a lady and a couple of police officers. They asked for permission to enter and I granted it. The lady was from the Department of Human Services (DHS).

As Jackie sat down, she began telling me of the forewarned complaint from the assistant pastor; she wanted to see Alexander.

After she saw Alexander, I took Jackie for a tour of the apartment, showing her the food pantry.

I explained to Jackie how Mary and I were doing all that we could for Alexander, but we did not feel that we were to take him to the doctor for religious reasons. To this, she said she understood, and that she and the police were there on peaceful terms; her main concern was the welfare of our son. I assured Jackie of how I could understand her stance in the matter.

The police gave me an ultimatum, "You can drive your son to the emergency room yourself while we follow you, or we will take him ourselves." The love for my son would not allow them to take him from my wife and me, so I drove Alexander to the hospital myself.

Now, please allow me to explain something to you before you stone me to death.

Although I believed God did not want me to take our son to the doctor, God had a higher reasoning for it. God was putting me in the fire of His love so that He could bring the old harmful way of love to the top. Once the old way of loving was brought to the surface, God could deal with that way of loving and bring me to the point of loving other people His way, this is the only true way to love other people. In the process of the fire, God was changing the old John Jackson into the image of Christ, His Son.

I loved Alexander, just not the way God loved Alexander. My love would not allow the authorities to take Alexander from Mary or myself. I was a protective father to him the whole time.

When a person as myself grows up not being loved as God loves us, there are mindsets that get engrained into the soul. Those "mindsets" do not just go away because a person reads, "I love you. I care for you. Come to me all you who are heavy laden, and I will give you rest" from God's Holy Word. In fact, because my father abandoned me before I was born, it took me several years after my supernatural salvation experience to fully understand just how much God actually does love me; I just could not believe it.

I am still learning.

Once at the hospital, we were booked into a room where they began analyzing and performing tests on Alexander.

The nursing staff was very kind in making Mary and I feel as if they were not a threat to us.

The hospital staff began nursing Alexander back to health, even bottle-feeding him in the room at his feeding time with us present.

The problem with Alexander's health was the simple fact that he was not getting any breast milk from Mary's breasts anymore due to the fact that Mary became pregnant with our third child and her breasts shut down the milk supply.

After a week's stay in the hospital, Alexander was a healthy, bouncing baby boy once again. At this point, I began asking the staff when we would be allowed to return home because I could not see any more reason for us to prolong our stay there. However, it was not the hospital staff that had the hold on us, but DHS.

Days later, DHS decided to strip our son from our lives and send us home, putting him in State's custody.

Victory Christian Center was good to Mary and me. It was during this time of hardship that the church hired Mary and I to work at the church; Mary in the nursery, and myself in the maintenance department.

As well, at the request of the church, a church member, being an attorney himself, agreed to take on our case and represent us in court free of charge.

I wanted our child back, immediately, and I did not want to jump through a bunch of DHS hoops to do it neither.

DHS began telling lies about Mary and me. All the while, the attorney acted as if he would do nothing about it.

Part of the fact that I hate lying, and the fact that I did not understand the process of law at the time, caused me to blow up at the attorney, asking him why he was not defending us against the lies of DHS. He told me, "John. Sometimes, you've got to pick your battles carefully." Then, he resigned from being our attorney.

My mind just could not fathom how this attorney was going to allow them to tell lies about Mary and me, especially with a casual attitude.

Yet, I was still learning how love works.

Mary and I could not afford to hire an attorney, so I entered the case Pro Se. From the trouble I had with the law as a criminal, I did not trust court-appointed attorneys; I felt as though they worked more for the courts, than for the clients. I felt as if I could do a better job for my own interests. I was correct in a way, but wrong at the same time.

I sought to plead the Fifth Amendment and not take the witness stand, but the judge denied my right to not incriminate myself and forced me to take the stand and answer the Plaintiff's questions.

I made no beef about my faith in answering the questions. I told of my love for Jesus Christ and how it was Him I sought to obey, not the law. Obviously, since I had no experience as an attorney, there is no doubt that the State's attorney took advantage of my inability to object to any questioning.

At one point, the judge leaned over to me and said, "Mr. Jackson. You may have a case here, but that is all I can help you with." I took it as a good indication that I should get an attorney and file against the State; my only concern at that moment was getting our children back; I thought they would understand my faith.

I was a young Christian at the time. You could say that I was a "baby" Christian.

At that time, I did not know as much about God and where He was leading me, as I do now.

I had read the Scripture that Jesus Christ taught, "If you were of the world, the world would love its own; but because you are not of the world, but I chose you out of the world, because of this, the world hates you." (John 15:19). Also, "Remember the word that I said to you, 'A slave is not greater than his master.' If they persecuted Me, they will also persecute you…" (John 15:20). However, I was not familiar with what Jesus meant when He talked about "the world." To my downfall, I thought the people who uphold the "law" was good people, not cutthroats. As well, the Apostle John wrote of Jesus Christ saying, "But Jesus, on His part, was not entrusting Himself to them, for He knew all men." (John 2:24). I did not take precautions in guarding myself from "the world."

By now, DHS had taken Angel into custody as well. That was very hard for me to deal with, considering how much I loved her. I loved Angel more than I loved Jesus

Christ.

DHS improvised a "treatment plan" (hoops) for Mary and I to complete in order for us to regain custody of the children. I despised the treatment plan from the start. There was not one thing in the plan that set well with me. I felt that a lot of the plan was about money (and it was); another part of it was on the part of DHS; it was an attitude of "We don't want this man having his children back".

Though I did not want to admit it, I kept hearing God say, "They are not going to give your children back to you."

You can consider it pride, ego, or whatever else you want, but I was not about to let them take my children like that, not without a fight.

It came down to God telling me to "stop doing the treatment plan." I kept hearing Him say it over and over, week after week. I finally quit working the treatment plan telling Mary, "God says that they have no plans of giving the children back, so I don't need to continue working the treatment plan." The battle was over, so I thought.

GOD CAN HEAL AT A COURTHOUSE!

During one of our court hearings, as Mary and I sat out in the lobby awaiting our turn, I overheard the woman sitting next to me explaining to another family member of one in their family who had cancer. That was music to my ears. My heart went out to the lady.

Thus, I asked the lady if we could pray for the victim of the foul disease; the lady agreed to accept our prayer. The lady accompanied Mary and I outside and right there in front of the courthouse, we prayed for the lady to be healed. I knew in my spirit that the God of Heaven and Earth answered our prayer; the lady was healed! Praise Jesus Christ forever!

OUR NEXT CHILD?!

One night, as Mary and I lay in bed, and before the problem arose with Alexander, I heard God say, "Your next child will be a girl, and you are to name her Ashley." God did not say exactly when "your next child" would be conceived or born. If He had given me that information, I might have discovered that to be the problem with Mary's breast milk.

This would be the last childbirth while Mary and I were together.

Mary's water broke one night as she sat on the couch causing us to rush to the hospital to give birth to Ashley. Thus, Ashley was born March 9th of 2006.

I was not given the chance to hold Ashley when she was born because DHS told the hospital staff that I was forbidden to have anything to do with my second daughter. The nursery staff was kind enough to hold her up so I could see Ashley through the plate- glass window of the nursery.

I went to work during the day and would go sit with Mary at night.

I was grateful when Mary informed me that the staff allowed her to hold Ashley.

After three days of this ill treatment, DHS informed us that they were taking Ashley from us as well.

I had enough. I told Mary that I was going home and asked her what she wanted to do, stay or go with me. She did not hesitate, but said that she wanted to go home with me. I informed the hospital staff of our decision and they acted as if I was some kind of control monster who was forcing his wife to leave the hospital. After they consulted with Mary, they found that she did not want to stay there any longer either.

The staff required Mary to sign some early release forms before they would allow her to leave. We signed the forms and vacated the premises as fast as we could.

It was not that I did not care for Mary; it was the fact that these people were so cruel. I just could not take it anymore. They acted as if I intentionally starved our son, and had intentions to starve our newborn daughter as well. That was not the issue with Alexander at all.

JOSIAH GEROME

As if Mary and I did not have enough to be sorrowful for, this story may as well put the icing on the cake.

After DHS took the children, Mary and I bought a brand new house in a small town about 10 miles outside of Tulsa. I was happy to have a fresh start in getting away from the apartment, along with the bad memories.

We found a new church that we could call home, along with some new friends. The church seemed to be a hundred times smaller than Victory.

I began helping the pastor with the maintenance of the church—mowing, painting and some light plumbing repairs.

Mary conceived again, and we went for check-ups and an ultrasound; the doctor said everything was fine and looking good.

One day, I went to town while Mary stayed home.

A short time later, Mary called me on the phone crying. Mary said, "I don't know what happened! It just came out!" With concern, I asked, "What just came out?" Shockingly to me, Mary said, "The baby just came out! I thought I needed to use the bathroom but the baby came out!"

I rushed home to find Mary lying on the bed.

When I walked into the bathroom and looked into the toilet, all I saw was bloody water.

In being more concerned with Mary at that moment, I called for some paramedics to come see about Mary. When they arrived, I showed one of them the toilet and asked him what I should do about the baby. I was appalled to hear him say, "Just flush it." I thought to myself, "Just flush my baby?! Are you kidding me?!"

The paramedics took Mary to the hospital by ambulance and I followed in the van. At the hospital, the doctor examined Mary and informed us that her body aborted the baby; for what reason, he did not know. We drove home in a sad, silent wonder.

Once back at home, I had no intentions of flushing the toilet. Considering how I do not like blood and guts, I braced my stomach and reached into the toilet to find our baby. We did not know what gender the baby was until I pulled the baby from the toilet.

The baby was a boy. He had eye, ear, and mouth sockets forming. He was as long as my hand with arms and legs. The hands and feet were webbed and undeveloped. As well, the part that told us his gender was also forming.

I laid our baby boy on the bathroom counter next to the lavatory so we could admire him for a moment. Even within that difficult situation, we felt the peace of God comforting our hearts.

We decided on the name Josiah Gerome.

We then found an airtight container to put Josiah in before we buried him in the flowerbed. We felt as if we would stay in the house for a while despite our hardships with the children; thus, we wanted his burial close by.

One day, the police came to the house, along with a medical examiner.

Mary had shared Josiah's story with a co-worker who in turn called the authorities.

The examiner said that it was "just routine that we check the fetus for a cause of death." I sought to detour the examiner from making me dig up Josiah's container, but the police left me no choice. The examiner assured me that he would be of utmost care with Josiah. Did I trust him?—No.

About three weeks went by before the examiner finally called to inform us that we could pick up Josiah, adding that he did not find anything unusual.

GOING TO TRADE SCHOOL

I applied for entrance as a student in the Tulsa Pipe Trades Training School. The students worked for various plumbing companies that signed on with the school program.

I had every intention of making a career out of plumbing; however, when it came to passing the math course, I failed. The school would not allow me any extended time for completion of the math exams.

Therefore, after attending school for a year, I dropped out.

THE SEPARATION

I felt as if Mary was messing around with another man behind my back. Thus, one day, I hid myself inside one of the bedrooms of the house so I could spy on her. The private eye speculation paid off. I over-heard Mary talking on the phone to one of her girlfriends saying, "Yeah. He said that I deserved a bigger rock than what I have on my finger now." Before it was all said and done, Mary showed up in court, pregnant with his child, even before we had a chance to get a divorce.

Her actions made me a firm believer in what some people call "Karma"; it was payback for what I did to Delilah's husband; what goes around, comes around.

On top of that, DHS began pressuring Mary to separate from me, enticing her with the promise that she would gain custody of the children if she abandoned the marriage. Thus, that is just what Mary did, with my help. I told her if she was going to abandon me, then for her to get to it. It was not long before she packed her belongings and moved in with a co-worker.

When Mary moved out, she was pregnant with our fifth child. The baby was born after I had moved out of the state. This would turn into another fight with DHS at a later time.

JESUS CHRIST APPEARS

At the start of 2007, Mary and I had been separated for a few months.

I decided that I wanted out of the area all together; thus, I called Danny back in Arkansas and talked with him about the situation. Danny agreed to come to Tulsa with his truck and flat trailer in order to help me haul my personal belongings back to Arkansas.

My heart was ripped out because of the battle that I went through with DHS. I was terribly saddened by the fact that these people could be so cruel.

I just did not understand that it was God's will for my life at the time.

I advertised a "moving sale" and set it for a certain weekend. My first customer was a policeman who stopped by in the wee hours on the first morning; he bought the deepfreeze and asked me to haul it to his house for him.

The rest of the furnishings sold like hotcakes.

I took some personal belongings over to where Mary was living and left it on the back of her friend's automobile. I also left a note telling Mary of my expected move and for her to come to the house and get anything else she wanted before it was gone for good.

Mary did not heed the note, but went to the courthouse and filed a restraining order against me. I laughed about it on my way to court. The restraining order backfired on her when I told the judge how I left her the note telling her to get her stuff.

The judge reprimanded her, telling her not to be wasting the Court's time with such silliness.

Finally, Mary came to the house with the police and got some of her stuff.

I continued praying to God and worshipping the Lord Jesus. Talking to God was the only thing I could count on to keep me sane now that Mary and the children were gone.

Now, with the house empty, all I had to do was wait for Danny to come get me.

I was on my knees in the living room floor, crying my heart out to God with tears uncontrollable, when I heard God say, "I want you to terminate your parental rights to your children." My response was, "You want me to do what?!" With no hesitation, God said it again, "I want you to terminate your parental rights to your children." I could not believe what I was hearing. With tears streaming down my face I cried out, "No! I can't do that! Why do you want me to terminate my parental rights?! You know how much I love my children!"

I was sitting on my legs and knees with my face to the floor as I continued crying tears uncontrollably.

Suddenly, I sensed a spiritual presence enter the room. I had enough experience with God to know that it was the presence of Jesus Christ Himself. I opened my eyes and looked at the floor directly in front of me and I saw the feet of Jesus, He was standing directly in front of me, and He was wearing sandals.

I continued crying tears uncontrollably when I heard Jesus say, "Look at Me." I said, "No. I can't look at You." He gently said it again, "Look at Me." I shook my head from side to side in a manner that said "No." Jesus reached His arms down and lifted my head with His fingers under my chin saying again, "Look at Me." This time, I looked at His face, which was shining as bright at the sun. When I looked at Him, He said, "I love you." I am sure He heard my heart say, "Oh no You don't!" because my mouth did not move with words.

Jesus said again, "I love you." My heart relented a little as I thought, "Yeah. Right." In a kindness only Jesus could have, again, He said, "I love you." Then, He was gone.

It was at that moment when I knew what I had to do, terminate the rights to my first three children.

GOOD JOB MR. JACKSON

I drew up the necessary legal documents for terminating parental rights and filed them with the court clerk. I was not allowed to file the case with the existing judge who presided over the DHS custody battle case. Therefore, a court date was set with another judge.

When I stepped into the courtroom and faced the judge, he said, "Mr. Jackson. I have looked over your case and you have done a better job than most court-appointed attorneys I have seen." I thanked the judge and he asked his next question, "Are you sure you want to terminate your parental rights? There is no turning back after this is final." I sadly replied, "Yes your honor, I want to terminate my parental rights to my three children." The judge responded, "Okay Mr. Jackson. It is final. After today, you will have no more rights to these children." With that, the battle was over; or was it?

CHAPTER EIGHT: My Spiritual Eyes Are Opened

*"Therefore, I say to you, all things for which you pray and ask,
believe that you have received them, and they will be granted
you." (Mark 11:24).*

About April of 2007, Danny came and moved me back to Arkansas with his pickup and flat trailer. I was surprised that he even came and helped me move back after my leaving and getting married to another woman a second time.

When I saw Susan again, her hair was trimmed short again; as well, an elderly couple bought her house. I wasn't too worried as to whether or not Susan still liked me; I just wanted to get back to a familiar place, away from all the heartache I just dealt with.

I moved back into the trailer I previously lived in and began helping Danny with the farm work again.

However, once again, something just did not feel right in being there and marrying Susan. I felt as if I would be choosing "the world" (people, places, things, and money) over the calling God had for me in Jesus Christ. I prayed with due diligence about what God would have me do about this confusion.

I was able to go back to work for Nick, the plumber I did work for previously. Nick was happy to hear that I attended a tech school, even though I did not graduate from the school with honors.

Life with Danny and Susan were just not working out like before; therefore, I decided to take a trip back home to Ada and visit EC and his family for the 2007 Thanksgiving holiday. I thought that getting away from things in Berryville would help clear my head so I could pray and think about Susan, as to whether or not she really loved me.

I stayed with EC for a couple of weeks before heading back to Arkansas. Life around his house was always fun and adventurous.

"YOUR EYES ARE HEALED"

This period in time began a season of supernatural activity in my life. Between this time and the end of 2009, I went through some good times, yet some very trying times.

After arriving at EC's home, I went over to visit EC's stepdaughter. Considering how EC had been my best friend since middle school, we were like brothers, and I considered his family to be my family as well.

His mother was like an adoptive mother to me; she always fed me and never turned me away if I needed a place to sleep.

After visiting with my adopted niece, I began the trip back to EC's house to turn in for the night. I was steering the vehicle with my left hand when suddenly, my left arm stiffened. By this time in my spiritual walk with God, I knew this was a spiritual experience.

I began feeling a pressure in my chest; the pressure continued down to the bottom of my crotch and then I felt a short span of heat at the bottom of my crotch as if someone took a cigarette lighter and lit it for a few seconds.

With my arm continuing to be stiff, I heard God speak, "I am in you." I answered His voice with, "Yeah, I know." He came right back with the same phrase, except this time, it was with a little more determination, "I am in you." I came right back with just about the same determination in my voice saying, "I know You are in me." As if I did not catch the seriousness within His voice the first two times, God spoke "I am in you" with even of a determination to get me to understand Him. This time, I softly said, "I know that You are in me Dad."

My arm relaxed as I pulled into EC's driveway.

I felt as if the flicker of flame under my crotch was an indication that God had delivered me from the sexual bondage for a second time. In consideration of that thought,

I told God that I wanted the 20/20 vision eyesight that I had been begging Him to give me for the past seven years; then, God spoke saying, "You don't need those eyeglasses anymore." I was overjoyed with excitement, too overjoyed if you want to know the truth about it.

However, one problem I have faced within my spirituality is the problem of spiritual pride. The book of Proverbs of the Holy Bible teaches: "Pride goes before destruction, and a haughty spirit before stumbling." (Proverbs 16:18). I can only imagine how many Christians deal with this same problem.

Up to this time, I had asked God to heal my eyes, but I only saw dollar signs, as if I would somehow become famous or something. It makes me sad to think about it now, but in November of 2007, I wanted 20/20 vision for all the wrong reasons—prideful reasons.

As with the time in 2001 when God said I was healed and did not need to take the medicine anymore, I asked what He wanted me to do with the eyeglasses I was wearing, I then heard, "You can do whatever you want to do with them." I could not believe what I heard and asked again. I heard, "Destroy them." I was a bit concerned at this point because without the eyeglasses, I was blind as a bat; I needed to make sure I was hearing correctly. Needless to say, I heard correctly.

I can hear some of you questioning me here, so please allow me to say something about this situation.

The Holy Bible teaches us this—it takes faith to please God. (Hebrews 11:6). I did not have faith in God for the eyesight; I had faith in the eyeglasses for the eyesight. God needed to remove the "crutch" from my face so He could deal with the unbelief in my mind.

When God sets something in motion, nothing can stop what God wants to happen (Isaiah 14:27).

Also, when God puts gifts and a calling on your life, God will not cancel your calling. There is nothing you can do to stop God from having His way.

I have found that God has unique ways to get you to where He wants you to be.

Not that it matters, but when I say, "God spoke", I really mean that the Holy Spirit is the One doing the talking. I did not realize it at the time, but it was the Holy Spirit who spoke to me in 2000 when He said, "You are going to attend this church."

Thus, when the Holy Spirit told me to destroy the eyeglasses, He in turn told me to "get the darkest pair of sunglasses you can find and wear them." Sadly, I did not take this command serious, nor did I listen very well. It would not be until 2013 when I actually bought the sunglasses. I will talk about that when I get there.

I began keeping a journal about the eyesight incident at that time, with the first date of journaling being "11-13-07". I felt as if I wanted to be ready to record exactly when the eyesight came into clear view, but the eyesight did not happen at that time. I will be writing more about the eyesight incident later.

Another thing about God is this—He has led me to face certain fears in life, and not being able to "see" without the eyeglasses scared me something fierce. I can remember driving home from Ada to Berryville scared to death that I would not be able to see the road signs; what was I going to do about work, would I be able to do my job? After the fact, I found that I could see better than originally expected.

As well, it was a big help having the Holy Spirit whispering in my ear; "You only need to see what I want you

to see." As time went on, it got easier for me to see, just not
crystal clear, as "I" wanted the vision to be.

A HUGE VISION

A night or two after the eyesight process began, I went
outside to pray so I would not bother EC and his wife.

As I stood in EC's driveway facing a satellite dish, I was
gazing out at the end of the roadway when I began seeing
heads of people appear. The heads were faceless and became a
very large crowd; to the tune of hundreds of thousands of
people large. At that moment, God's voice boomed inside my
spirit saying, "You will go worldwide and heal the masses." I
gasped for air from the shocking statement. As I stumbled
backwards I exclaimed, "Oh no! It will not be me but You
doing this through me!" Then, I went in and shared the vision
with EC.

The Holy Spirit spoke several things to me concerning
both the eyesight (which runs parallel with the "vision") and
the vision: "Just as you do not know how I am bringing about
the eyesight, you will not know how I will bring about the
vision of healing the masses." "How determined you are in
receiving your eyesight is how determined you will be in
fulfilling your vision." "You don't need to see clearly to fulfill
the vision; you just need to be obedient." "You don't need to
'see', you need to obey." "Through you, I will show the world
My glory." "You don't need to 'see', I need to see through
you." "Just as clear as you hear My voice, is as clear as you
will see."

What I did not realize at that time was the fact that God
takes His sweet time in brining things to pass. I mean, just
look at how long Isaiah, a prophet of old, prophesied the birth
of Jesus Christ before He was actually sent to earth and born
of the Virgin Mary; try 700 years!

BACK IN ARKANSAS

I drove back to Arkansas blind as a bat. In fact, I had to do everything from then on mostly blind.

I had an old pair of eyeglasses stored away because my mother always told me to keep a pair "just in case." I knew her advice was hindering my faith for the eyesight. The extra pair of eyeglasses had a nosepiece missing; it was a pain in the nose to wear them. I believe that God planned it that way so that any time I wanted to turn back on the eyesight and put the old eyeglasses on, I would be faced with the broken nosepiece and change my mind. I could have repaired the eyeglasses, but I really wanted the eyesight more than anything else. Thus, I left the eyeglasses in a box, and kept praying.

It got to where I needed to find some work. Danny helped some with this aspect by asking his oldest son to give me a job. His son operated an electric business and put me to work as an electrician's helper. I lasted one day because Danny's son said I was "too slow." Then, the youngest son hired me on in his carpentry business as a helper. I bombed that job because I could not see well enough to do the work.

I told the younger son about my eyesight issue, to which he showed some sympathy, but finally said, "Well John. Maybe you should put your eyeglasses back on. I'm just saying." Just as I could not take my son to the doctor, I just could not put the eyeglasses back on; I wanted 20/20 vision in each eye without eyeglasses, corrective lenses, or surgery by any man's hand, period.

One thing I failed to mention earlier. Back in about 2003, before God spoke to me about the eyesight, causing me to destroy the eyeglasses, Mary and I went to one of those laser surgery doctors so I could have my eyes checked. We wondered if God would give me 20/20 vision in each eye that way. It was to no avail. The doctor said, "Your left eye would come out just fine, but your right eye is on the border; you could come out blind in your right eye, and that is a chance I will not take." With those hopes dashed, it was back to believing God for a miracle.

"GO FIGHT FOR YOU SON"

Along about January of 2008, I got a knock on the door from a sheriff's deputy. He was there to issue a summons from the Department of Human Services back in Tulsa; DHS was suing me for custody of David, the fourth child that Mary was pregnant with when we separated in 2007.

David was born on September 14th of 2007.

I knew enough about the law to know that I did not need to show up for the summons; I could let it go, and let DHS win. Thus, I prayed to my Father about the situation so I could find out what He wanted me to do about the summons. He replied, "I want you to go fight for your son as if you were fighting for Kind David." (King David was the ruddy teenage boy who God chose to be king of Israel in place of Saul. Read about it in the book of First Samuel, from the Holy Bible.).

When God told me to go back and fight for my son, I actually thought that I had a chance of winning the battle with DHS. Nothing could be farther from the truth.

LET'S GO SOLDIER!

At some point, I had bought a Ford F-150 pickup. The clutch quit working in the transmission. It was a pain to drive because I could not push the clutch in before starting the engine. I had to put the transmission into first gear without the engine running, and then turn the key over to engage the starter with the flywheel. This allowed the transmission to start the engine with the first gear. I could then easily shift the transmission without the clutch while driving down the road. The only problem would be when I was forced to come to a complete stop; then, I had to do the process all over again. This was nerve racking because it could result in the starter breaking a tooth off of the flywheel, or cause the starter to quit working due to the added strain of turning the engine.

I went to church and told my Christian friends about my
trip to fight for my son.

One friend agreed to take a look at the transmission and
determine what the problem was; he informed me that the
slave cylinder was the problem, but for some reason, he could
not fix the problem.

I packed the furnishings that I could not take with me and
put them in a storage unit there in Berryville. I then packed
the pickup with the personal belongings that I would need in
Tulsa. I tied a tarp over the belongings to protect them from
the weather.

I said personal goodbyes to all but Danny and his family.

However, before leaving town, I went to Danny's only
daughter and talked with her about my relationship with Susan.
After we talked, I felt better about my decision to leave Susan
for the last time.

I wrote everybody in Danny's family a personal letter. In
the letters, I told them about the call to preach that God had on
my life, then, I dropped the letters into their mailboxes as I
headed out of town.

I headed for Ada to visit EC, and pray to find out just
exactly how my Father wanted me to go fight for David.

I was hoping I could stay in Ada, get a job, fix the pickup,
and travel to Tulsa for the court battle, but, as usual, God had
a different idea than my little brain did.

I arrived at EC's house on January 5th of 2008 and settled
in with my trusting friend.

TULSA BOUND

I stayed with my faithful friend, EC, during my stay in
Ada.

I was constantly praying about whether to stay in Ada, or
go on to Tulsa.

Although EC was trying to get the money together so he could help me get the transmission fixed, I was sensing my Father wanting me to go on to Tulsa. I knew I had my answer when EC's plans fell short.

My mother and I were not getting along well enough for me to ask her if I could stay with her for very long.

She asked for her house key back while we had crossed words with each other. I returned the key with a letter, telling her how I had given up everything for Jesus Christ, including my children, how I was not ashamed for it, and that I was headed for Tulsa.

I headed for Tulsa on January 18th of 2008. I arrived in Tulsa homeless and with $150.00 in my pocket.

GOD DID WHAT FOR YOU?!

I had no idea where I would stay, nor where to begin looking for work. Therefore, I drove to the only familiar place I knew, Victory Bible Institute's parking lot. I slept in the parking lot that Friday night. I remember it being very cold outside, thus, I would start the pickup and run the heater for a little while before turning the engine off to save fuel.

Sometime in 2007, before I moved back to Arkansas, I met with a realtor name David, who agreed to short sale the house Mary and I bought. He had helped me tremendously, so I drove to his house on Saturday to see if he had any ideas for work or a place to stay.

His wife would not allow me to stay in their home with them but he invited me to attend church with them the next day. I felt as if this was the next step in God's plan, so I agreed.

We talked a lot about God and supernatural activity. Before David sent me away, he told me a supernatural story about a miracle that happened to him. He said he had a mouth full of bad teeth. The teeth were so bad, that they kept him in constant pain. David pleaded with God as to what to do about his teeth. God told him to put his hand in his mouth and pray for new teeth and God would heal him. When he went to bed that night, his teeth continued to hurt him something awful, but when he woke up the next morning, he had a mouth full of brand new teeth. God had healed him and given him new teeth!

From that moment on, I began asking and believing my Father for brand new teeth as well!

GOD SAID WHAT?!

After hearing the supernatural story about my friend's teeth, I was pumped and ready to go to church.

The next day was Sunday, so I drove to the church, arriving about eight A.M.

I was the first person to show up.

Shortly after, a lady drove in and parked across the parking lot.

Before long, this same lady, named Sharon, walked across the parking lot and informed me that there would be someone there to unlock the door shortly. Approximately fifteen minutes later, someone did open the doors.

Sharon invited me inside and led me to the Sunday school classroom where class would be held.

David came in and sat with me to make small talk for a few minutes; as well as the assistant pastor, who was also the Sunday school teacher.

After the lesson was taught, David led me into the sanctuary for the main service. After talking for a few minutes, David excused himself and I found a place to sit for the service.

Sharon came and spoke with me for a few minutes as well; I then excused myself to the men's room.

I prayed in the Spirit for a time during the praise and worship part of the service, and then the offering plate was passed. I sensed my Father asking me to give $100 of the $150 I had in my pocket. I knew this to be a test because my Father always puts me under pressure with money to squeeze the self-provision mindset out so He can replace it with His provision mindset.

I hum hawed around about giving the money because I had a motel room reserved for that night and was looking forward to a relaxing evening after a shower. The motel bill would be a little over $50; if I gave the $100, I would be short. My Father spoke to me saying, "If you release your hundred, then I can release My thousand, ten-thousand, one-hundred thousand, one-million." By the end of the service, I decided that it was best if I gave up my hundred.

After the service was over, Sharon came to me and pulled me into a classroom, with a very serious tone in her voice, she said, "I don't know you or what is going on with you, but while I was singing in the choir, I kept hearing God say He is going to restore your children back to you." Goose bumps rose up on my skin and I exclaimed, "He said 'children'?!" After Sharon answered yes, I blurted out, "That will be a miracle because you don't know that story!" We parted ways from there.

After service was over, I asked my Father what He wanted me to do next; He said to "wait." Therefore, I went outside to the pickup and sat inside waiting for further direction.

It was not long before a lady drove up to my pickup and asked if I wanted to go eat lunch with several others from the congregation. I informed the lady about my pickup being a pain to drive and said I would be happy to ride with a gentleman to the restaurant. She asked her husband Ed, if I could ride with him and he obliged.

Once at the restaurant, the pastor, Kyle, came and introduced himself; he wanted to talk with me for a few minutes so he could get a better understanding of what my spiritual state was, as well as, where I was going with life.

As we talked, Pastor Kyle told me that he felt as if I was being honest with him, and that God had great things in store for me.

Pastor was very nice to me in that he paid for my dinner that day; said he would see about having someone fix the transmission; he would also see about getting me into a little trailer house which sat on a small plot of land for a reasonable price; and that he would allow me to be a part-time maintenance man at the church.

My Father showed good on part of the "If you release your hundred, then, I can release My thousand, ten-thousand, one-hundred thousand, one-million." promise with having the pastor pay for my lunch. As well, Ed gave me $50 during the ride back to my pickup. Before it was all said and done, I got the $100 back, and then some!

As well, as I sat in my pickup during the early evening hours, the police drove up and asked me about my situation, saying that someone called the police station concerned about me sitting at the church overnight.

The police were very nice to me in that they gave me a motel and fuel voucher worth almost $100 itself.

The help from the police is a testimony of God's grace in itself.

In order for me to get the voucher, I was required to follow the police to the station. I told the police about the problem I was having with my pickup transmission but it was no big deal to them, because one of the officers led me through two red signal lights by turning on his emergency lights. After we arrived at the station, the officer asked me if being led through the red lights helped with the pickup, to which I happily said yes.

God's grace also helped in the fact that the officers never asked me if I had insurance on the pickup, which I did not.

As well, as we drove to the police station to get the motel/fuel voucher, I informed my Father that it would be a great time for me to receive the 20/20 vision He promised at EC's house the past November, because I surely would need the eyesight to fill out some paperwork in front of the officers at the station. In kind of a laughing manner, God said, "Stop worrying." Once at the station, I did not need any eyesight because the paperwork was ready for me.

If that is not God's grace, I don't know what is!

HEALING ANOINTING CONFIRMED

I went to church the following Wednesday night, which was January 23rd, the day before my first day at battle in court for my King David.

The anointing was very strong during praise and worship, allowing me to enter into the presence of the Lord. While there, the Holy Spirit spoke to me about the ministry I was called to be a part of, saying three times in a row, "I want all the sick, maim, crippled, blind, deaf, dead, and all wheelchairs up front. They will all leave whole. If one of them does not leave whole, I will hold you accountable."

What He said did not fully register in my brain at first.

It was "Question and Answer" night in church. David (the man with the new teeth), asked this question, "Who is to have the faith, the one praying or the one being prayed for?" The assistant pastor gave this answer, "It is totally on the shoulders of the person praying." Then, the pastor told David this story: "John G. Lake once said that if you pray for someone and they do not get healed, then it is your fault."

You would have thought I was choking on something by the way that statement took my breath away, because John G. Lake is my hero. I was fascinated with Mr. Lake, and I wanted to be just like him. With that, I knew I was on the right track because of what I had just heard the Holy Spirit say to me.

LET THE BATTLE BEGIN!

That same night, the Lord also spoke "Do not fear tomorrow." "Tomorrow" was January 24th, 2008, the first day of the court appearing for David.

I rented a motel room so I could have a place to freshen up and put on my Sunday suit of clothes.

Basically, DHS did not think I would show up to answer the summons, due to the fact of how I previously filed and had my parental rights terminated to my first three children.

I made the appearance in court and supervised visitations with King David were set.

GRACE FOR WORK

It just so happened that there was a metal building company hired by the church in order to construct an activity center next to the church.

I could not have asked for a better deal than to have everything I needed right there at my fingertips; the company hired me on the spot.

GRACE FOR A PLACE TO DWELL

Some people in the church were ready to loan their tent and sleeping bag to me so I could pitch the tent on church property in order to have a place to sleep at night.

As well, Pastor Kyle gave me permission to string an extension cord from the church to the tent so I could have electricity at night.

However, Jerry, a foreman for the metal building company, invited me to stay in his horse trailer camper that he had on his property. He did not use the camper often, and said I could stay as long as I needed.

Although he lived a good ways away from the church, I could ride with him to the jobsite, thus, saving the wear and tear on my pickup, which I had not been able to get fixed as yet.

Jerry was a very nice man.

We met because he let me sit in his pickup and keep warm while we ate lunch. I was able to save money because I did not need to idle the engine in my pickup to keep warm.

Therefore, I decided to live in Jerry's camper verses the tent; the camper was a warmer dwelling. Jerry strung an extension cord to his camper so I could have the comforts of home.

I was also blessed by Jerry's family. His wife invited me into their home for dinner every night.

They had two young boys who were involved with FFA, and they invited me to a farmer's event where one of the boys had an animal entered into the contest.

FINALLY! A NORMAL PICKUP!

With Jerry's help, I was able to get the pickup fixed.

However, the repair was short lived, and the clutch went out.

I called the mechanic, and he came and towed the pickup back to the shop.

There was a different problem with the clutch this time; the bill was more than I could pay.

One night, I sat alone after a church service wondering what I was going to do about the mechanic's bill.

Once again, God's grace shone through His servants in the church. A wonderful lady, they called Mama Joann, came up to me and asked what the matter was. I told her that everything would be okay.

After she insisted I talk, she took me by the hand and led me to the church's secretary. She proceeded to tell her that I needed help. The secretary agreed to pay the mechanic's bill the next day. The pickup was fixed once again.

She gave me $150 dollars cash on top of that!

God was proving His promise to me!

FINALLY! A PLACE TO CALL HOME!

Amazingly enough, the little trailer house that Pastor Kyle told me about was still available. I saved $500 for the down payment. I then gathered the money together for the first monthly payment and moved in to my new home. What a blessing it was to have a place to lay my head.

I could tell that an anointing rested in this mobile home. Somebody living there before me was a prayer warrior. The peace was thick inside the home.

I took advantage of this anointing and spent hours in prayer myself. I would get up early to pray and read the Holy Bible out loud, despite not having received 20/20 vision in each eye without eyeglasses yet. I continued to not wear eyeglasses as well. Then, ending the day with a couple of more hours in payer and reading of God's Word.

Ironically, I was able to listen to the same fifteen-minute preachers I listened to back in 2001 when I lived in Berryville.

WALK IF YOU MUST

David was between six and eight months old now, as well, a spitting image of me.

The command from God was to "go fight for your son…" That was exactly what I planned to do, regardless of what I had to go through. I wanted to show DHS that I was a good father.

The DHS headquarters are about a fifteen-minute drive from where I lived in Sapulpa. Therefore, having the pickup operating again was a blessing.

However, once again, the pickup broke down, leaving me walking for three weeks in a row.

I felt as if I had no choice but to walk to see David.

The first week that I walked the fifteen-mile trek, I caught a ride for part of the trip, but there was no such grace on the way home. My body hurt so bad, all I wanted to do was to lie in the bed for two days while my legs healed.

By the time I walked the second trip to see David I was getting frustrated with life.

The vehicle problems were caving me in. Thus, the second week, I walked to the visitation angry with my Father. I questioned Him, and His techniques. Why did He allow this vehicle problem? Doesn't He know how important it is for me to be at the visitations? Where is His help in this fight for my son?

Suddenly, as my feet beat the pavement towards the visitation with David, I was crying tears of frustration when I heard God speak, "March on soldier!" "How much do you love your son?!" Do you love your son as much as I love My Son?" The words pierced through my soul, leaving me to think about what Jesus Christ did for me on the Cross, and how He took stripes on His back so I could be healed in my body.

At that moment, I heard sounds of footsteps behind me. It sounded as if the footsteps were of someone marching behind me as I walked. As I looked behind me, I saw nothing but angels marching behind me. The sound of their synchronism in step still brings goose bumps on my neck! I was shocked to see that many angels!

I had no more complaints for God.

The third and final week that I walked to visit David, I completed it with a joy in each step, because God had taught me some more about His love.

In the Holy Bible, the Apostle John said, "The one who does not love, does not know God, for God is love." (First John 4:8)

Jesus Christ was the Godhead in body form (Colossians 2:9). Therefore, when we study and examine how Jesus Christ conducted Himself, and how He exerted His love towards people, we get a good idea of exactly what real love is; and we can express that love towards other people, even if they hurt us.

By the end of the court trial, I was not frustrated because DHS won the battle and had my parental rights terminated. I was happy to be able to walk in forgiveness—love.

David was adopted by an African American lady. I had impressed DHS to the point that I was allowed to meet David's new mother, and walk them outside to the parking lot of DHS headquarters in order to say my last goodbye to David. The lady was very nice, and I have no doubt that David is growing up in a good home.

VISIONS

As I continued to attend the church, the Lord showed me visions during praise and worship. The visions were about money. Paper checks, in various amounts, would fly through the air in front of my face; close enough that I could read the amount of the checks. Amounts as in $800, $1,000, $2,000, $5,000, $8,000, $10,000, and $250,000. The Lord did not tell me from where the money would come from; He only showed me the amounts.

As well, it was about this time when I received the revelation of how much money the Lord had stored in my savings account of Heaven, just waiting to be released at a later time.

At home, while in deep prayer, I would read a devotion from the book called Sparkling Gems From the Greek by Rick Renner. It was during a reading of one of the devotions when

the Lord gave me a revelation saying, "You are a millionaire."
At the time, I might have had $10 in the bank, so I questioned
"…are a millionaire." as in being a millionaire today?

God, being a God who calls things that do not exist as if
they really do exist, was teaching me the same principle He
uses in confessing things into existence. Then, all the
prophecies made about Jesus Christ made sense to me. God
began speaking Jesus Christ into existence in the book of
Genesis of the Holy Bible (Genesis 3:15).

With that in mind, I felt led to begin confessing what I
heard the Lord saying to me about being a millionaire.
Confessions as in, "I am a millionaire." "I have more money
than I know what to do with." "I can walk into any place of
business and buy anything I want. I don't need to ask the price,
I just say, 'Wrap it up. I'll take it.'" "I have a brand new
Cadillac." I have a brand new Harley Davidson Heritage Soft-
tail classic." "I have an eight passenger jet; I can fly anywhere
in the world I want."

You may think it all to be a pipe dream, but to me, it is
real, and I believe every word the Lord says to me.

I have heard one preacher say it this way, "Doubt your
doubts."—Jesse Duplantis

THE SECOND VISITATION

I knew I was not too far off the spiritual tracks, because
supernatural activity was happening. Supernatural activity as
in Jesus Christ appearing to me for the second time.

While I was down on my knees deep in prayer one night, I
sensed two angels standing outside on the porch. The angels
looked like one of those thin-metal iron worked cowboys that
people stabilize on the corner of a house. The iron cowboy
causes people who are passing by to think that someone is
actually standing there, leaning up against of the house.

Suddenly, I sensed the presence of the Lord, I opened my
eyes just in time to catch a glimpse of a spiritual figure come

171

through the front door without even opening the door. I knew it was Jesus and buried my head in the floor in reverence of His presence. Jesus walked straight up to my face and said, "Look at Me!" I opened my eyes and saw Him standing there with His feet in sandals. I reached out and put my hands on the top of His feet while I raised my head up to look at Him. His face was shining as bright as the sun, yet the brightness did not blind me. I could see His long hair flowing and bouncing on top of His shoulders as if He was walking in a breeze. As I beheld His face,

Jesus said, "Never cut your hair." I thought to myself, "What?" In questioning Him, Jesus answered, "I don't want you to cut your hair." Then, He, along with the angels, were gone.

Except for trimming the dead ends, I have not had a haircut since.

CJ! I GOT IT!

With the visitation from Jesus Christ and all of the revelation coming forth about the money, the spiritual realm felt more real than the natural realm did.

For instance, there was one point during this time, where I would sit in my living room recliner and literally feel the weight of my king's robe resting on my shoulders. As I would look behind me, I could see the train of the robe lying on the floor behind me. The robe was red and white with blue stars, and a big fuzzy fur lining as the border.

Also, at this time, the spiritual realm was so strong in the house, that I literally felt as if the eyesight would manifest in my eyes at any given moment; yet, I continued each day with not wearing any eyeglasses.

The spiritual sensing about the eyesight was so strong, I called my brother CJ on the phone, and with tears rolling from my eyes, I informed him with a choking voice, "I got the eyesight!" I can still remember his resounding question, "You got the eyesight? You mean you can see without your eyeglasses?" At the time, I thought I would be lying if I told CJ "Yes. I got it!" while continuing to be blind. Therefore, I sadly and softly spoke, "Well. No. I can't see without the eyeglasses, but I got the eyesight in the spiritual realm."

As we ended the phone call, I could hear his mind reeling with "Johnny is going nuts." I must admit, I kind of felt as if I was going a bit crazy myself; yet, I believed it.

JULY 4TH WEEKEND

My Father showed up with His own fireworks the weekend of July 4th, 2008; supernatural fireworks.

Again, all of the supernatural stories I have chosen to tell here, are true. For the sake of time, I have only chosen stories that are no doubt from the supernatural God.

I needed to get away from the grind in Sapulpa and be around some friends for a change.

Thus, I traveled to EC's home for the holiday. As usual, EC took me in and allowed me to sleep on his couch.

EC was always my trusting friend. I could always count on him to feed me and shelter me.

I began the trip to Ada around noon, arriving that early afternoon, before EC completed his workday.

As I usually did, I stopped at Beth's house, my adoptive mom. She, as EC, always invited me into her home with such a loving heart and sweet loving way. Beth never hesitated to feed me, or allow me a place to lay my head if I needed it.

TAKE AUTHORITY!

After arriving at Beth's home, we sat outside and talked about what had been going on in each other's lives. Beth spoke up and said, "John. I have been having blackouts.

One blackout made me fall the other day and hurt my leg." An anger towards the devil rose up in me and I snapped, "Oh

no! We are not going to put up with you having blackouts!" I
added, "And we demand that your leg be healed, in Jesus
name. Amen."

She agreed in saying amen and commented, "I know you
don't put up with bad stuff like that. You always did take care
of me. I appreciate you watching out for me like that. You
remember when something was wrong with my wrist, and you
said a prayer for me. The wrist never hurt me again." I shied
away from the praise of a loving mother and said, "Well.
Praise God. I don't know why He uses me to heal you like
that." She agreed with, "I don't know why neither."

Beth said she needed to go inside the house for a moment;
I walked her to the front door and opened the door for her.
After she was inside, I closed the door behind her and turned
to walk back to the bench we were sitting on. Before I got to
the first step, I began to feel a blackout coming on my body;
the blackout was forced out of Beth and attacking me.

At that precise moment, I felt a pair of hands grab my hips
and shake me. When I felt the shaking, I heard the Lord say,
"You take authority over the blackouts." I said "Okay" and
attempted to proceed down the steps, but the Lord shook my
hips again and sternly said, "You take authority over the
blackouts!" I could still feel the effects of the blackout trying
to come into my body, so I snapped, "Blackouts! I take
authority over you now! I take authority over you in the name
of Jesus!" The blackout obeyed my command and left me
alone, for the moment.

DEPRESSION! YOU HAD BETTER RUN!

Back in Sapulpa, I met a lady name Lori, who had two
daughters. Lori was a single mother.

When I met Lori, I was hired to do some landscaping
around her house, as well as, her father's house.

When I did some work, Lori would invite me in so she
could talk with me. I felt as if she just wanted a friend to talk

to due to some tense relationships she was having with some family members.

As Lori and I talked, I sensed that she was depressed most of the time. I was usually an upbeat positive guy, and I believe she liked talking to me because it lifted her spirits.

The day before I made the trip to Ada, I offered to take Lori with me to EC's house, but she indicated that she did not feel up to the trip because she was having a depression bout. I asked her if she wanted delivered from the depression, to which she replied, "Oh. I don't know. I'll have to think about it." I replied, "Okay. Let me know when you are ready and I will take care of it."

I then gave up on coaxing her to make the trip with me and left her house, heading for Ada.

The next day, I went to pray and read the Holy Bible in a block brick building, that was located on EC's property, next to his home. The building was .a good one-hundred and fifty feet in length.

I chose a spot to pray about one-hundred feet down from the entrance of the building and paced back and forth in deep prayer.

As I prayed, I felt as if my Father gave me the authority to rebuke the depression and make it leave Lori's mind. Thus, I rebuked the depression and commanded it to leave

Lori, and not come back. Suddenly, I sensed a presence enter the building through the front door. I was facing a wall with the doorway on my left hand side. I looked up from the Holy Bible, which was in my hands, and looking towards the doorway, I saw a grey cloud filling the building, making its way down the building towards me. Immediately, I knew that it was the depression trying to come and attack me. I took two steps towards the depression, then began running towards it. The depression turned around and moved quickly back to the doorway where it exited the building. I was astonished that my Father allowed me to chase the very depression that plagued my dear friend Lori.

I shouted and hollered praises to God for performing such a wonderful miracle for Lori through me. I marveled as to how my Father was allowing me to see such supernatural miracles.

YOU NEED TO GET OUT OF THERE

During the holiday weekend, I went over to EC's, youngest stepdaughter's house, to visit her and her family.

There were other people there who had come to visit for the holiday as well. As I sat outside with these people, they talked about some sort of health complication that one of them was going to have surgery in order to fix the problem in the days ahead.

I sensed God wanting me to do something about their problem, thus, I asked the person what he desired, to have the surgery, or for God to heal him supernaturally. He was content in having the surgery. I prayed for him to have a successful surgery.

The conversation turned to another lady's two children.

One child, an eight-year-old boy loved to walk around and preach about God but was having health issues in the form of kidney failure; he also had a cyst on one kidney. My ears perked at the sound of the little boy preaching, so I asked the mother if I could get the boy a toy and lay my hands on the toy as I said a prayer, cursing the disease. She agreed and I told her that when she gave the boy the toy, he would be healed. I asked the mother what toy or TV show the boy liked to play with and watch. She said he liked to watch wrestling on TV. I agreed to get him an action figure toy.

The little girl was about five-years-old at the time. She was not having health issues as her brother; her issue was that she was acting out in a hateful demonic way; saying things like "I have a demon. I have horns on my head."

The mother said that her husband drank alcohol and did spiteful things.

I began to pray about what the Lord would have me do about the little girl.

As I drove to buy the toy for the little boy, the Holy Spirit showed me of how the demonic spirit was actually coming from the husband and acting out through the little girl. He instructed me to take a $5 dollar bill and lay my hands on it in prayer for the little girl and she would be fine.

However, before I left to go buy the toy, the guy who was to have the surgery said, "Can we stop talking about this? I am drinking beer and talking about this is making me feel funny." I was flabbergasted and appalled at his attempt to hinder the power of God from flowing.

The guy went into the house and told my niece that he did not like what I was talking about. In turn, she called her father-in-law who called me and said, "You need to get out of there. They don't like what you are talking about." I informed EC that I would be leaving shortly thereafter.

I took the toy and the money back to the house and knocked on the door. They were reluctant to open the door to me, but the lady, who had the children, opened the door and as I gave her the toy, I told her to give the money to her daughter and the little girl would be fine.

I want to say something here about one thing I have learned about the gifts of God. When God anoints you with a gift, He does not expect you to go save the world with His gift, He expects you to use the gift at His command, not your leisure.

In my walk with the gift of healing, I have wanted to jump out and heal people at random. However, I have heard the Holy Spirit say so many times, "Let the people come to you. Do not go in search of people to heal." It is a guard against pride.

In my study of when Jesus Christ walked the earth, He did exactly what His Father told Him to do in the area of healings. Yes, you will read in a couple of places of the Gospels where the Scriptures say, "...and He (Jesus) healed them all." However, there was more times, where not everybody was healed.

One example is the Scripture talking about the man, who laid paralyzed by the pool of Bethesda for thirty-eight years (John 5:1-15), waiting for the water to stir so he could somehow roll into the pool and get his healing. Jesus Christ came by one day and told the man "Pick up your bed and walk." because the man was healed. Jesus Christ did not heal every sick person there lying by the pool. He only healed one person.

That is what God expects you to do with your gifting; be obedient.

HEALINGS CONTINUE BACK HOME

After the holiday, I traveled back home for preparation to go back to work.

A Sunday or two later, I was walking through the church before service was to begin.

The pastor's fifteen-year-old son, who played the guitar in the choir band, met me at the sanctuary doors. I saw how he had a wrist brace on his hand and a sling on his arm. With major concern, I asked him what happened to his arm. He told me of how he had a skateboard accident and broke his wrist. I asked him if he wanted his wrist to be healed and he answered yes. I placed one finger on his wrist and commanded it to be healed in the name of Jesus. We parted ways.

During the service, he took the sling off of his arm, and by the next Sunday, he had removed the wrist brace and was on stage playing the guitar again! Praise Jesus forever!

DON'T CALL YOUR MOTHER THAT NAME!

Here is a beautiful story of the power of God.

It was the month of August, and Big B's fifteen-year-old stepson was working with us through the summer months, because his mother was teaching him how to be responsible in paying for some of his living expenses.

One day, the teenager came to work spitfire mad. I can't stand anger and asked him why he was so angry. He snapped back, "I am so mad at my mother! I just want to go home and call her a b***h because she is making me get a job and work during this coming school year!" At that statement, I became very serious with him and told him that he better go home and respect his mother in doing everything she told him to do.

The young man asked me why I was becoming so defensive with him and I told him that it was because I hated the word he wanted to go call his mother. He answered, "I can't help it! I just get so angry!" At that moment, I seen his resolve and asked him if he wanted to be rid of the anger. He said he did indeed want rid of the anger. I told him "From this day forward, you will not have the anger anymore." I continued telling him that anger was from the devil and that I commanded the anger to go to hell. As a startled look came across his face, I walked away.

A little bit later, the young man came to me and asked me what he was supposed to put in the place of the anger. I told him to "put love, joy, and peace in its place."

He then asked where he could go get some lunch, so I told him to walk across the street to the convenient store. There was a big field between the jobsite and the store.

After lunch, this healed young man came to me and with exclamation in his voice, he said, "John! As I walked back across the field from lunch, a joy came over me!" We praised Jesus together.

I instructed the joyful young man to "Now. Go home and respect your mother by doing everything she tells you to do." He agreed that he would do just that.

I also asked him how the job search was going back home. He told me of how there was only one grocery store in the whole town and that he had applied for a position as a bag boy. We prayed without delay in belief that he would get the job. He got the job! Praise the Lord!

JOHN! YOU NEED A TAN!

When I moved back to Tulsa in order to fight for my son, my daily dress attire was work boots, blue jeans, long sleeve button up shirt, and suspenders. Needless to say, without clothes on, I was white as a bed sheet.

After I began hanging iron with the guys, who I worked with, they gave me a hard time about my skin color, saying, "John. You need a tan on that body!" I argued with them for several weeks, reluctant to give in to their requirements.

However, I gave in one day and surprised the crew when I showed up to work only wearing shorts with tennis shoes. Oh, and a bunch of suntan lotion!

YOU SORRY NO-GOOD BLACKOUT!

In working with the iron hanging crew, it was my job to sort out the metal pieces in preparation for the crew's next move.

One day, as me and my helper (the young man delivered from anger) sorted the iron, I picked up on one end of a 20' long steel girder. Suddenly, the middle part of my lower back popped, and pain shot through my back. I knew I had hurt my back real bad.

I walked about one-hundred and fifty feet to where Big B was looking at some blueprints. When I walked up to him, I said, "Hey boss. I just hurt my back real bad, but I don't go to doctors." Before I turned to walk away, he answered, "Okay JJ."

I no sooner turned around to walk away when the blackout attacked me. I fell flat on my face and hit the hard concrete floor like a ton of bricks. A dimple continues to scar my nose from where I hit the concrete.

When I came to, I was sitting on my butt with Big B was holding me in his arms like a baby. He was asking me if I was okay. I told him to give me a minute.

I began assessing what was really going on in the spirit realm. A verse of Scripture came to my mind—"For our struggle is not against flesh and blood, but against the rulers, against the powers, against the world forces of this darkness, against the spiritual forces of wickedness in the heavenly places." (Ephesians 6:12). I knew the blackout had attacked me again.

By this time, the other guys were gathering around me as I lay on the ground. One co-worker spoke up and said, "Maybe we should call an ambulance!" I piped back, "No! Do not call an ambulance! I do not go to doctors! Just give me a few minutes and I will be fine."

I asked Big B to help me stand up, so he helped me up and walked me about five feet to the front of his work vehicle that was parked on the concrete floor.

As I stood there, I began praying in the Spirit under my breath. However, even then, the blackout continued to attack me, causing me to lose consciousness again. I grabbed the brush bar on the front of the work vehicle and sank to the concrete, landing on my butt again. At this point, I spoke under my breath to Jesus, saying, "Jesus. I am not sure what is going on here exactly, but You better get me up off this concrete, and help me with this before these guys call an ambulance." I rebuked the blackout and commanded it to go to hell. Then, I shook it off.

After I got back to my feet, I told the guys that I would be okay.

The owner of the company had a company picnic planned at his house for that afternoon. The guys were very nice in driving my pickup to the picnic, and then to my house afterwards.

I told the owner that I would be okay, that I just needed some time to heal. He said he would pay for any medical attention I needed, but I declined his offer.

I spent two weeks at home, then, I went back to work and performed light duties for a couple more weeks after that.

From that, I learned how serious the spirit realm really is. It is not to be messed with.

I learned to stand strong and tell every problem or disease to "Go to hell in the name of Jesus! And don't come back!"

I learned to stand strong in faith, and don't back down.

"WE DON'T NEED 'YOUR KIND' HERE."

I continued attending the church and working as the maintenance man.

There was some spiritual activity, as well as revelation, continuing during the services.

Spiritual activity as in the time I felt I should pray for a man who wore hearing aids. One night, as I prayed in the spirit during service, I felt as if I should go pray for the man to receive his hearing. After the prayer, I told the man that he could take out his hearing aids when he was ready, and he did just that.

Unfortunately, the next Sunday, the man had put the hearing aids back in his ears, showing that my prayer had failed. The man treated me with scorn each time he saw me after that.

During this time, I saw a vision of people who were crippled, maimed, blind, deaf, with crutches, on stretchers, and dead lined up at the front door of the church, waiting to get into the service. The line went as far as the eye could see.

I told several people in the church about the vision I saw. Some agreed with me, others stayed silent.

As well, at one service, the anointing was very strong on the pastor. He called people to the front for prayer, and I went forward. The pastor grabbed my hand and entwined his fingers with my fingers. He raised my arm to the sky and prayed something like, "I pray that the anointing of God flow to John and through John." At that moment, I felt a surge of electricity shoot from his hand into my hand, and go through my arm to my armpit. After the prayer, I asked the pastor if he had felt the same electrical current shoot through his arm, and he agreed to the fact that he had indeed felt the electrical current.

Unfortunately, even with all this spiritual activity happening, persecution came my way.

One day, I went to the church to do some routine maintenance, but the door combination was changed. When I asked the pastor about this, he informed me in not such a pleasant way, "We don't need your kind here." I was appalled at his response. I did not press the matter further because I was hurt enough as it was. I felt as if the pastor could have discussed the issue further, but I did not want to be hurt any more than I was.

AW MAN! NOT AGAIN!

Life began deteriorating from this point.

It started with the pickup breaking down again, leaving me stranded.

I began to give up on life.

My prayer time and Holy Bible reading time dwindled to little or none.

I became discouraged with people, and my Father. It was a huge test that I failed, miserably, making me miserable.

I walked to the church in order to participate in the services. I was amazed at how many people could see me walking, yet they never offered to give me a ride. I asked the assistant pastor if he knew of anybody who would be willing to come pick me up for the services. Thus, he gave me a name of a gentleman. This gentleman gave me a ride for the morning service, but was not returning to the evening service, therefore, leaving me walking again. After asking the assistant pastor if he knew anybody else, he hung his head and declined. I knew that his desire to help me was slim to none.

After all this time of being in the church and receiving so much revelation, even being a part of so much spiritual activity, I just could not believe that life had taken this down turn.

I was learning how to be "...content in whatever circumstances..." (Philippians 4:11). I found myself to be involved with. It was not easy, and I did not like this learning curve. This would not be the last opportunity I would have in living content.

OH! I'M SICK OF THIS

I was able to get the pickup fixed.

I continued working with the iron building crew, continuing the twenty-mile drive one-way to work. Even the drive was becoming a dreaded way of life.

However, the slave cylinder malfunctioned in the transmission again. This was the last straw. I had enough of a Christian life gone sour.

The more I thought about how miserable life had become, and how life was crashing down around me, I became increasingly angry with God. Thus, as I drove to work one morning, I had a heated conversation with God. I just could not get Him to see things my way.

I usually kept a paperback Holy Bible on the dash of the pickup. This particular morning, as I became vehement with

God, I rolled down the passenger side window of the pickup, grabbed the Holy Bible, and flung it out the window. I looked at Heaven and exclaimed, "Now are You happy?!" I did not get a response.

Flinging the Holy Bible out the window did not help life much. What did help was the fact of how God continued to be good to me in that I still had a place of employment, a shelter to sleep in, food on the table, and clothes on my back. God's goodness at that point in life gave new meaning to the verse of Scripture which reads, "...knowing that the kindness of God leads you to repentance." (Romans 2:4).

PICK UP THAT HOLY BIBLE

I talked with Big B about the problem with the transmission in the pickup. He told me of a small Mazda car that he had, saying that he would trade his car for the pickup, and give me $500 to boot. I thought that it was a good deal and traded vehicles with him.

It was not a good deal. I traded one problem for another problem; and the extra money on top of the deal did not do much to help me.

The car had a water leak coming from the engine. I could not figure out where the water was coming from, or how to fix the problem. This added more frustration to an already frustrating season in life.

I drove the car to work each day, stopping about three-quarters of the way to put water in the engine so I could make the rest of the trip to the jobsite. This worked for a few weeks.

The leak became increasingly worse and worse, to the point where the car overheated one morning, leaving me stranded about five miles from the jobsite.

Grabbing my lunch box, I left the car on the side of the road and walked the rest of the way to the job.

As I walked, my heart was softening towards the will of God for my life again, and I began repenting to God for my attitude that had transpired over the past few months.

I was nearing the exact area where I flung the Holy Bible out the window just a few weeks before. I felt sorry for flinging God's Word out the window in frustration. Thus, when I neared the place where the Holy Bible laid, I heard the Holy Spirit say, "Now. Go pick up that Bible that you threw out the window." I obeyed His gentle command and walked directly to the place where the Bible lay. I was amazed at how I walked to the exact spot. I picked up the Holy Bible and put it in my lunch box.

The Holy Bible had laid there through the weather elements, and came apart in the middle, making two pieces. I keep that Holy Bible on my bookshelf to remind me of my childish arrogance.

The car sat on the side of the road until the state department came and hauled it off. I just did not have any way to get the car home, or get it fixed.

I AM OUT OF HERE!

With no automobile, I had no way to make the twenty-mile trip to the jobsite. I did not want to be a burden in asking any co-worker to make the extra trip in order to give me a ride to work.

I looked for a job closer to home, but with the burden of having to walk everywhere, I did not find any work.

This became a low point in my life because the church seemed to turn on me. As well, the eyesight was not manifesting. I even felt as if God had turned His back on me, for what, I just did not know.

One thing I have learned is the fact that when something is frustrating us, it is because we are not getting "our" own way. Then, the devil comes with a temptation in order to get us to fall for his "feel good" medicine. That "medicine" can be food, sexual acts, alcohol, drugs, other people, or material possessions. At this point in life, I was frustrated, and playing right into the devil's hands. However, God always has a plan.

Frustration stops faith because all you can think about is what is frustrating you.

The way we combat frustration, which I was ignorant of at the time, is to put our faith in the peace that Jesus Christ gave us (John 14:27). Because, His peace is not like the peace the world tries to give us. The world's peace only comes from the "medicines" I mentioned above.

The bills were piling up and I needed to get out of there before I found myself living on the street.

Therefore, I called my trusty friend EC and told him of the situation; he agreed to come rent a U-Haul and help me move back to Ada.

One thing about EC, I was always amazed at how he loved animals, and people. I witnessed to EC about Jesus Christ after I got supernaturally saved, but I could not get him to admit that he was saved and going to Heaven. He did make this statement to me once: "Do you know how I know God Kilroy (that was his nickname for me), because of my love for animals. I admired his ability to be "real"; he never could stand a fake person.

Another thing about EC was that he was successful in life; just about everything, he set his hand to do, prospered. I asked him what the reason was for his success; he admitted, "When I do something, I just make my mind up, then jump in with both feet."

That was good advice for someone like me who froze at doing things like a cow at a new gate stops and will not go through the gate. As I have written about previously, I had a healthy fear of making mistakes.

CHAPTER NINE: You Want Me To Do What?!

"...My grace is sufficient for you, for power is perfected in weaknesses..."

(Second Corinthians 12:9).

t this point, December of 2008, the walk in the supernatural was over. I was just trying to survive now.

As proven so many times before, EC was a good friend in my time of need. My mother and I were still at odds with each other, so EC allowed me to stay in a camper he had bought and set next to his small trailer house. The roof leaked when it rained, but it was a place to lay my head.

One thing that I was learning about myself at this point in life was the fact that I wanted everything to be perfect; I was a perfectionist. However, God would not allow me to have anything that was not blemished in some way. I could buy something brand new and it would still have something wrong with it. This mindset carried over into judgment of myself, as well as others. This was a process where God was teaching me to accept my flaws, and other's flaws as well.

BACK TO WORK

It was time to look for work again. I landed a job with the local Solo Cup factory in Ada. It was a good job for a while.

Amazingly enough, I was able to get past the application process without any eyeglasses or manifested eyesight.

I worked on the assembly line for a time, then, management moved me into a machine operator position. I was concerned about operating a machine blind as a bat, but I was able to handle the task fairly well. There were times when I was required to read some fine print involved with the operation of the machine. I was relieved that another manager did not ask me about my eyesight, because I was reluctant to tell anybody about the miracle I was waiting for.

Day after day, my daily routine was go to work, then come home and wait for the eyesight, but day after day, that is all I did was wait because the eyesight never came. This was aggravating to me. I knew God's power, I just did not understand why, or what, He was waiting for in manifesting the 20/20 vision. Day after day, I grew more and more frustrated with God for not allowing the eyesight to manifest.

Inside the building was very hot during the summer months. As a result, I overheated, causing me to have a heat stroke. I was very sick, and I laid in bed for two days recovering.

About February of 2009, I began working for Solo Cup, and I worked there for about nine months before management did me dirty, which caused me to walk off the job.

How it all went down was due to management placing an assembly worker on my line to pull product off the line and pack it in a box. This worker was being difficult, as well as, not cooperating with my instructions. He wanted to go slow in pulling the product off the line as it came out of the shrink-wrap oven, causing the product to back up into the oven and melt. After I insisted the worker speed up his performance, he became hostile and threw some product at me, hitting me in the chest.

My manager was walking by the production area just as the product hit me in the chest. I thought for sure that I had this guy dead to rights, but somehow, the situation became my fault.

After an argument ensued in the supervisor's office, I was reprimanded and sent back to my line. As I worked, my manager and her manager stood at a distance watching me work. The more they watched, the angrier I became. I finally snapped. After grabbing my tools, I walked off the job and quit.

"JOHNNY! IF YOU BELIEVE THAT, YOU'RE STUPID!

Sometime around February of 2009, my oldest uncle past away.

CJ, my brother, rode his motorcycle from Arkansas in order to attend the funeral.

One day, as I stood at my mother's kitchen table washing some dishes, CJ and I had a conversation. At that time, he was on his way out the door to go visit some family.

The conversation concerned my spiritual beliefs in God's healing power. The conversation turned to my eyesight. I explained to CJ that my eyes were healed because Jesus Christ took stripes from a Roman soldier in a scourging. CJ asked this question, "Why aren't you wearing your eyeglasses?" I responded with, "Because my eyes are healed." CJ's attitude went to anger; raising his voice, he shouted, "Johnny! If you believe that, you're stupid!" He then turned and stormed out of the house.

After his departure, I broke down and balled like a baby. I could not understand why my Father delayed in granting the 20/20 vision in each eye, thus, in turn, allowing me to be ridiculed by someone whom I expected to love me and understand my stance of faith.

It reminded me of something Jesus Christ taught—"A prophet is not without honor except in his hometown, and among his relatives, and in his own household." (Mark 6:4).

I knew I had 20/20 vision in the spirit realm, I just could not understand the reason why the eyesight was not manifesting in the natural realm; and that caused me to doubt.

I NEED A DRINK

With all the pressure from Solo Cup, and waiting around for the eyesight to manifest, the frustration grew to the point of no return.

I did not have a prayer life anymore; nor did I indulge in the reading of God's Word. I just existed, day after day.

After almost nine years of sobriety due to God supernaturally setting me free from alcohol, I decided that I needed a drink. Thus, I bought a six-pack of beer, then, it was off to the races.

On a side note—for a long time, I never wanted to think of myself as an alcoholic. It would be several years before I really understood what an alcoholic truly is. Now, to me, an alcoholic is a person who cannot control how much alcohol they drink. Once the first alcoholic beverage is drank, there is no stopping; they must drink until they get their full. I did not understand this concept until later years. Now, I know what will happen if I drink just one beer, I will not be able to stop drinking. Unfortunately, this bout with alcohol would not be my last.

That is the sad part about the devil's medicine; he makes it sound like such a good deal, until he has you hooked. Then, misery sets in, and you can't stop drinking alcohol (or taking his medicine) until disaster strikes, forcing you to beg God for help.

Another problem with taking the devil's medicine is that it opens the door for the devil to come in and control your life with the alcohol as a stronghold. This leaves your life open to other stronghold areas as in sexual and emotional.

Jesus Christ teaches about being a "slave to sin" in the Holy Bible, saying, "Truly, truly, I say to you, everyone who commits sin, is the slave of sin." (John 8:34).

Now, what is "sin" to you may not be sin to someone else. The Apostle Paul taught about this in the book of Romans, and chapter 14, when he said, "But, he who doubts is condemned if he eats, because his eating is not from faith; and whatever is not from faith, is sin." Paul is teaching about food here, but since Paul uses the word "whatever", then it can apply to anything that you do not believe you are supposed to be doing. Maybe you can have a drink of alcohol with a dinner; other people can't (that would be me). I don't believe I can drink alcohol socially. Therefore, drinking alcohol is a sin for me.

So many people are caught up on what "sin" is. When you read the story of the first sin ever committed, found in the second chapter of the book of Genesis, of the Holy Bible, you find where God said, "The LORD God commanded the man, saying, 'From any tree of the garden you may eat freely; but from the tree of the knowledge of good and evil, you shall not eat…'" (Verse 16-17). One command, one sin—disobedience. When God tells you to do something, or not do something, whether that command is in His Word, or in your prayers, and you disobey God, you are sinning. When God supernaturally set me free from alcohol the second time, I should have known that drinking alcohol again would be a sin to Him. However, in that despairing moment of 2009, I wanted some "feel good" medicine. Unfortunately, I would not be able to stop until a disaster happened.

YOU'VE GOT TO BE KIDDING ME!

After I walked off the job from Solo Cup factory, work was hard to find in Ada.

My mother and I began to be on better terms; I was able to go visit her without our conversations breaking out into an argument.

During one such visit, my mother suggested that if I could not find any work in Ada, she would take me to my brother's house, where I could look for work there. I worked in Berryville a few times before, so it might be possible for me to find work there again.

My mother also suggested how I might be able to go to work driving an eighteen-wheeler with the company where my brother was employed. I told her that I would pray about it.

I did just that, I went home and asked God what He would have me do about my mother's suggestion. My Father's reply still stings to this day. God answered, "I want you to put those eyeglasses back on your face." You could have hit me upside the head with a baseball bat and I would not have been as angry with you as I was with my Father at that moment. In an attempt to persuade God to relent on His decision, I argued, "I don't have a pair of eyeglasses to put on my face." My Father calmly reminded me of the pair of eyeglasses that I had packed away in a box, which was in the rented storage unit. He had me there. Once again, I was spitfire mad with my Dad because He made me put the eyeglasses back on my face instead of healing my eyes. At that moment, I had no idea what the future held for me; I just knew life was taking me where I did not want to go.

BERRYVILLE. HERE I COME.

When you are walking in disobedience, you can't expect to walk in God's authority. Disobedience opens the door to the devil and allows him to have the authority over your life instead of you having authority over the devil.

Thus, God decided to take me on a trip around the United States. I assure you, it was not a trip I enjoyed. Although the countryside was beautiful, life was still miserable.

I pulled the eyeglasses out of the box and put them on my face. When I looked in the mirror, I could not believe how bad I looked. I could not stand to look at myself. My hair and beard were horribly un-kept. I was shocked at how nobody said anything to me about how terrible I looked.

CJ was kind in allowing me to stay with him while I looked for work. I secured a job working with a sanitation company. They wanted to train me in driving a trash truck. I wasn't for sure if I would be able to stay with that company because the smell of the rotting trash was unbearable.

I traveled with my brother on one of his company trips when he went to pick up a load (I think we went from

Arkansas to Illinois). CJ showed me some of the pros and cons of driving an eighteen-wheeler. Being on the road was not so bad, except when you needed a bathroom, or a shower. Getting something to eat on the road was fun as well.

Then, my brother suggested that I apply for a position within a truck driving school. I was not favoring the deal because I knew my eyesight was not good enough to drive a big rig. However, my brother insisted saying, "You never know unless you try." Try I did, and accepted I got.

I argued with my brother with the fact that my eyesight was not good enough to pass the eye exam, which was a must in order to get into the school, get the driver's permit, and get the Class A CDL driver's license.

The problem was that I needed at least 20/30 vision in each eye in order to pass the necessary eye exams in school. My brother was generous in taking me to an eye doctor in order for us to see what we could do to enhance my vision. Unfortunately, the doctor said, "I can get your left eye corrected to 20/20; however, I can't correct your right eye any better than 20/60. I'm sorry." Once again, I had high hopes of having 20/20 vision in each eye, but once again, my hopes were dashed. At that moment, I knew that the eyesight was in the hands of God; only He would be able to correct my eyesight to 20/20 vision in each eye without eyeglasses.

It was back to square one with the question of how was I going to pass the eye exams. CJ came up with the idea of me memorizing the 20/30 line on the standardized eye chart. I argued with this idea because my conscience was tearing me up inside. My mind raced, "What if I get caught?" It came down to what other choice did I have. There was not another choice. Either memorize the 20/30 line, or drop out of school and collect smelly trash.

However, collecting smelly trash came to a halt when I informed them of my acceptance into truck driving school. I gave the company three weeks' notice of my intentions in going to school. I asked if I could continue working until the time for my departure to the school, but the company declined my notice and termed me on the spot.

A NIGHTMARE FROM THE BEGINNING

CJ and our mother took me to the bus station in order for me to travel from Springfield, Missouri to Salt Lake City, Utah, where the truck driving school was located. We went to eat at an Olive Garden, and took some photos before dropping me at the bus station.

I dreaded the long bus ride. There is always the concern of thefts, missing the bus on transfers, or your luggage being lost on such a long trip. It seemed as if the bus ride was about 20 hours long.

When we arrived at the school, there were not enough beds to go around for all the students. That's when I really got the hint that this was a good deal gone bad. The school put the extra students up in some sort of motel type place.

On top of the problem of more students than beds, the school had to make two shuttle trips to the school in order to get all the students to the school. This caused some of us to be late for breakfast, or miss the meal all the way around. Thank God, the school term was only three weeks, then, the students were out on the roads with their driving trainers!

THE FIRST PROBLEMATIC EYE EXAM

It was time for us to go to the driver's license facility in order for us to get our driver's permit.

We took a number and filed into the waiting room in order to wait our turn in getting our permits.

When my number was called, I went to the counter. After a few questions, it became time for me to look into the binocular tubes and read the letters. I did great with seeing the blinking red lights on each side of my eyes. As well, when the license associate asked me to read the letters, which I saw in the binocular tube with my left eye, I read them well.

However, it did not go so well with the right eye, because when I looked into the right side binocular tube, I could not see any letters. The associate said, "You need to read the rest of the letters." I shrieked as I had to inform the person, "I can't see any letters." I was sure they held me guilty for failing the first eye exam. However, they told me that I needed to get a doctor's clearance before they would grant the permit.

The shuttle driver raced me back to the school facility, where I was examined by the doctor they had on staff. The doctor asked me some questions, had me read an eye chart, and wrote me a clearance slip. I was wiping the sweat from my brow as I was shuttled back to the license facility to get my permit. God's grace was sufficient for me, that time.

THE FIRST ROAD TEST

The students were taken out in a big rig for their first road test.

The big rig had a manual shift transmission, and the students were required to shift the transmission with a double clutch motion. That meant that when we shifted the gear, we were required to push the clutch in, pull the shifter into neutral, let the clutch out and then push the clutch back in before shifting into the next gear.

I did not fare so well on this task. My tendency was to shift the transmission without using the clutch at all because I could not get my body members to coordinate with my brain fast enough in order for me to double clutch the transmission. The instructor told me that I better get it figured out, or fail. I took a back seat and when my turn came around again, I had it figured it out.

WELL. THAT WAS EASY!

When it came time for the students to take the backing test, I had no trouble with this part of the course. For some reason, backing the big rig with a trailer was no big deal; I aced the test.

Why backing the rig was easy in school, I don't know, because after I was on the road alone, I had two backing accidents. Ooooopsie. Driving in the real world was so much different than driving the rig in school. I was scared to death for the first month or two.

CALIFORNIA! HERE WE COME! AGAIN.

The school had a program that allowed the best students to hit the road early for a special trip during the third and final week of school, with one of the company's over-the-road drivers.

How I qualified for this trip, I don't know.

Although nerve racking, it was a fun trip. The trip took me from Utah to California, and back.

During the trip, we drove through some snow and ice. Therefore, I was able to get some real-time experience before I hit the road on my own. I did not mind getting the "experience" from the passenger seat; it was in the driver's seat where I was scared spit-less.

WHAT ARE YOU DOING?!

Driving a big rig is a bit different than driving a regular size vehicle. There is much more weight involved; it takes several more feet to stop the enormous vehicle, especially if you are pulling a load. Learning to drive with the extra weight takes some time.

I went traveling across the country with my first trainer towards Texas from Utah. He had grown to trust my driving enough so that he could crawl into the sleeper and get some shut-eye; thus, it was my turn to drive. As I drove through a town in route to our destination, I was cruising fairly well when a signal light changed to yellow. I did not feel as if I could make it through the light before it changed to red, therefore, I pressed on the brakes in order to stop the truck at the light. However, I forgot that I could not stop a big rig on a dime. As I pressed on the brakes, I realized that I needed to press the brake pedal with a little more leg power than I was applying. When the brakes caught, the truck came to a screeching halt. In the process, the force of the stop rolled my trainer out of the bunk, and into the floor. I heard the thud of his body on the floor and knew I messed up.

Needless to say, the trainer was not very happy and stuck his head out of the curtain and exclaimed, "What are you doing?!" I could do nothing but hang my head and apologize.

Although it should not have been funny, I still laugh about how I rolled the trainer out of the bunk and into the floor. He was not a small man neither; he weighed about 250 lbs.

YOUR WHEEL CAME OFF!

On another trip with this same trainer, I was driving down the highway as fast as the rig would go (top-end of 62 MPH). Suddenly, a man driving a pickup came up beside the rig, waving frantically and pointing at the back of the trailer we were pulling. The trainer told me to stop on the side of the highway.

The man in the pickup stopped behind us, the trainer went back to talk with him and see what the problem was. In a few minutes, the trainer came back and informed me that a trailer wheel had shaved clean off and went rolling down the highway, almost hitting the man in the pickup; the man in the pickup was extremely upset about it as well. This man was nice enough to take the trainer back to the point where the wheel lay and allow the trainer to load the wheel into his pickup in order to bring the wheel back to the rig.

I had no idea we had lost a wheel, and this worried me greatly. From then on, I paid more closely to the mirrors, watching for any more trouble.

The trainer called for a mechanic. When he got there, he could not do anything except chain up the axle on the trailer so we could pull the trailer to a shop and have it fixed.

GET OUT OF MY TRUCK!

The school program involved two drive-training sessions with two different trainers. This session was nearing its end.

We were parked in one of the company's truck-waiting yards; we were waiting for a load to haul.

This particular trainer and I had trouble with each other because there were things we did not agree on; there were times we had to agree to disagree.

While we waited in the company yard, we had few choices of what we could entertain ourselves with; therefore, we were sitting in the rig having a conversation about God, which turned into a disagreement before long.

I was telling him of how I know God and how I was supernaturally saved. Somehow, the conversation turned to how I got past the eye exam, and he went off on me in anger. He then said he would report me to the company, and for me to get out of his truck because I was not allowed to ride with him anymore. I became very worried when he said he would report my secret.

I got out of the truck and went into the trucking facility to await my fate. The trainer came and got me, telling me that we got a load out, and that he would not report me, but that he would sign off on my training as soon as he could, passing me off to the next trainer. I climbed into the truck relieved that he would keep his mouth shut about my eyes.

He did just that, passed me off onto the next trainer as soon as he was able. I was somewhat glad to be away from the first trainer due to the friction we had between us.

AW! A BROTHER!

The second trainer was African American (I am not sure where he originated from, but he was a black man). I did not mind training with a black man, because I actually gel better with black people than I do with white people (Oh, by the way, I am a white boy).

Some of my best friends have been black. I will be writing about a time in my life where I listened mostly to rap music. Artists as in Biggie Smalls, Tupac, Dr. Dre, 50 Cent, Snoop Dogg, Ice Cube, Ton Loc, Jay Z, Lil Wayne, Lil' Kim, and of course, Eminem.

Biggie Smalls was my favorite rapper. I was fascinated with his rags-to-riches story.

As well, when I refer to people as "black", I mean no disrespect to them whatsoever.

Before I tell a little about my experience with this black trainer, I want to tell a story about an incident that happened when I was about nine-years old, just after I was shipped by Greyhound bus to live with my mother in Little Rock.

My mother had a PA system in her house that she used to call me with when it was time for me to come home.

One night, a male co-worker/friend of my mother's came to the house for a visit. They worked together at the same company. The man was there for maybe an hour or so. My mother noticed that the neighbors, who lived across the street, were peeping through their curtains on their windows. We could see the curtains being held in a V-shape. Thus, my mother took the mic of her PA system and hollered, "What are you looking at?!" Just after my mother said this, we saw the curtains jerked closed very quickly. We all laughed and laughed about that for years, and I still laugh about it today.

What were the neighbors peeping at us for? My mother's friend was a black man.

The second trainer was cool and laid back. We got along great.

There is not much here to write about. We drove and drove and drove.

One point of interest is this: when it came time for me to turn in my permit and get the real Class A CDL driver's license, I was very scared that I would not be able to pass the eye exam and get the license. I expressed this concern to the trainer; explaining to him about my eyes, and how I cheated the eye exams thus far. He actually understood, agreeing with me of how we must do what we must do to survive. When we stopped in the Oklahoma town where I was to get the license, he reassured me that everything would be fine; to go in confidence. That is what I did, with the help of my brother as well.

Up to that time, I had spoken to my brother about not being able to read the letters in the binoculars. He came up with a brilliant idea (he is good at that). CJ said, "Just tell them that you can't read through the binoculars, but you need to read the eye chart." Thus, with that bit of advice, I passed the eye exam and received my Class A CDL driver's license.

The one thing that disappointed me about the second trainer was that he was required to take me back to the company's home base in Utah so I could complete the second training session. However, we were all the way across America when I completed training, and he was ready to push me out of the nest and make me fly on my own. I wanted to go back to the familiar place where I started, not be dropped off in some foreign land where I was lost. He won the argument, and I was out on my ear. It was cool with me though, I understood that he did not want to drive the hundreds of extra miles just for me to be in a familiar place when my session was complete. So, we said goodbye.

OH! YOU DIRTY SCOUNDRELS!

The nightmare continued when I walked into the company's sister office.

When I applied for a position in the school, the advertisement read something to the effect of, "Upon completion of your training, you will have the choice between being a company driver, or taking a lease position." Well, obviously, I was in it for a "company position", not a lease. Take a guess as to what happened next. Yeah. I walked in and the company said, "Oh. We don't have any company positions open at the moment, so you will need to take a lease." I was so aggravated with that company that I could have went postal on them. However, what choice did I have?

It would later turn and bite the company in the behind as someone filed a class action lawsuit against them, netting me a settlement worth a little over $1,500.

MOM! I'M BEING RIPPED OFF HERE!

The whole time I was in the leased rig, I grew more and more frustrated over the deal. I wanted out.

I called my mother and told her that I wanted to come home because I was being ripped off with the lease. She agreed to help me, and although the company tried to talk me out of my decision, I turned the lease rig over to the company.

I was so relieved to be out from under the lease. I could not believe how the company finagled me into signing a lease. What, was I supposed to somehow, be happy with the idea that I owned my own rig, and pulled freight for myself? There was nothing "happy" about the whole deal from start to finish. It was a rip off from the start. However, then again, who was the bigger swindler, them, or me?

UGH! I MUST GO THROUGH THE EYE EXAMS AGAIN?!

I stayed with my mother for a month or so before I got an offer to drive for another trucking company.

As with the trucking school, I had to compromise the eye exam with this company as well; as if my having the Class A CDL was not enough for them.

Thus, I went to work for the company, but it was short lived as well, because they did not want to give any time off from driving. The deal was for me to drive for three weeks and then be at home for about three days. Yet, the company kept me out on the road for five to six weeks at a time. Therefore, the last weekend I went home, I never returned.

YEAH! I CAN LIKE THIS!

In 2010, after leaving the previous trucking company, I landed a driving position with a prominent trucking company. It was a company that my late eldest uncle drove for when he was still alive; his wife also drove with him as a team.

I was set now. I found a good company where I could be happy.

However, the first trip out, I was almost terminated for being late with the load. My first load was actually two loads in one, and I was dispatched to the state of Michigan.

When I got to the town where I was to drop the loads, I got lost. I was very scared, and my anxiety level was screaming at me. My mind went blank, and my palms went sweaty.

I called my dispatcher and told them that I could not find the place where I was to drop the loads. They were nice about it and gave me a phone number to call in order to talk to the receiver who was waiting on the loads. Due to the confusing roadways, the receiver assured me that the place was hard to find, and that was why I got lost. After I was straightened out on what roads I was to take in order to get to the receiver, I called the dispatcher back and told them how difficult the place was to find. I still remember the dispatch saying, "It is company policy that you are to be termed if you are late for two loads in a row, but we are going to override policy and give you another chance. Don't be late on the next load, or you will be termed." I was not late for any more loads after that.

JESUS!

During this time, I was cruising through South Dakota, where an ice storm was blowing into the state.

Most trucks were pulling off for the night, but I kept moving because I enjoyed driving at night when traffic was low.

As the road began to ice over, I felt as if I had enough experience that I could continue to navigate through the ice. I was hoping I could drive out of the storm. Suddenly, I felt the rig begin to loose traction and slightly slide sideways. At that moment, I grabbed the steering wheel and screamed "Jesus!" As soon as I said His name, the rig straightened up and I kept on trucking.

I marveled at how quick I was to call on the name of Jesus, even though I was living in the sin of alcohol. That moment gave me a lesson of God's grace. It helped me to understand just how much God, my Father, actually loves me.

Let that encourage you to call on the name of the Lord Jesus, even if you are deep in sin. It does not matter what your sin is. You could have just murdered someone, and now you are running scared. Turn around; Jesus Christ is right behind you with open arms.

A MORE POWERFUL STRONGHOLD

Up to this point, I still had a drinking problem with alcohol. However, the thing about it was, I didn't get to drink any alcohol through school or training.

I knew that it was also against company policy to consume alcohol while being out on the road driving the rig. I was free to drink as much alcohol as I wanted when I was home on leave, but not on company time.

However, the devil had me in his grips with alcohol. I could not stop drinking alcohol without God's help; and God was not helping me.

A couple of side notes here:

One—Jesus Christ taught, "Now, when the unclean spirit goes out of a man, it passes through waterless places seeking rest, and does not find it. Then, it says, 'I will return to my house from which I came'; and when it comes, it finds it unoccupied, swept, and put in order. Then it goes and takes along with it seven other spirits more wicked than itself, and they go in and live there; and the last state of that man is worse than the first." (Matthew 12:43-45).

When God supernaturally saved me, and set me free from alcohol in the year 2000, I fared well for many years, seeking Him in prayer, and walking in His power. However, I gave in to doubt. I quit praying and reading the Holy Bible, and that left me open to sin, and the devil's hands. Therefore, God had backed up and was letting my poor decision to return to alcohol take its course; thus, it was as if the demon of alcohol returned with seven more evil spirits and took up residence in my soul. The devil had his stronghold back on my life, and he would not let go until his "medicine" brought disaster again.

You see, God cleaned my "house" in 2000, but I gave up on keeping the house "clean" after tests and trials began to happen in 2008. This left my "house" vulnerable to "dirt" that collected and defiled my house. That is why I could not stop drinking alcohol.

Two—when we continue to fall into the same sin, God turns us over to the "desire of the flesh" (Galatians 5:16-21). in order to have the acts of the flesh destroy what is bad in us. There are two Scriptures I use to apply this principle. They are found in First Corinthians 5:5, and First Timothy 1:20 of the Holy Bible.

The Apostle Paul is talking in both passages of Scripture: "I have decided to deliver such a one to Satan for the destruction of his flesh, so that his spirit may be saved in the day of the Lord Jesus." (First Corinthians 5:5). Also, "Among these are Hymenaeus and Alexander, whom I have handed over to Satan, so that they will be taught not to blaspheme." (First Timothy 1:20).

One would think that I learned my lesson the first two times when God set me free from alcohol, but I had not. Therefore, God backed up, and let the devil have his way.

It is sort of like reverse psychology. When a child wants to eat candy all the time, instead of good food, the parent may set the child down with a table full of candy in front of the child and say, "Eat all you want." Then, when the child has had its full, the parent says,

"No. You sit there and eat more." The child may sit there and eat candy until the child gets sick of eating candy. In the end, the idea is to cause the child to not want as much candy as he/she wanted in the first place, thus, curving the child's craving for candy.

Although my mother tried this with my brother and cigarettes, it did not work.

As a teenager, my brother (like me) would sneak around and smoke cigarettes behind our mother's back. My mother found a pack of his cigarettes hidden, and sitting him down, she made him smoke cigarette after cigarette after cigarette, until he was sick of smoking cigarettes.

I last saw my brother during Christmas of 2019, and he is still bound by the bad habit of smoking cigarettes. He did quit for a time, but the addiction was too overbearing.

At the time when I was driving the rig for the prominent company, my Father had turned me over "for the destruction of the flesh." Unfortunately, it would take a couple of more times of being turned over to the devil before the flesh finally was crucified.

UHOH! YOU MESSED THAT ONE UP!

The seven demons were not finished with my flesh.

The sad part about this story is the fact that I had built a good rapport with my dispatch, to the point where I was granted a brand new spanking big rig. I mean, this rig was so new, that it still had the plastic sleeve on the gear shifter when I climbed in the cab. For a short time, I felt really blessed; I had every intention of taking good care of this opportunity for long-term employment. However, it did not end that way.

I was becoming a good driver of the big rig. Other than a couple of minor backing accidents, I was at a point where I was getting the loads delivered on time, every time.

However, I allowed pride to get in the way of the reality that it was God's goodness that was excelling me, not my minor accomplishments.

I pulled a load up into the Northeast region of the United States and arrived in a nearby town of my destination. Thus, I parked for the night, planning to make the drive to the receiver the next morning when I had plenty of daylight to find my final destination.

I began drinking beer after I found a comfortable place to park, as I did so many times before then.

One thing about driving a big rig, there is plenty of money to be earned. I was bringing home a net of about $900 per week. I was earning such good money, that I paid for a $3,500 motorcycle with two, back to back, payments. Therefore, I would indulge in a few beers in the truck in order to unwind, then, I would go find a good restaurant and get something to eat.

I did just that on this particular evening.

However, the demon of hard liquor, sexual lust, and show-out showed up and made me look like a fool.

I went inside a restaurant and sat at the bar. I ordered a beer, and then, I thought I may as well have a shot of liquor. Before I knew it, a pretty girl was sitting next to me and I was buying her alcohol as well.

The liquor took affect and I fell asleep with my head on the bar. I woke up to the bartender telling me that I should leave a tip and go home. The fact that they asked me for a tip did not set well with me, therefore, I pulled a bunch of change out of my pocket and as I slammed the change down on the bar, I arrogantly and sarcastically spouted, "Here! You want a tip! Here is your tip!" Then, I staggered out the door and continued staggering to my rig. The restaurant called the police as I exited the premises.

All would have been well that night if I had just stayed in my rig, but I decided to stagger back to a convenience store and buy, of all things, some chewing gum. I made it to the store and got the gum, then, on the way back to the rig, the police showed up.

Unfortunately, and sadly, I could barely walk. It made the arrest by the police easy, because they did not need to give me any kind of field sobriety test; they could see that I was drunk.

WHERE DO I GO FROM HERE?

As mentioned, I was arrested and taken to jail.

The next morning, my stupid self was hoping I could get back to the rig in order to deliver the load, which was late by that time. The problem was that I had no idea where I was, nor where I needed to go to find the rig. I honestly had no idea where to begin, so I began with walking. Although I was drunk, I did remember riding down a highway for what seemed like ten minutes or so. Therefore, I found the highway and began walking in a direction just by pure grace.

At one point, I grew very tired of walking, and my heart began to develop a desperate cry out to God to help me find the rig.

I stopped inside a business along the way and called a taxicab, asking the cab to come and take me to the rig. I almost did not want to wait for the cab, but I was so tired of walking, I felt I had no choice.

I assure you, it was totally by the grace of God that I found that rig. As I rode in the back of the cab, I told the cabby, "I am looking for a white semi-tractor trailer rig." Sure enough, I saw the rig and hollered, "There it is!"

My heart sank when I saw the rig, because there was a semi-wrecker parked next to it with a man was trying to jimmy the door of the cab so he could get inside the rig. I jumped out of the cab as it pulled up and started questioning the man trying to get into the rig. The man asked, "Is this your rig?" I spoke a quiet "Yes." I told him that he did not need to jimmy the door because I had a key. His words still hurt to this day; "Oh. You have a spare key?" Good. I can drive it to the barn instead of towing it." I asked the man if there was any way I could call the company and see if they would allow me to resume the trip. The man said, "No. The company told me to tow it and they would have someone come pick it up later." I knew then that my job was doomed.

I rode in the cab with the man driving the rig to his shop building. My mind was racing as to how I was going to explain this to my mother. When we arrived at his shop, he gave me a box and a trash bag, telling me to pack what I could because he was instructed to take me to the bus station; and take me to the bus station he did.

Telling this story still hurts my feelings, even after ten years gone by.

I can remember calling my mother while I was traveling on the bus. When she answered the phone, I busted out balling like a baby (It brings tears to my eyes even now). I told her that I was terminated from the driving job, and that I was on a bus headed her way. She agreed to come pick me up at the bus station, and we went home.

BACK TO JUST EXISTING

I had all my stuff packed into a storage unit that I was renting; and I had my motorcycle.

I felt really, really terrible about losing the great job I had with the trucking company. I felt so ashamed, that I did not even want to stay in my mother's house, even though she told me that it was no problem if I stayed with her in her house.

Therefore, I made a bed inside the storage unit and slept in there with the motorcycle.

CHAPTER TEN: Living in Sin!

"Marriage is to be held in honor among all, and the marriage bed is to be undefiled; for fornicators and adulterers, God will judge." (Hebrews 13:4).

(READER'S DISCRETION IS ADVISED)

Once back in Ada, I began hanging out with EC and his family again.

I was invited over to the house of EC's sister, Dora, for a birthday party. There were several people there, including a short woman, name Ann. I don't remember much about Ann at the party, but...

One day, I got a phone call from Dora. She wanted me to come over to her house for something that she did not specify.

When I walked in the front door, Ann was sitting on the couch; she began making butterfly eyes at me right from the moment she laid eyes on me.

Dora said, "Hey Kilroy! You remember Ann from the party, don't you?" I shamefully admitted that I really did not remember Ann, because there were several other people at the party besides Ann.

After I sat down on the couch with Ann, the chemistry between us went through the roof. It was all I could do to keep Ann off me. She continued with the butterfly eyes towards me as she lay on the couch with her head towards me. As well, Ann was placing her hands on me in a flirting manner. I knew then, that Ann and I would be having sex with each other at some point in the near future.

Ann and I decided to leave Dora's house and drive around to continue our conversation (and flirting), which had begun in Dora's living room. We decided to stop at the local area Wintersmith public park so we could visit in a more intimate way. Thus, once at the park, it did not take long before we were in the back seat getting naked; then we were having sex.

The devil, with the use of his seven demons, had placed another stronghold on my life, in the form of fornication with Ann.

After Ann and I finished our "business", we laid in her back seat naked, just talking. Suddenly, there was a knock on the side door window. After the window was rolled down, a member of the Ada police department shone a flashlight in our eyes; snickering, he told Ann to "get dressed and come out here." Ann got dressed and met the officer at the back of her vehicle. After a few questions from the nice officer, she climbed back into the vehicle and informed me that it was past the park curfew of midnight, and we needed to leave. I was dressed by then, and we exited the park, thankful that we were not ticketed.

I THINK I SHOULD MOVE IN

Ann continued our sexcapade at her house from time to time.

As well, I continued to sleep in the storage unit where I housed my motorcycle.

On one of our sex-occasions, Ann's son, Clarence, poked his head in the door of his mother's bedroom and discovered me lying in the bed with his mother. I can still remember the look of amazement on his face when he saw me.

Clarence, a teenager, was informing his mother that he was going to town with his sister.

I apologized to Ann for being there in the bed with her when Clarence stepped in. Ann brushed it off in saying, "Oh. They don't know how to knock on the door before entering." I indicated my concerns in not wanting to cause her any trouble with her children (Ann had another older son, and two daughters). Again, Ann brushed it off and said, "Oh well. It's my life. The only problem they will have is with their faith in God. They are very religious." That gave me the relief and boldness in saying, "Okay. I really think I should move in with you. We can help each other out; I can help you with the bills and housework, while you help me with a place to live while I find a job." After that, it was settled, I moved in with Ann, Clarence, and her two daughters (One daughter was 20 years old, while the other was a teenager).

ME! A CARETAKER?! OKAY.

Ann worked in the kitchen as a service attendant in a mental hospital. At times, I would go to the hospital in order to pick Ann up from work, and in the process, I would help her carry out the trash from the kitchen.

I finally landed a job with a caretaking company, which was responsible for taking care of "special need" individuals. I was not sure I wanted to work at such a place where I was responsible for the care of other human beings. However, I needed to go to work.

Having a job as a caretaker was not so bad, just as long as I was working the overnight shift where the special individuals were supposed to be in the bed sleeping. I was glad to work the night shift because I did not want to be responsible for cooking the special individual's meals. There was enough stress in making sure they got their own medicines, along with the correct dosages.

At times, the special individuals would be difficult. In turn, with my lack of tolerance, the need for me to control myself would arise, and I would find myself gritting my teeth in order to keep the individuals under control, and in a safe environment. It was not easy.

RRRRRR! NOT MY MOTORCYCLE!

In order to work for the caretaking company, I needed a vehicle as an added security for the special individuals during the night, as well as, for transporting the individuals to their daily destinations the following morning.

The only transportation Ann and I had was her vehicle and my motorcycle. Ann needed her vehicle for transportation to the hospital in the early mornings, which did not suit my schedule.

That left my motorcycle as my transportation, and that was not a suitable vehicle approved by the caretaking company. That meant I had to trade the motorcycle for an automobile that would transport at least three other individuals. Thus, I traded the motorcycle for a four-door automobile.

That was a disappointing time for me because I went through a lot of turmoil to earn the money to purchase the motorcycle, as I drove the big rig. I had my first experience in riding a motorcycle at the age of sixteen, and I loved it!

THE FAITH JACKET

Along about the time that I was forced to trade off the motorcycle for the automobile, a man gave me a black leather jacket. I was not sure why the man gave me the jacket, because I did not have a motorcycle at that time. As well, my hopes to have another motorcycle were dashed when I traded my prize motorcycle away. Motorcycles are not that easy to come by, due to "motorcycle fever". If a motorcycle enthusiast has a motorcycle, they are not as quick to give up their therapy machine. Plus, the price of a motorcycle is usually not cheap. Thus, I hung the jacket in the closet in an act of faith that

I would one day have another motorcycle.

IT WORKED!

By now, you may be thinking that I'm crazy. You may say, "Pffff! A faith jacket! This guy is off his rocker!" However, the Holy Bible teaches, "Now faith is the assurance of things hoped for, the conviction of things not seen." (Hebrews 11:1).

Hold up. Let's analyze this verse of Scripture for a moment. "Now faith is the assurance of things hoped for..." The jacket was my "assurance" of what I "hoped for", my "conviction" of "things not seen", which was another motorcycle.

With that in mind, Ann had a male friend with an "extra" motorcycle, which he allowed me to purchase with small payments each month. Thus, the faith jacket worked! Ann and

I loved to go for rides on the motorcycle from time to time (especially me!).

This taught me a thing or two about "faith", which I continue to use today. In the upcoming pages, I plan to write about some of the things I use to ensure my faith today.

RATS! THEY TURNED ME DOWN!

During this time, I applied for work at one of the distribution warehouses of the retail giant, Wal-Mart. The position was a great opportunity for me to increase my income substantially, which is something Ann and I needed in a desperate way.

However, although I was called in for an interview, I did not make the cut.

This, along with other pressures of life, aided in my desire to drink alcohol again. I had not drunk any alcohol since the embarrassing moment of being terminated by the prominent trucking company, and landing homeless in the storage unit. Thus, I began drinking beer again. Ann was not overly pleased, however, I was still in the devil's hands.

YOU SET ME UP!

It was July 3rd of 2011, and I desired to spend a little party time with EC for the 4th of July holiday weekend.

As well, EC's birthday had just passed two weeks before. I did not get to spend much time with him on his birthday, so I planned to spend some time with him for his birthday.

Ann was not favorable in going with me to the party, or wanting me to spend time with EC that evening.

Ann and I were on one of our bike rides when I decided to stop at Wal-Mart and get a six-pack of beer for the party. We argued about the issue inside Wal-Mart before exiting the store. In seeing that she was not talking any sense into me, she called her oldest daughter and asked her to come pick her up from the Wal-Mart parking lot, because she refused to ride with me to EC's house. I had only planned to drink the six-pack, then, we would go home.

However, since Ann threw such a fit about the party, and her not wanting to go with me, I decided to stay longer, and drink more. It would turn out to be a bang of a holiday I would never forget.

Sadly, as I write about this moment in time, I am reminded of the 4th of July in 2008, where supernatural miracles were happening, and how drastic a difference it was between this 4th of July weekend, where I wanted to go party.

After the party, I hopped on the motorcycle (which I was really too drunk to ride) and headed home. Everything was just fine until I neared home and saw the flashing blue lights of the police cars, which were lined up on the highway that passed by our house.

Upon approaching the scene, I discovered that it was a roadblock, and the police were checking motorists for any illegal activity. Unfortunately, I fell into the category of being an "illegal motorists" because I was riding a motorcycle while being over the legal limit for alcohol consumption. Once again, I found myself in the back of a police car, headed for jail for yet, another DUI.

EC heard that I was in jail and hired a bondsman to come bail me out. When I thanked my trusty friend for the help, he replied, "I figured you had the money, and that nobody else would help you." He was correct in saying.

Considering how the police checkpoint was almost directly in front of the house Ann and I were living in, I had a sneaking suspicion that Ann had something to do with the checkpoint; although she denied it, and I could not prove it.

Because of the DUI, my Class A CDL driver's license was suspended for six months. Thus, due to financial hardship, it would not be until December of 2015 before I was able to obtain the license again. By that time, I decided to drop the Class A, but kept the motorcycle endorsement.

ANOTHER DEVIL'S DEMON

Ann's children did not want me to stay in the home with them anymore. I found out because I snuck up to the home one night and over-heard them talking about me. I then snuck inside the home, hid in the closet of our bedroom, and waited for an opportune time to confront Ann about the police checkpoint, and to see where she and I stood in our relationship. Ann was not being very cooperative in standing up for me against her children. Therefore, I told Ann I was going to hang myself in a tree behind the house.

I had a long logger's rope in the trunk of my car, which I retrieved and went to fulfill my promise I made to Ann. I took the rope to a huge tree, climbed up the tree, tied the rope off, and put a hangman's noose around my neck. I had every intention of ending my life that night, but, the thought of taking care my mother when she is old, kept me from following through with the horrifying act of death.

Ann called the police and a deputy came to the house in order to help her look for me. I stood in the tree with the rope around my neck, watching as the deputy's flashlight scanned the trees. They never found me.

I decided to face my stupidity and climb down. I left the rope hanging in the tree to be a reminder of just how close the devil came to claiming one of God's children. In guarding against a future attempt, I did not want to climb the tree again just to keep the rope.

WELL! THAT BACKFIRED!

Ann and I patched things up between us, and I agreed not to drink any more alcohol.

We also began talking about getting married. In preparation for the marriage, Ann suggested that we counsel with a big-time Christian counselor who practiced in the big town of Oklahoma City. I agreed to go for the counseling, although I did not see the counseling doing us much good.

On the day of our first counseling session, Ann and I arrived at the counseling office and filled out some paperwork, then, we waited for the counselor to invite us into her office. Once the lady invited us in, I sat on the opposite end of a long couch from Ann, facing the counselor. The counselor wasted no time in getting down to the nitty-gritty of the Christian faith when she looked us square in the eyes and asked, "Are you too living together and having sex?" We had nothing to answer with but the truth of "Yes." The counselor looked straight at Ann and said, "You know that you have been using this man, don't you?" Ann shrieked and answered with a sheepish "Yes." Ann figured out real quick that her batting butterfly eyes was not going to charm this lady. I spoke up and claimed, "For the past couple of weeks, I have been feeling as if God wants me to move back in with my mother." In wasting no time again, the counselor focused her attention on me and said, "Well then, you know what you need to do." The counseling session ended; Ann and I quietly got up and headed back home to Ada.

Once we were back home, Ann and I had sex for the last time; it was like screwing a dead person because Ann just laid there looking at the ceiling. After that, I knew that I was living in sin, and I needed to run from my wicked ways as fast as I could.

Besides, it was the time of year for Thanksgiving, and the tension between me and the other family members were as thick as a pumpkin pie, you could cut it with a butter knife.

It seemed as if everything I tried in order to smooth my mistake over, and clear my name, hit the brick wall of everybody's heart.

As well, it seemed as if Ann's usury of me was showing brighter and brighter as the days crawled by. The counselor had nailed both of us to the wall with her keen spiritual senses. With each passing day, the Holy Spirit of the Living God was pounding my heart with, "Get out! Get out! Get out now!" It gave new meaning to the Scripture that says, "…do you think that the Scripture says in vain, 'The Spirit, who dwells in us, yearns jealousy'"? (James 4:5; NKJV). To think that God's Spirit is jealous over us! Whoa is me!

WHAT ARE YOU DOING?!

I began packing my rocks in boxes in preparation to move out of the house and back in with my mother. Ann saw me packing and exclaimed with wide-eyes, "What are you doing?!" I shockingly answered, "I am moving out. You heard what the counselor said. It was your idea to go to the counselor in the first place. Now you don't want to accept her advice?" She continued trying to inject her charming poison in me with, "What about me?! You are just going to leave me here with no vehicle to drive?!" (Her vehicle was in a mechanic's shop). I defensively answered, "I have no choice. I don't want to live in sin any longer. Clarence has an automobile. He can take you to work until you get your automobile back." With that, I finished packing, loaded the car with my belongings, my rocks, and then, I headed to my mother's home. It was over, and I was relieved to be gone.

I WILL NOT BE DISRESPECTED!

While working for the caretaker company, I was assigned to a different house, working a different shift, with different special individuals. One individual living in the home had a devious attitude, which caused him to act out when he did not get his way.

One evening, this particular individual informed me that the day worker promised him he could go out and get some ice cream. I was not up to taking the individual out into the public, unless it was necessary. The other worker needed to keep the promise, not me.

As I informed the individual of my decision, he attempted to warp me on the leg with a crutch (he broke his foot). I took his crutch away from him and pinned his arms to his chest in order to keep him from hurting me any further. The company said I should not have touched the individual and terminated me. My appeal was denied, so I went my way.

I WILL NEVER SPEAK TO YOU AGAIN!

Living back with my mother was, as times past, nerve racking.

My mother is the type who gets worried if there is not a steady income coming into the home. Thus, she is the type who holds a job for years, and I mean ten years at a time. For instance, the job she has now, she has worked for this company for somewhere around ten years or more. Before that, she worked for another company for about the same amount of time, and before that, the same.

However, with me, I have only had one job in my lifetime where I stayed with one particular company for five years. Most of the other places of employment, if not all, have only lasted for a year or so. Ever since I was supernaturally saved, God has led me to every place of employment I have ever worked. That is just the way He does business with me. This bothers my mother to the extreme. She thinks I should jump out and get a job as quickly as possible.

This does not set well with me, as it puts me under pressure, and takes my peace. The way I work is to pray, then, I wait and see where God wants me to apply for employment. It has worked time after time after time. As well, there have been times when I have not even needed to hand a company an application. I have worked for several people just by word of mouth. As with the company, I am preparing to write about, in the coming pages.

With that said. I was doing just that, praying and waiting on God to point me in His direction. However, my mother kept pressuring me to "Go find a job!"

EC worked at a body shop where he detailed the automobiles, which were repaired after it was damaged by either an accident, hail, or any other mishap. I was only working part-time with EC at the body shop when he needed help detailing an automobile. As usual, my mother grew impatient with this schedule. However, God had a bigger plan.

One day, my mother started in on me about looking for a steady job. I informed her that I was doing the best I could while working part-time with EC. At times, EC's boss, Kenny, was taking note of my cleaning abilities and allowing me to clean some of his shop. However, when my mother started in on me with her nagging, I blew a gasket and we had some crossed words. The argument escalated into a shouting match, my mother demanded her house key, and that I get out of her house, for the umpteenth time. I shouted, "If you take my house key, I will never speak to you ever again!" And I meant every word I shouted. I stormed out of her house with one of her portable dinner tables, and, in a fit of rage, threw the table over her house, into her back yard. Before I stormed off to enter my homeless state, I screamed at her saying, "I will never speak to you again."

I had traded my car for a covered, four-door jeep; therefore, I at least had a place to sleep, while being homeless.

I drove to Kenny's body shop and spent the night there, in my jeep.

CHAPTER ELEVEN: What Kind of Name is That For a Business?!

"But, you shall remember the LORD you God, for it is He who is giving you power to make wealth, that He may confirm His covenant…"(Deuteronomy 8:18).

I woke up to EC and the other workers showing up for work.

EC questioned me as to why I was sleeping in the parking lot. After explaining to him about the disagreement with my mother, he just snickered about it because it had happened so many times in the past.

Kenny questioned me about my overnight stay in his parking lot, so I shared the same story with him that I told EC.

Kenny welcomed me into his home and allowed me to sleep in his spare bedroom; giving me access to a shower.

I remember being very humbled at how Kenny invited me into his home, allowing me to stay with his family. As well, I knew that Kenny was a member of the Ada First Baptist Church; his generosity to me proved his Christianity.

MORE WORKING HOURS

Kenny allowed me to work more hours cleaning his body shop. This work entailed sweeping and mopping his office, as well as, sweeping the shop area and keeping the trash hauled out to the dumpster. As well, as needed, I continued to help EC detail automobiles from time to time.

Kenny was very impressed with my cleaning skills. I told him that I had to give that credit to my mother, because she required my brother and I to complete chores as we grew up, which entailed washing the dishes, sweeping, mopping, and vacuuming the floors, dusting and polishing the furniture, making up our beds, and doing the yucky part—cleaning the bathroom.

The chores were divided between my brother and me. The set of chores that one brother cleaned one day, the other cleaned that set of chores the next day, and vise-versa.

My mother taught us boys to be detailed cleaners by putting a quarter of a dollar under some object in the bathroom, then, if we did not find the quarter, we were required to clean the bathroom again and again until we found the quarter. I learned to move everything in the bathroom every time, so I would not be stuck cleaning the bathroom a second or third time. As well, she inspected the dishes as we washed them; if we did not get the dishes clean to her satisfaction, it was the same as the bathroom, wash the dishes again.

Although I am not very fond of cooking food now, my mother also taught us how to cook food; my brother and I would alternate nights with cooking the evening meal as well.

Kenny asked me to go out to his house and do some detail cleaning for his wife, because I was a detailed cleaner. She was equally impressed with my cleaning skills as well.

A NEW BOSS

Kenny had a very good friend name Mickey.

Mickey would come to the shop and visit with Kenny from time to time, especially if he wanted some type of work completed on one of his vehicles.

Kenny introduced me to Mickey, who in turn hired me as one of his business helpers.

Mickey owned a landscaping business where his workers performed lawn mowing and various other landscaping tasks around the customer's home.

THIS WORK IS EASY

As I previously wrote, I spent several years in the plumbing field up to this time; approximately seven years straight to be more precise.

Another part of Mickey's business was in the area of installing irrigation systems (sprinkler systems). Kenny had shared that I had some plumbing skills with Mickey, and suggested that I would probably make a good sprinkler system hand.

That is just what Mickey hired me to do, take over the operations of his sprinkler system empire. I remember Mickey telling me, "John. This is what I want you to do. It's real easy. Just watch me and I will show you how to do it." Up to that point in my plumbing career, I had no experience with sprinkler systems whatsoever. Mickey was confident in my abilities to perform the work; I was not so sure.

Mickey taught me what I needed to know about installing a sprinkler system. Once I got the hang of what the job called for, I found the work to be some of the easiest plumbing I had yet to work with. For me, installing a sprinkler system was much easier than installing a plumbing system in a house.

It did not take long before I was handling the sprinkler system extension of the business on my own without needing Mickey's assistance. If I had trouble with any area of the operation, I just needed to ask Mickey, and he would school me on what to do next. Otherwise, Mickey bid the jobs, and then, he mapped out the systems groundwork. Then, it was my responsibility to cut the ditches and install the system. Before long, I was handling the operation so well, that all Mickey did was bid the system, then, he turned the rest of the operation over to me and the worker assigned to help me.

FINALLY! ANOTHER PLACE TO CALL HOME!

Mickey had a mobile home on a hillside, which he invited me to take up residence in. Considering how I was homeless at the time, I was much obliged.

The mobile home sat off the road on a hillside. As well, it had an adjacent one-car garage.

I loved living at this location because it was out in the country where there was not a lot of traffic going and coming on the roadway. This afforded me the leisure of being the nudist I was. For whatever the reason, I took after my natural father in lounging naked around the house.

There were trees around the mobile home as well, huge beautiful trees, which I thoroughly enjoyed.

Living in this place was serene, and special.

From 2008 (when I threw the Holy Bible out the pickup window) until now, I had no interest in seeking God or His will for my life. Yet, He continued to apply His grace to my life. I actually built a rock altar in the office of the mobile home in honor of Him. As well, I began taking time to pray, although it was nothing as it was back in 2007 and 2008.

However, I was still bound by alcohol. Day after day, I begged my Father to help me stop drinking; yet, swig after swig, He refused to set me free. The drinking was as bad as ever, if not worse. At one time, where a six-pack of 12-ounce beer would give me the desired results I wanted, it now took at least six, and at times eight, 16-ounce beers to give me the buzz I sought. Even with knowing I should not be drinking, I could not stop.

YOU ARE NOT BEING OBEDIENT

Even through the drinking problem, the Holy Spirit was right there with me the whole time.

One day, while I sat in my vehicle pouting about not receiving the eyesight, the Holy Spirit spoke, "You are not being obedient with the sunglasses." This command was given in 2007, when I was told I did not need the eyeglasses anymore. God said, "I want you to get the darkest pair of sunglasses you can find. Keep them on your head at all times; even within reach while you sleep."

I did not take the command serious because I felt that the eyesight should just pop in, and then, I would wear the sunglasses. I answered the Holy Spirit back with, "Are You serious? Why can't the eyesight just happen?" In His gentle voice, He answered, "You are not being obedient. Remember when I said, 'You must be very obedient in doing everything I tell you to do before you receive the eyesight'." I had to admit that I did in fact remember Him saying that back in 2007.

From then on, I got a pair of sunglasses and put them on my head. At times, I have felt like a complete idiot wearing the sunglasses, because I must even wear them on my head at night. However, for several years after this, I treated the sunglasses with disdain and as non-important; I continued to be disgruntled about not receiving the eyesight, because, as previously written, I have been somewhat of a spoiled spiritual brat.

I also believe that the Lord was concerned about the stronghold of sexual lust that continued to hand onto my soul. I felt as if He would not grant the eyesight as long as I was bound by the sexual demon.

Maybe you are thinking, "Could not God deliver you from the sexual demon, opening the way for the eyesight to come into focus?" You answer is "Absolutely"! However, we must take my "will" into account. The fact remains of how God set me free of the sexual demon twice before; 2002 or so, and 2007. However, like a dog returning to its vomit, I let the demon back in by not keeping the authority God gave me over it. God's "will" would not override my will.

You see, Jesus Christ had a "will" of His own as well, yet, He chose His Father's will over His own desire. (See John 6:38 and Matthew 26:39). I want to quote from the book of Mark, chapter 14, and verse 36, "And He (Jesus) was saying, 'Abba! Father! All things are possible for You; remove this cup from Me; yet, not what I will, but what You will.'" We can see from the verse in Mark where Jesus Christ denied Himself of what He wanted and accepted what His Father wanted for Him. My soul wanted to look at pretty girls and lust after them; my Father could not let me have the eyesight until I stomped on the lustful demon. However, I had to stomp the alcohol down before I could stomp the lust.

YOU CAN HANDLE THIS AS WELL JOHN!

At this point in my walk with Jesus Christ, I was learning of how God was leading me to do things that I was absolutely scared spit-less to do (As in drive an eighteen-wheeler across the United States).

Another extension of Mickey's business was tree trimming.

As a teenager. I had a small amount of tree work experience due to working with my oldest uncle. Although my uncle never taught me how to use a chainsaw, I learned rather quickly working with Mickey.

It was not long before I was Mickey's #1 chainsaw man. This was about the same as the sprinkler business; Mickey bid the tree work, and John (I) took on the responsibility of laying the trees down.

It was crazy. Even before I was confident in my ability to lay trees down, Mickey would meet us at the jobsite and show me the tree, or trees, he needed laid down and cut up for haul off. In the beginning, I would express my concern about my abilities and Mickey would say, "Don't worry, you can handle it." Then, he would jump in his Jeep and drive off. Never mind if there was a chance of me laying the tree down in the living room of the customer's home.

I got fairly confident with my tree cutting abilities, and, I laid down some huge trees. I am talking about trees that were 3-4 feet in diameter huge. I remember one tree where Mickey rented a 24" chainsaw just for the tree I was to lay down.

I was still hoping the eyesight would pop in at any moment. Thus, one day, I decided to lay down a tree and cut it up only wearing the sunglasses, without the eyeglasses. However, I was putting the crewmen and myself in danger by not wearing the eyeglasses. It did not take long before I put the eyeglasses back on my face, and the sunglasses back on top of my head.

Laugh out loud. On a side note. My mother and I drove to my brother's home to watch one of his daughters get married. As I sat in my brother's living room with my sunglasses on top of my head, my brother asked, "Why are you sunglasses on top of your head?" In order to guard against a conversation as the one we had in our mother's kitchen in 2009, I excused it off with, "Where else am I going to keep my sunglasses? I can't put them in my pocket because I might crush them, and I don't want to set them down anywhere or I might lose them." He didn't say anything else about it. I breathed a sigh of relief because the conversation did not become about my eyesight.

COME TO CHURCH WITH ME

Somewhere around December of 2012, Mickey invited me to attend church with him, the same church where I met my brother Estell.

I decided that church might be a good idea; it might even help me stop drinking.

I attended Sunday school with Mickey as well.

I began attending the Celebrate Recovery meetings in an attempt to stop drinking. The meetings helped for a while, but I had a sinking feeling in my gut that told me I was depending on the "meetings" to keep me sober, not Jesus Christ. That bothered me, so I quit attending the meetings.

GOD SAID DO IT

About a year after I had been with Mickey, I bid my first sprinkler project for my first customer.

It came about one Saturday as I worked on an existing sprinkler system for Mickey. A man stopped and asked me if I could come to his home and give him a bid for a sprinkler system installed in his yard. At the spur of the moment, I blurted out, "Sure. I suppose I could do that." I had never bid a sprinkler system in my life; yet, I was about to bid one.

When I showed up at the man's home, I had no idea what I was doing. In being the honest person I am, I informed the man that his system was my first system to bid, and I had no idea what I was doing. At the same time, I felt as if my Father was directing me to start my own sprinkler business. Therefore, because of my ignorance in how to bid a sprinkler system, I called Mickey on the phone and asked, "Hey Mickey. A man asked me to give him a bid on a sprinkler system. How much do I charge per zone?" (I was very familiar with the rest of the process). You could hear a pin drop from the silence that overtook Mickey in that moment. When he finally spoke, he said, "I usually charge $650 per zone John." I tried to make small talk with Mickey, however, he abruptly said, "I am out camping with my boy John. I got to go." He then hung up the phone, and I was on my own.

When I believe God wants me to do something, I don't care who it offends; I just do it. Therefore, that is what I did. I went to Mickey and asked him if I could work my business on Friday through Sunday, and work for him in his business Monday through Thursday; I thought Mickey was going to have a cow with the way he acted. It did not go over well with him. I told him that I felt as if God wanted me to do my own business. He said, "John! I taught you everything you know!" I reacted with, "What part of 'God wants me to do this' do you not understand Mickey?" He just could not get it. We went around and around about it. He spouted off, "You are stealing from me!" I reiterated again, "What part of 'God wants me to do this' do you not understand Mickey?!" His final answer was, "No. You can't work for me and do your own business." There was no need to pray about it; God had spoken, therefore, I was gone.

ARE YOU SERIOUS?!

I was buying a small pickup from Mickey, to which he demanded that I pay the balance off in full. He knew my financial situation, yet he still demanded the $700. Thankfully, the money from the sprinkler system was enough to pay off the vehicle.

Mickey also requested that I move out of the mobile home that he allowed me to live in. I stalled on him for a couple of months while I got my finances to a point where I could afford to rent another place.

I was hurt. I thought Mickey would help me; however, I was wrong.

WHAT KIND OF NAME IS THAT FOR A BUSINESS?!

My Father began speaking to me about naming the "business". As I continued to pray about the name of the business, I was thinking about something along the lines of "John's Sprinklers", or "John's Sprinkler Systems", or even "John's Irrigation." However, that was my selfish pride thinking. My Daddy had a different name in mind—"John's Investments".

My usual way of following what I believe God is saying to me is to pray, and then let it ride for a time, then, if what I hear keeps ringing in my ears, I do it. I argued with my Father about the name, saying, "What kind of name is that for a sprinkler business? It may be confusing to people (and it has been for some).". He did not relent, but said, "Everything you do is an investment into your future, as well as other people's future." That made since to me! Therefore, when I ordered my first set of business cards to be printed, I put the phrase, "INVESTING IN YOU!" on the cards.

Although I have made some money with the business, I have not made a profit; every penny earned has gone back into the business, or has paid the bills. I have sat back and been amazed at how God brought work to me when I needed to pay some bills.

CHAPTER TWELVE: Whaaat? I'm Going to College?!

"My people are destroyed for a lack of knowledge..." (Hosea 4:6).

The man whom I installed the first sprinkler system for had an apartment for rent in town; thus, in early 2014, I moved to town and rented the upstairs apartment, which was located in an alleyway.

John's Investments did well for a time before business fell off to a trickle, then stopped all together.

Another man, who lived across the street from my first sprinkler job, asked me to bid his yard for a sprinkler system. He accepted the bid and became a faithful customer for a few years. Then, the trickle-down effect took place with the man next to him hiring me to install a system in for him, and his neighbor hired me to install a system in the front yard and flower beds only.

Things could have gone very well for me financial wise if Mickey would have kept me on as an employee, allowing me to work my business at the same time. However, the money I made with the four sprinkler systems was eaten up with bills as in renting the apartment and such.

As well, the man across the street introduced me to the man responsible for the upkeep of his lawn and landscape, which in turn, brought me a couple of more sprinkler systems to install, a slew of sprinkler repair work, along with some regular sprinkler maintenance work.

When I moved to the upstairs apartment, the drinking problem subsided for a bit; for some reason, I just did not feel like drinking any more beer for a while.

THE TRAIN!

I enjoyed living in the apartment due to the location in town. Without the need to drive, I was within walking distance of most anything I needed.

That was until I heard the most awful sound any person could ever hear—the train horn. When I moved into the apartment, I did not realize that it was only a half a block away from two railroad crossings, with several more crossings down the line from the apartment. When the conductor blew the horn, it blew for blocks at a time, and for all hours of the day and night. The train horns became the most annoying thing to me. Before I was able to move from there, I hated trains!

AN ENEMY TURNED FRIEND

You remember the man, EC's stepfather name Kevin, who weighed in at about 400 pounds? He lived two blocks down the street.

I met up with Kevin again because I noticed a second hand shop, where someone would set out nick-knacks for sale. Upon closer look, I saw that it was Kevin. At times, I went and sat with him when he had his shop open.

I told Kevin where I lived and he would ride his powered wheel chair to the apartment. He would holler at me to come to the window so we could chat a moment.

I began going to his apartment to sit with him and watch TV, just to keep him company.

Kevin was a nice man. He never hesitated in offering me something to eat when I came for a visit.

After Kevin and I became good friends, I saw that he was a changed man, not the man he was when I was growing up as a teenager. Thus, I asked him if he was a Christian going to Heaven when he passed from this life to the next. With tears in his eyes, he assured me that he was a Christian well on his way to Heaven to be with Jesus Christ one day. I was relieved that I would see my friend in Heaven one day.

Then, a sad day came.

I went to Kevin's apartment for a usual visit. After I sat down, Kevin said, "You remember how I have this sore on the calf of my leg that will not heal?" I agreed. He went on, "The doctors want me to go to a nursing home so they can monitor the sore and see if they can get it to heal there." As tears began to fall from his eyes, I sadly extended my condolences. I did not know what to say. What do you tell a man who is losing his freedom?

I continued my weekly visits with Kevin after he moved into the nursing home. I kept with our regular TV time. Although I did not like having to go into the nursing home, I could tell that he enjoyed the time I came and spent with him. Kevin had been such a hard man during his younger years, it caused several people to disown him; they just did not want to visit him in his later years, and I believe that hurt his feelings more than anything else did.

One day, I strolled into the nursing home ready to see my friend. When I got to his room, he was not there. After inquiring of his whereabouts with a nurse, she informed me that they took him to the hospital that day, via an ambulance.

I raced out to the hospital fearing the worse. I walked into his room and found him lounging on the bed watching TV. I watched some TV with him for the rest of the thirty-minute visitation time.

Kevin was closed mouth about his condition, not wanting to give me very many details of what the doctors diagnosed. He just said that he was okay.

My friend informed me that he would be back at the nursing home the next night, which was a Monday. He asked me to come and visit him the next day. I thought it odd that he would ask me to come back the very next day. I am not sure now, but I seem to remember saying I would come back on Monday; however, Monday came, and I decided to visit him in a week or two.

I missed our visit the next Sunday, but I went in to see my friend the following Sunday. After I walked into the nursing home and headed towards his room, a nurse caught my attention and said, "Sir. Are you here to see Kevin?" I answered a quizzical "Yes." By now I was growing concerned about the new I was about to hear. The nurse continued, "You may want to talk to his nurse." I asked her where to find Kevin's nurse and she volunteered to go find her. I choke up as I write this. Kevin's nurse came and informed me, "Kevin passed away." I could do nothing but sigh in grief.

I went home and balled my eyes out (I still cry about his death today) because I had let my friend down in not coming to visit him for a couple of more visits.

I believe the doctors told Kevin that he only had a few more days to live, and that is why he wanted me to come back that next night. I felt very sorrowful about missing our regular visit the following Sunday as well. I can hardly wait until I step into Heaven so I can hug his neck and tell him how sorry I am for not coming to visit as he asked me to do; although it will not matter much then anyway.

I attended my friend's funeral; he had a good turnout of friends and family. At the funeral, I asked if I could say a word on Kevin's behalf. I told of how we became friends, of how Kevin was a born-again Christian, finishing with, "Now Kevin is sitting in Heaven with Jesus Christ, eating anything he wants."

I miss my friend. It was a difficult lesson about love to learn.

If you have a loved one cooped up in a nursing home, by all means, please go visit them. Just spending time with them means so much. Then, you will not regret it as I do.

A BEAUTIFUL MINISTRY OPPORTUNITY

After the separation from Mickey, with the exception of changing Sunday school classes, I continued serving at the Ada First Baptist Church, because that is where I believed God needed me to serve.

I committed to greeting at one of the doors with a wonderful man name Jack. We became very good friends.

I felt as if I could share my eyesight trip with him. I told him about the sunglasses, how God was requiring me to wear them on my head, no matter what. Jack had no hesitation in saying, "Hey! He (God) can do it!" That encouraged me in believing that I was in fact, hearing from God, and being obedient.

On the other hand, at one point, I attended a prayer meeting with a few other men in the church. After one prayer meeting, I felt as if I should get up in front of these men and tell that God healed my eyes (It was only in the spirit at this time). I did this because of what the Apostle Paul preached about in the book of Romans, chapter four, and verse seventeen—"…God…calls into being that which does not exist." I had a legit reason to say that I had 20/20 vision in each eye; I was calling the eyesight into being before it existed in my eyes.

When I finished the testimony, the prayer meeting was over, and we walked out. On the way out, one elderly man asked, "I just want to know; how did it happen?" I did not know exactly how to answer the man quizzical question, so, I swallowed hard and said, "It has not happened in the natural yet, it has only happened in the spirit." I had the faith for the eyesight. However, once again, I had no idea "why" the eyesight had not manifested in the natural realm. I should have just told the man, "Jesus Christ healed my eyes." Yet, I did not want to mislead him either.

One Sunday, while I waited for the service to start, a man name Bert came to me and told me about a prison ministry that he was involved in. He asked me if I would be interested in participating. I felt as if I should answer the call, thus, I did.

When God wants you to do something, there is always a fight from the enemy. Sometimes, that "fight" can make a person feel as if it is not God who is sending the call. However, it is the enemy wanting us to quit because he does not want us advancing the Kingdom of God.

With that said, Bert said there was an application process we must follow. I filed three applications with the Department of Corrections. The first application was denied. The second application was lost. When I filed the third application, it needed more information due to my own criminal record. Finally, I was permitted to enter the prisons.

IT'S THE ANOINTING THAT BREAKS THE YOKE

The ministry is called Kairos Ministry (Kairos for short). Kairos is not your usual ministry, where you go into a jail on Sunday and visit with the inmates. No, Kairos is much, much more than that. Kairos really changes the lives of the inmates through the love of Jesus Christ.

For starters, there are forty inmates who are hand-picked by the Chaplain. These inmates must meet a certain criteria before they can be permitted to join the meeting. The inmates must also be approved by the Warden of the prison; the Warden is the final authority in the matter.

The motto of the Kairos Ministry is "Listen, Listen, Love, Love." Loving the inmates is the main focus. Therefore, when the ministry team goes into the prison, the inmates are not considered "inmates" any longer, they are referred to as "participants", because the team wants the participants to understand that they are important, not just somebody locked in a cell and forgotten. As well, the team does not, in any way, care about what any participant does, nor do we ask any participant about their crime or crimes.

The ministering takes place over a weekend, three and a half days to be exact (there is another half day that happens a couple of weeks after the weekend ends in order to follow up with the participants; making the weekend four days). The team goes in and introduces themselves to the participants on Friday evening, has a bite to eat with them, and takes time to fellowship with them; causing the participants to become comfortable. That in turn, causes the participants to let their guard down a little. The team exits the prison after saying goodnight that first evening.

The one thing that makes Kairos a success, is the love of Jesus Christ. Every team member that you meet, has the love of Jesus Christ thriving in his or her heart (There are women who go into the women's prison under the Kairos name as well). Therefore, most of the team bring their sleeping bags and pillows and camp out in a local area church, which has opened their doors to allow the team to sleep in over the weekend. Foam pad mattresses are provided by the Kairos Ministry for the men or women to sleep on. This helps the team bond with each other in the expression of love.

That is the one thing that makes a Kairos Weekend a success—unity of the brethren in the Spirit. The Psalmist expressed it this way: "Behold, how good and how pleasant it is for brothers to dwell together in unity! It is like the precious oil upon the head, coming down upon the beard..." In the Old Testament, when a priest poured oil upon a person, the "oil" represented the anointing of the Holy Spirit. That is what happens within a Kairos Weekend; the anointing of the Holy Spirit flows through the team and onto the participants, changing their lives for the better.

Another success of the Kairos Ministry is the cookies. Team members bake or buy dozens of cookies in order to take into the prisons, making them readily available for the participants to eat, as many as they can eat. It's an amazing thing to watch the participants become like children when they are told they can have as many cookies as they want in one setting.

In most prisons, the teams are allowed to take food in from the outside, food that is cooked and prepared by wonderful ladies of the team. This, on top of the cookies, breaks down the participant's stubbornness and unbending attitude of the heart. Most inmates in any prison act tough to keep other inmates from taking advantage of them. We want the participant's hearts to soften, so they can receive the love of Jesus Christ, with the ending result being either salvation, or a miracle of some sort.

There are several other aspects of the ministry weekend, but I will not give it all away in case there is any inmate (future participant) who may read this. The team is sworn to silence about the events that happen over the weekend in order for the participants to be surprised.

One thing I can tell you is that the participants are led through various teachings that help them to see the error of their ways. In turn, they can change their lives for the better. We want the participants to follow suit and take what they learned back to their living space in hopes that their changed lives can be examples that help change the lives of other inmates.

It is the prayer of every team member for the participants to see Jesus Christ, not the team members, because it is only Jesus Christ who can truly lead the participants to true freedom.

THE INVISIBLE MIRACLE OF SALVATION

God has performed several miracles for me and in me; allowed me to see several miracles happen, and has worked through me to perform miracles in and for other people. However, my Father never let me see a genuine miracle of salvation take place in an individual until the first Kairos Weekend He allowed me to attend.

My Department of Corrections application was approved just days before the November 2014 Kairos Weekend #15 was to begin inside this particular Oklahoma prison.

During the three and a half days of ministry, the large group of participants and team members are broken down into seven smaller groups called "families". There are four participants and three team members who sit at each of the seven round tables.

Each team member sits at the table with a participant sitting on each side of him or her.

The participant sitting on my right hand, name KP, was fifty-two years old. He looked like the cartoon character named Shaggy, who played in Scooby Doo.

At that time in 2014, KP had been incarcerated since 1985, except for a brief three-year break of freedom. Unfortunately, he picked a fight with a guy over a girl.

KP's story is a mouth full of miracles in itself.

To start, KP told me of how he was "tired of shooting dope and wanted to change." Thus, he began asking for permission to attend the upcoming Kairos Weekend. Although the Chaplain wanted to allow him to be a part of the meeting, the Warden was reluctant to allow KP to be a part due to his habit of drug use. Thanks to the support of a fellow participant graduate of a previous Kairos Weekend, and the assistant Chaplain, the Warden agreed to allow KP the opportunity to take part on one condition, pass a drug test before the meeting was set to begin. KP informed me that he found the power within himself to stop shooting the dope just three weeks before the officials surprised him with the drug test. KP added, "It was the first drug test I passed without manipulating the results."

Although KP was a humble man, he did not know Jesus Christ as his Savior.

He was a loyal type of guy. If KP said he had your back, he would give you the shirt off his back if you needed one yourself.

I formed a love for KP from the start; he was just a lovable type of guy.

I saw a hunger in him to change and began working with him, softening his heart to accept Jesus Christ as his Savior before the weekend ended. I would say to him, "KP. You are a good guy." Hanging his head, he would respond with, "No I'm not John. I will haul off and knock a guy upside the head at the drop of a hat." I would lovingly say with a smile, "Aw. It is okay KP. Everybody makes mistakes."

During one of our Saturday conversations, I questioned KP about his salvation, was he saved and going to Heaven. I strictly said, "KP. I can't let you get through this weekend without making sure you are saved so I can see you in Heaven one day." He simply said, "John. I don't know anything about that." I came back quick with, "Well. You have two days to accept Jesus Christ as your Savior."

At some point of the two days, my true brother did indeed accept Jesus Christ as his personal Savior. Thus, on Sunday, when the Chaplain took the microphone and asked if there was anybody who had accepted Jesus Christ, KP was the first one to jump out of his seat to show everybody his decision. I was the second one out of my seat applauding KP with ecstatic enthusiasm.

There are two Kairos Weekends held per year in most prisons. Thus, I went back to this particular prison for the spring of 2015 ministry weekend. I was very excited to get to see my brother KP once again. However, as the team assembled at the prison in anticipation of greeting the spring weekend participants, we got word that the Warden cut KP loose and gave him his freedom with an early release. Although I was happy to hear about KP's long deserved freedom, I was disappointed because I did not get to see him just the same.

THE SAINT WENT HOME

I was able to get word to KP with my contact information through his caseworker. I wanted to meet up with him and encourage him to stay strong as a new Christian.

KP was living in a halfway home about a three-hour drive from me, so, I made arrangements to meet with him. After making the drive to his home, we visited a while and I then went back home. I was well pleased to see that he was staying strong in faith.

I got a phone call from him another time after that; he was down and having a hard time. He had somehow been booted from the halfway home and was homeless. I took him to a nice restaurant and then paid a motel bill so he could have a place to shower and rest for a couple of days.

Sometime after that, he came to my home for a visit with his girlfriend. He was doing much better than the last time I saw him. He told me of how he was hired by a lawn-mowing outfit that took care of a cemetery's landscaping; he was being prepared for a promotion to the supervisor's position within the company as well.

Sadly, a tragedy struck a few months later.

KP's girlfriend called and informed me that KP was dead. I could not believe what my ears heard. It was a cold-blooded murder by a family member during a family feud that ended his life.

I was sad. KP came so far, changed so much for the good, and was making something of himself. He had a girlfriend who loved him; he just got his driver's license back and bought an automobile; as well, he was promoted to the supervisor's position he worked so hard to secure.

Although I miss my dear brother, he is in Heaven with Kevin, chatting it up with Jesus Christ. With his comical attitude, I am sure he is keeping the both of them laughing.

A DEMON POSSESSED ROOM

A man came to me and asked me to paint a couple of his rent houses. I was grateful for the work.

After finishing the first rent house, I moved on to the second rent house and began the work. As I worked, I became aware of a "presence" in one of the bedrooms. I sensed that the presence was that of a terrible demon; a vicious demon. I just knew that something awful had happened in that bedroom; I did not want to know what that terrible thing was. I did not even want to enter the room; however, I had to paint the room in order to get the job finished.

I prayed about the evil demon, which lingered. I sure did not want the demon to attach itself to me and cause me trouble. As well, being as how I knew that I had spiritual authority over demons, I did not want to leave the demon in the house so it could bother other people. Thus, the Holy Spirit told me to speak to the demon and command it to go to hell, in the name of Jesus Christ. I obeyed, and the demon obeyed, ridding the room of its presence.

The owner of the house got a bewildered look on his face when I told him, "There was a demon in one of the bedrooms, but I told it to leave; it is not there anymore."

I DON'T KNOW WHAT TO SAY!

Business was slow; I barely made enough money to pay the bills. God was faithful up to that point to send just enough work to keep me a float. However, business slowed down so much that I had no choice but to sit on a street corner and sell off some equipment. This was humiliating to me.

I also went to work at a customer support center answering calls from customers who needed help with various cell phone problems or just wanting to complain.

I seemed as if God was leading me into another situation where I must face a fear; the fear of answering the phone, talking to a stranger, and deciding what step was best to take after hearing their issue.

It was a good deal for a time. I had a full time job for about six weeks where I was paid during the training process.

The fist training night on the phone was not that bad. I was scared of answering the phone, yet I made it through the night. Then, training was over, and it was a full shift of constantly answering the phone.

I did not do that well on the live calls. It was one thing or another with the supervisor; I took too long to come up with a solution; I let too much time elapse between statements; I did not attempt to up-sell the customer. If the truth be told, I never did like trying to sell something to someone who did not want to buy it. Thus, after about three weeks of giving it my best, I was terminated, because I just did not know what to say from one phone call to the next.

It was okay with me. God never gave me the gift of gab. I am a straight to the point type of guy; you want it, you got it; you don't, let's move on.

FINALLY! A GREAT PLACE TO WORK!

After the let down by the Wal-Mart distribution center in 2011, I was finally hired by the company in March of 2015. I was so relieved because the position's beginning pay was about $16.50 per hour, and on top of that, some excellent benefits starting at ninety days.

The work schedule was Saturday through Monday. Although the technical hourly schedule was set for eleven hours each day, I found myself working from four o'clock in the morning until the work was complete, which was usually about three through five o'clock in the afternoon. The weekend schedule afforded me time during the week to do the work that I needed to do within the business.

From working with my oldest uncle, I learned not to shy away from hard work. I cut wood with my uncle from morning until dark at times because my uncle was a hardworking man.

As well, I worked with my uncle hauling hay. I loved hauling hay. I loved the smell of the fresh cut hay as we stacked it on the truck and into the barn. At the age of fifteen, the money was good at $.07 cents for every bail that was bucked onto and off the truck.

That was the case with the Wal-Mart distribution center—hard work. The job was hot, fast paced, and the lifting heavy at times. When I began working in the distribution center, my arm muscles were skinny; however, before long, I was growing muscles that looked like a miniature Estell Kauffman!

I AM GOING WHERE?!

The Holy Bible teaches, "You will also decree a thing, and it will be established for you…" (Job 22:28). Thus, while I lived in the upstairs apartment, the Holy Spirit said,

"You need to put a map of the world on the refrigerator. Every day, confess each country that you wish to travel and visit." I questioned this while at the same time, I obeyed.

As I obeyed the Holy Spirit, one place that became heavy on my heart is the Philippines. There is just something about that country that attracts my attention. For some reason, I like the people; and the women are some of the most beautiful in the world. I decided then and there, I want my next wife to be a Filipino.

As with the millions of dollars revelation I received back in 2008, I began telling people of how I planned to travel to the Philippines one day. Estell and my mother can testify as to how many times I have told them I would indeed one-day travel to visit the Philippines. I circled the name "Philippines" on the map; it is my faith in action.

YOUR UNCLE IS DEAD

As I previously wrote about the big argument I had with my mother in early 2012, and how I told her I would never speak to her again, I had kept my promise up to this point in mid-2014.

One day, I received a knock on the door. Upon opening the door, I was faced with my mother and brother staring me in the face. Even though I lived on the same street as my mother, just eight blocks away, she had no idea where I lived. She had to go ask of my whereabouts from my old friend EC.

My mother informed me that my favorite uncle, her second oldest brother, had passed away.

My uncle's death was grieving to me. I learned quite a bit from him as I grew up, the good along with the bad. He was a very intelligent man. He was an accomplished music drummer; singing and playing in a music band with his older brother for several years. A heavy equipment operator, a refrigeration repairman, a great water navigator with his boat, a good mechanic, an awesome father figure, and he loved to make jokes; he loved causing people to laugh. My uncle lived a full life with many more accomplishments.

I WANT THE FIRE!

For some time, I asked God over and over to baptize me with His holy fire. From my study of the Holy Bible, I could see that there is indeed a baptism in God's fire.

My belief comes from my study of a few people from the Holy Bible as in Jesus Christ, Elijah, Elisha, the Apostles of Jesus, and the Apostle Paul. Since those people, I believe people as in John G. Lake, Smith Wigglesworth, Kathryn Kuhlman, John Dowie, Reinhard Bonnke, and Benny Hinn, just to name a few, all were baptized in God's fire.

There are two of the Gospel writings that mention how Jesus Christ baptizes with "…the Holy Spirit and fire." (Matthew 3:11; Luke 3:16). From these two Scriptures, we see that there is a baptism with "fire". Now, I understand that this fire may mean judgment in the end time; however, I believe there is a baptism with fire that empowers a believer in order to enable them to raise the dead.

Fire is a "consumer". There are situations that come about in our lives that are meant to "consume" bad habits, attitudes, thoughts, and acts of the flesh in order to purify us for the work of God that He has called us to do through Jesus Christ.

There are levels of the Holy Spirit that a believer can attain within the Spirit of God. I believe this is expressed in the book of Ezekiel, chapter 47. There, in this passage of Scripture, a man led the prophet along a journey of the temple of the Lord. In chapter 47, a river is flowing from under the doorway and out through a gate. At the gate, the water is but a trickle; however, the man measures distances of about 1,500 feet at a time and leads Ezekiel through the water in these intervals. Each time the water becomes deeper than the last interval—ankles, knees, waist, finally too deep to walk, so the prophet had to swim through the waters of God. The water of God is the life of the Spirit flowing through a believer. The Christian life is a "walk". As we progress in God's Spirit, we are taken to a place where we can no longer walk; we must swim in God's current of His life flowing river. Once a believer is purified with God's fire, or baptized in fire, he or she is able to be effective witnesses for Jesus Christ, and walking the earth as He did, in the fire of God.

We progress through the river of God by the leading of the Holy Spirit. The Apostle Paul put it this way: "For in it (the Gospel) the righteousness of God is revealed from faith to faith…" (Romans 1:17). As we acknowledge God in all of our ways, He directs our paths (Proverbs 3:6), thus, taking us from faith to faith, deeper and deeper into His river of life.

BECOMING DESPERATE

In early 2014, I became desperate to receive the 20/20 vision in each eye that I had been waiting so many years to receive.

I heard of a healing and teaching meeting by Pastor Benny Hinn, being held in the nearby state of Texas. The drive would take about three hours.

There was not anything bidding my attention, so I made the trip to Texas the night before and slept in my car that night. As some of you may know, a Benny Hinn crusade can be packed to the hilt, therefore, I wanted to be there when the doors opened and get a good seat as close to the front as possible.

Once inside, I found a seat and waited for the service to begin.

Although I am sure I looked stupid, I wore two pair of sunglasses through the service. I was hoping to get God's attention of how desperate I was in receiving the eyesight; I wanted Him to see my faith. My efforts did not work; I went away empty handed, and blind, continuing to wear the eyeglasses.

YOU SHOULD BE AN ATTORNEY

In March of 2015, I took part in a historical event where a prison was hosting its first Kairos Weekend. In fact, this prison management system is an international prison system, and this was the first prison of the system to host such an event.

As I sat at one of the round tables chatting with a few participants, waiting for the meeting to begin, I shared with the participants that I had a desire to be an attorney and help inmates with legal advice within the prison system. The guys thought it to be a great idea and gathered around me to pray for me, asking that the wisdom of God lead me on the path to become an attorney. One guy said, "You should go to college!" I blurted back, "I don't know what the process is to becoming an attorney, but when I get home, I will be search and find out what the steps are for me to take!"

After the weekend was over, that is what I did, I searched and found that I needed to earn a Bachelor's Degree in Science, then, earn a doctorate degree in law; oh, let's not forget about passing the bar exam.

Enrolling in college was not an easy task. There were finances to secure, time-frames to consider, and a mountain of red tape to cut through. Part of my application process dealt with my past criminal record. The college wanted to be assured that I would not be a menace to the campus. Another part of the process dealt with my low high school GPA of just 2.5. As a result, I was required to be tested to see if I could qualify to enroll. The tester said I did better than most others who had taken the test before me.

Finally, I was allowed to enroll in the college; however, I hum-hawed around about securing the necessary finances needed to begin my first college semester in the fall of 2015, thus, at the age of forty-eight, I began my college adventure.

Attending college was fun, yet difficult at the same time. I enjoyed being there. The professors gave me all the help I needed, and before my early, forced withdrawal, I was on the President's Honor Roll with an overall GPA of 3.6.

The one problem I saw with working at the distribution center, and attending college full-time, was that I worked a regular shift at the Wal-Mart distribution center on Monday, the first day of my weekly classes. I went to the plant manager at Wal-Mart and asked him if he would allow me to leave work early on that day in order to keep my full-time schedule. Fortunately, for me, he agreed, and I was thankful for his generosity.

CHAPTER THIRTEEN: That's It! NO MORE!!!

*"When you walk through the fire, you will not be scorched,
nor will the flame burn you. For I am the LORD
your God…" (Isaiah 43:2-3).*

O ut of all the chapters in this book, this chapter is the most difficult to write, because it reveals some of the most personal information about me to date. Maybe you ask, "Then why are you revealing such personal information about yourself?"

The devil hates truth. At this present moment, I have the devil on the run. He is afraid of me because I walk in boldness of raw truth. Nowadays, there is a false truth and there is the real truth. I am concerned that there are a great number of people, Christians alike, who believe it is okay to tell those "little white lies." (What those types of lies are, I have no idea) I don't believe in telling ANY lies. One may withhold information and only tell what is necessary, but never tell a lie.

God's Word has plenty to say about truth. The Psalmist penned, "Behold, You (God) desire truth in the innermost being…" (Psalm 51:6). The Apostle John wrote, "If we confess our sins, He (God) is faithful and righteous to forgive us our sins and to cleanse us from all unrighteousness." (First John 1:9). Again, the Psalmist gives us some inside information to living on God's holy hill—"…He who walks with integrity, and works righteousness, and speaks truth in his heart." (Psalm 15:1-2).

The Apostle Paul taught, "…I do not regard myself as having laid hold of it yet; but one thing I do: forgetting what lies behind and reaching forward to what lies ahead, I press on toward the goal for the prize of the upward call of God in Christ Jesus." (Philippians 3:13-14). I strive to please Jesus Christ. Walking in truth pleases Him.

Each of us has a testimony of our good points, and our bad points. God uses our testimony to overcome the enemy, and set other people free from that same enemy. When we hold our testimony in, it actually holds us in bondage, and, the devil is able to use that bondage to drag us back into the bondage God has set us free from. The book of Revelation reveals this: "And they overcame him (the devil) because of the blood of the Lamb, and because of the word of their testimony..." (Chapter 12:11). Also, revealing our "bad" testimonies helps us to be accountable to other people. When our "secrets" are known, we know that there are other people watching us to see if we are going to mess up again. As Don Henley sang: "People love it when you lose; they love dirty laundry." After our secrets are revealed, we are fools in their eyes if we return to our vomit like dogs. Thus, this gives us strength and power against the bondage God set us free from.

Now, that does not mean that I go around town spouting out what I am about to tell in this chapter, because I refuse to allow the past trouble label my future. I know who I am in Jesus Christ. I know what Jesus Christ did for me when He took the stripes on His back, when He hung on the Cross, and when He triumphantly walked out of the grave, alive. I only accept what God's Word says about me, not what the world judges me by. I am forgiven by God, and I have forgiven myself. With that said, here we go.

THE MOVE CLOSER

After my mother came to the apartment to inform me of her next to the oldest brother's death, our feelings toward each other subsided. I extended my help toward and told her, "If you need me to help you with anything, just ask." Sometime later, she s her tested me and sent a message asking if I would go to the grocery store and buy something that she needed. I kind of snickered at the request, went and bought what she requested, and took it to her. Our relationship has progressively become better ever since then.

As I continued working at the Wal-Mart distribution center, the finances improved greatly; I was able to breathe a sigh of relief and actually sit back and enjoy life.

In the spring of 2015, an opportunity to rent a house a half
of a block down the street from my mother became available.
I felt that it would be a good idea if I lived closer to my
mother, thus, I rented the house and moved from the upstairs
apartment, the totally annoying train tracks, and the mind
blowing train horn.

PEANUT BUTTER

The house I moved into sat on the corner of the street, I
could see my mother's home from my bedroom window.

To the side of the house, in the alley, sat a duplex
apartment. The people who lived in one side of the duplex had
two good size puppies; one of a grayish-white color, and one
of a tan color. These were not your ordinary puppies because
they were of a Heinz 57 mix of Rottweiler, Bullmastiff,
Labrador, and German Shepherd. For puppies, they were
already bigger than a small breed dog. The owners of the
puppies did not feed the dogs very well, and it showed in the
puppies' rib cages. One could tell that the puppies were of a
sad state due to them not getting enough food, and no
attention.

The grayish-white puppy would always get loose and I
would pet it and then take it back to its chain. I liked this
puppy and informed the owners of my desire to acquire the
puppy. However, they expressed their interest in keeping the
puppy.

The owners informed me of their upcoming move, and
that they could take only one puppy with them. Considering
the fact that they intended to keep the grayish-white puppy,
that left only one other puppy for me to acquire, the tan puppy.
I told them that I would take the tan puppy off their hands
upon their departure. The owners moved without telling me,
and after about a week, I moved the tan puppy over to my
place and began grooming him into a healthy young pup. As
well, the owners told me of how they preferred naming their

animals after food products, thus, the tan puppy took on the name of Peanut Butter.

Peanut Butter trimmed out very nice as he grew into his adulthood stage. His tail bushed out like a foxtail, his fur became thick as a bear's coat, and his ears were as perky as rabbit ears. His paws were as big as the palms of my hands; Peanut Butter grew into a big beautiful animal. One could tell that he was happy as well.

Peanut Butter was as big as a lion, yet he was afraid of just about everything, except anybody who would play with him.

I miss Peanut Butter because he was a good dog.

UGH! THIS ROOMMATE!

A guy name Willie began working at the Wal-Mart distribution center. This guy was different from me. He took his time and moped around as if he was one-hundred years old. I honestly do not know how he kept pace at the distribution center because of how slow he worked.

However, Willie was an okay guy. He was intelligent, dependable, faithful, and very orderly. He always kept his area clean and in top shape.

Willie did not have a vehicle that he could drive to and from work at the Wal-Mart distribution center. The drive was a forty-five minute drive one-way. Therefore, I began giving him a ride to and from work.

Attending college is a financial strain. As the business continued to dwindle away, I needed some help in paying the bills. Willie was in the same boat with the apartment he lived in; he was paying more for his rent than I was. We agreed that it would help both of us out if he moved into the house with me and paid half of the rent. Thus, I allowed him to become my roommate and sleep in the living room.

Although it was a good thing financially, his presence within the home was a strain on my nerves. I, like my mother and grandmother, had grown accustomed to being alone. With there being only one bathroom in the house, this caused problems, especially with his slow moving antics. However, Willie was good friction for me. Considering how the Holy Bible teaches, "Iron sharpens iron, so one man sharpens another." (Proverbs 27:17), I am not sure which was getting sharper, my teeth from constantly gritting them, or my soul from Willie's antics.

One thing, which helped relieve the pressure, was when Willie bought his own vehicle and began driving himself to work. I could not ride with him to work due to our differences in timely ideas.

The relationship with Willie continued to deteriorate as our "iron heads" kept bumping together. His disrespect of my household requests did not help matters any. I asked him not to feed Peanut Butter; he fed him anyway. I asked him not to allow his girlfriend to stay the night; she stayed anyway. He lost his job at the distribution center, adding financial pressure. He found another job, then, he moved in with his girlfriend.

UGH! NOT ALCOHOL AGAIN!

The demons of alcohol continued to plague me, causing problems with my school lessons, and work at the distribution center.

Alcohol had been a hit and miss problem since 2009; nine-years after God set me free. I just could not shake the stronghold.

I read back in my journal and almost became depressed at how easy it was for me to pick up the bad habit from time to time. I was able to quit drinking near the end of 2012 when I began attending church with Mickey, and took part in Celebrate Recovery. However, I went to visit EC on his birthday in late June and his niece asked me if I would drink a beer with her; that was all it took to get me hooked again. Then, as previously written, I was able to stop in 2014 when I moved to the upstairs apartment. I never drank any alcohol while living there. With the added pressure from the roommate, I began drinking beer again. I picked up right where I left off in 2014 with drinking at least eight 16-ounce beers each day. The financial strain was killing my pocket book.

FINALLY! I AM LEGAL AGAIN!

In late 2015, about three o'clock in the morning, as I set out to make the forty-five minute drive to work, I was stopped by the police as I was driving through town. It would be a nightmare turned into a blessing.

I rolled down the window as the policeman walked up to the side of my car. I had a funny feeling that I was going to jail when he asked to see my driver's license. Because, as previously written, my driver's license was suspended when I foolishly rode the motorcycle drunk back in 2011. Through all the trouble since that time, I was never able to pay the cost for all the red tape in order to get the driver's license back.

Sure enough, I found myself riding in the back of a police car, with handcuffs wrapped around my wrists, on my way to jail, one more time.

For some reason, the officer never took my cell phone out of my pocket. I suppose it was due to my showing them my security badge for the distribution center, and lunch sack; they could see how I was on my way to work at the distribution center. I begged them to allow me to continue on to work; that was not an option. Therefore, while riding in the back of the police cruiser, I slid my handcuffed wrists under my feet, took out my cell, and sent my mother a message; explaining everything to her about my trouble. Amazingly, my mother actually answered the text message in the middle of the night.

Thankfully, I had enough cash in the office safe at home to bail myself out. My mother went to my home and got the money, came to the jail and got me out that very night.

We went to the impound yard where my car was and bailed the car out. The man in the impound yard said, "I am not supposed to let the car go, but as long as I don't see you drive out of here, I don't care if you have a driver's license or not." That is what I did; thanked my mom and made the forty-five minute drive to work as fast as I could. Even though I was late for work, I made it. As well, I kept my job, at least for a little bit longer.

Through that process, I decided to pay the money that was required to reinstate my driver's license. It was here that I had the chance to continue holding the Class A CDL endorsement on the license; however, I had no intentions of driving a big rig again, so I opted out of that endorsement and kept the motorcycle endorsement instead.

IT WAS THE MANAGERS FAULT!

In November of 2016, during my second semester in college, I was terminated from the Wal-Mart distribution center due to a managerial error.

Halloween was coming, and with all the pressure I was already dealing with, I did not want the added strain of dealing with the so-called holiday at work. As with every year, I have a hard time dealing with that time of year, due to the traumatic experience I dealt with during Angel's birth on Halloween of 2002. Therefore, I asked for the day off, which was on a Monday. Unfortunately, Wal-Mart implemented a new computer system in order for an employee to ask for time off. Once the employee docked the day off in the computer system, the time off needed to be approved by the Human Resource manager, which my day off was approved. The step I missed in the process was in asking the shift manager for the day off as well. In my mind, I was finished with the process when my day off was approved.

The Saturday before Halloween, and my approved day off, I went to the shift manager and reminded him of my upcoming day off. He was surprised at my confidence in my day off and said, "No. You did not put in for the time off back here." I asked for him to explain what he meant. He continued in telling me that, although I was approved up front, I must be approved with him. I about threw a hissy fit and told him of how I had already made plans. At that, he motioned to the assistant manager and said, "Go ahead and put him on the list." I rode off on my power jack and went back to work.

Our regular four days off (my five days off) went by and I returned to work that following Saturday as normal. When I entered the building and headed for the time clock, the security officer called out to me and said, "I think you are on the terminated list." I gasped and asked, "What for?" For what reason, he did not know. He agreed to allow me to try and clock-in to find out if my time card would work. To my disappointment, the card failed. I returned and told him I wanted to see a manager.

When the manager came to the front, he was apologetic and said he would see what he could do about the problem. After some deliberation with another manager, they decided that there was nothing they could do; it was out of their hands; I was fired.

I appealed to the plant manager in trying to keep my job. He had about the same response as the shift manager in that they had been lenient with me in the past with days missed and unexcused absences. Although it was a manager's fault, I was out in the cold.

THE WINNER OF THE APPEAL

I applied for unemployment in response to being terminated. Wal-Mart fought, of course, and for a time, won the battle.

I filed an appeal with the unemployment security commission and after explaining my side of the story on the phone, the appeal was granted in my favor, I won the appeal.

Thus, due to Wal-Mart's strict one-year no re-hire policy, I lived on the unemployment and maxed out several credit cards I had acquired throughout 2016. Considering how the business was dead, I focused my attention on my college studies, along with the stock markets.

UGH! THIS IS NERVE RACKING!

Before Willie moved out, and I was terminated by the distribution center, I learned a few things from Estell about the stock markets, enough for me to try my own hand at trading.

As it usually goes with most "green" traders, I lost more money than I earned. However, I learned that I actually do have a knack with trading.

I remember several meetings with Estell in his office, after hours, where we would show each other a stock or two that we believed would do some good for us if we could buy and sell at the proper intervals. My problem was that I was usually too late with the buying, thus, causing me to lose money on the sell-out.

If I learned one thing, it was that I can soon be a "day-trader" in the stock market.

AWW! WAL-MART AGAIN!

I waited out the, "no re-hire year", according to Wal-Mart's termination policy, and was rehired by the company once more.

In the year and a half that I worked for the company the previous time, I became one of their top employees. It was not easy because it took a while for my body to get to the point of handling the gruesome workload required to be at the top. When I began employment there, I told one of my new-hire co-workers, "I will be in the top ten. Watch and see." When I made it to the top ten, he was not there to see it because he resigned his position; I made it into the top three, taking third place.

When I was called in for the initial interview, I told the Human Resource manager that I was a top employee the previous time I worked there and he said, "That is the only reason you are sitting in that chair." I was very thankful for being back in his presence.

However, I was not thankful enough, because this term of employment would end in bitter embarrassment, and defeat on my part. The devil had his way with me once more.

ALCOHOL AGAIN

By now, I am sure you are thinking, "Does this guy ever learn from his mistakes?" The answer is, up to this point, no. Unfortunately, I have suffered from stubbornness for many years. There are times when I believe that if I could just turn that stubbornness against the devil, and the spiritual realm, then, I would see more miracles. However, life happens and we must continue getting up after each fall.

King Solomon wrote, "For a righteous man falls seven times, and rises again…" (Proverbs 24:16).

As well, the Apostle James wrote, "Consider it all joy, my brethren, when you encounter various trials, knowing that the testing of your faith produces endurance." (James 1:2-3). There are times when we all encounter various trials and fall into the devil's trap; however, we must rise above and soar like eagles.

The demon of alcohol grabbed me again at Christmas time of 2017. Just as all it took was for a woman to ask me if I would drink a beer with her for the last bout of alcoholism to begin, so it was this time. I took my mother out to eat at a restaurant and decided to have a glass of wine with the meal; that was a bad idea.

Unfortunately, all of my life, the problem has been impulsiveness; a spur of the moment decision to do what gratifies the flesh. Instead of praying through the temptation, I jump at the first thought of gratifying the appetite of my desires. The thought is, "I will just have a drink or two and then, I will not drink anymore." However, it never has worked that way. The drinking always got worse.

There is only one thing I have found that keeps me sober—devotion to Jesus Christ.

Neither Alcoholics Anonymous meetings, nor Celebrate Recovery has ever kept me sober.

LIFE OR DEATH

King Solomon penned, "Death and life are in the power of the tongue…" (Proverbs 18:21).

Up until this point in my life, I never fully understood how to apply this verse to my life. I understood how we were to speak positive, but it was just not sinking into my brain.

That was until I got into the trouble I am about to share with you. Now my eyes are wide open to the power of my tongue. If I want something, I speak it into existence; if not, I keep my mouth shut.

WATCH YOUR CONFESSION OF FAITH

The writer of Hebrews (It is debated who penned the book) wrote, "Let us hold fast the confession of our hope without wavering…"

After I began drinking alcohol again in December of 2017, the demon of sexual sin got ugly. I was looking at things on the internet I should not have been looking at; talking dirty to women online; and masturbating at a profuse rate, every day. I could not quit drinking alcohol, therefore, the sexual sin raged in my members. I begged God over and over to help me stop all of the sin. Yeah. He helped me stop it all right.

For several weeks, I confessed from my mouth, "I am going to jail! They are coming for you!" I did not want to go to jail, yet my confessions of that "death" were at work in the atmosphere.

The more alcohol I drank, the more the sexual demon raged, making me do horrible things that I had never done before. As well, I continued attending college fulltime.

WHAT WAS THAT NOISE?!

My mother asked for a single gate to be installed in her privacy fence on the side of the house that did not have a gate. Since I had weekdays off, I worked on the gate during the week; finishing on Friday, March 23rd, 2018. How I would love to forget that date.

I drank the normal 8-pack of 16-ounce Budweiser beer while I put the finishing touches on my mother's gate. Then, I went home about five o'clock that afternoon. I should have went to bed in order to sleep off the alcohol and be able to get up in time to make the forty-five minute drive to work at three o'clock the next morning. However, my flesh was not finished drinking alcohol.

While at home, I delved into some more beer, and sexual sin. While I sat naked at the computer, I heard some voices outside my front door. I got up to look out the window and saw a group of teenagers standing in my driveway chatting and laughing with each other. Considering how I had not seen any woman naked since late 2013 while I lived in the upstairs apartment, I got excited at seeing the teenage girls standing so close outside. Thus, I could not control myself because of the alcohol and opened the door a crack to get a better look at one of the girls. I let the sexual demon drag me too far this time, and one of the girls looked my way and saw me naked. I closed the door for a moment, then, I opened it to a crack again, this time, two of the girls looked my way and saw me naked.

I went to bed for some sleep then. I never thought anything would come of it.

I woke up to a loud bang, then, I saw light and heard footsteps in the house. Before I knew it, there were four policemen staring at me with their lights in my eyes, guns drawn.

One officer was saying, "Get up! You're under arrest!" God's deliverance had struck.

I hate to write this part of the book about myself. Yet, I am not writing this book for me, I am writing it for God.

PROBATION AGAIN

Calling my mother from jail once again was very difficult, especially baring the charge I was under. I hated to call her at all, but she was the only person I had on the outside; I could not just let her figure it out for herself.

My mother was a sweetheart in clearing my belongings out of the house and putting them in a storage unit. I felt sorry for bringing that added problem on her. She also deposited money into my jail account so I could call her on the phone, and get some food to eat while cooped up in the jail cell. Mother and I have a good relationship now.

The justice system is corrupt nowadays. Judges do what they want, regardless of a person's rights; simply because they know the poor man, or woman, can't do anything about it. For instance, when a person commits a crime, the courts leave that person in jail for extended periods of time with a high bail; then, demands that the criminal get a court appointed attorney who does little to nothing for the "criminal". God forbid the person get bailed out of jail, because then, the court appointed attorney is dropped, and the person is forced to hire an attorney, or be threatened by the judge in having the bail revoked. The person can forget representing himself or herself, because the judge does not want to deal with someone who is ignorant of the law and its process.

Thus, I sat in jail from March 24th until July 13th of 2018, because I did not have the $5,000.00 bail money to post on the $50,000.00 bail that was set.

Yeah. I committed a crime. Yeah. It was a part of God's great plan. Yeah. I repented.

I plead no contest on July 13th of 2018 and was released from jail on three years' probation; two years supervised probation with one year unsupervised probation. The original

plea deal was for five years' probation; I argued for three
years' probation, and got what I wanted.

GOD IS IN JAIL TOO!

After I was jailed on the sex charge, I knew God wanted
me to deal with the alcoholic and sexual demons. It was the
confessions of my mouth, along with the sinful flesh, that got
me there in the first place.

There is not much to do while sitting in jail. That is one
reason so many people "find God" while sitting in jail—you
have nothing better to do than pray and read the Holy Bible.
That is what I did.

I was reluctant to even face God at first. God helped me
by sending me an angel, disguised as a newborn baby
Christian. He offered me a Holy Bible to read. I knew then
and there, that God wanted me to come back to Him, no
matter how reluctant I was to return. I knew that the only
place to start was on the knees of my heart. Therefore, I began
by repenting for my sins against God; I also began by opening
the Holy Bible, turning to the first chapter of Genesis, I began
reading; I did not stop reading until I finished reading the last
word of the book of Revelation. Then, I read the Holy Bible
completely through five more times. After I finished reading
the Holy Bible completely through the sixth time, I began
reading the New Testament over and over, until the day I was
released.

The newborn baby Christian's testimony, who handed me
a copy of the Holy Bible, is a beautiful testimony. He was
innocent, and his charges were dropped. When he was booked
into the jail, he had been shooting dope. A preacher man,
inside the same cell block, who was being charged with a sex
crime himself, began talking with the young man about Jesus
Christ. The young man accepted the truth of God's Word,
dropped to his knees, and accepted Jesus Christ as His Savior.
He was then baptized in the Holy Spirit with the evidence of
speaking in other tongues. I watched this young man separate

himself from the group of other inmates to pray (Not an easy task to do in there). He was praying in the Spirit.

I too began praying in the Spirit. As prayer set in, the devil got pushed out.

GOD SENDS ANOTHER ANGEL

This particular jail has open bullpens, with up to twenty-four open cell bunk beds, which houses the inmates. When a new inmate comes into the bullpen, the bunk choices are usually the top bunk; sonority in the jail is highly important.

When I was booked into the jail, I took a top bunk. Later, I gained enough sonority to be worthy of a bottom bunk.

As well, the inmate who has been in the four-bunk cell area the longest wears the title of cell boss.

One day, a new inmate name Darnell came into the bullpen. He walked straight to our four-bunk cell area and looked straight at me. The bunk above me was available, and he wanted to move in. However, before Darnell got to our area, the cell boss said, "Don't look at him (Darnell)." I did my best not to look at Darnell, but when he looked at me, I looked back and shook my head in a side-to-side motion, which indicated "No. You can't have that bunk." He turned to look at the cell boss, who gave into Darnell's begging eyes, and allowed him to take the top bunk over the boss.

After Darnell moved into the top bunk, I somehow knew that God directed Darnell to the bunk over me. I can only imagine that God was sending Darnell to my area for both of our benefit.

Darnell was a skeleton of a man due to his recent stretch of drug use; he shot dope. As well, he was well known. Some remembered him from a prison term he served where he was a body builder; they remembered him because of the size of his muscles back in prison. It did not take Darnell very long before he was doing pushups, sit-ups, and lifting a water ball

(doubled up trash bags full of water). Before I was released,
Darnell had arms as big as my legs!

I traded bunks with another guy who wanted to bunk with
the cell boss. Then, the new area cell boss was shipped out,
leaving me as the new cell boss. Darnell wanted to move over
to my area and take a bottom bunk, thus, I agreed to his move.
After his move over, I apologized for not allowing him to
have the top bunk over me in the old cell area.

Darnell was a strategic move of God in order to get me
more involved in reading and teaching the Word of God
because after Darnell moved over to my area, he asked me to
read the Holy Bible to him. I did not mind it knowing that
God was behind Darnell's motives. The reading of the Word
to Darnell was comforting to him, and a test to me to see if I
would be afraid of the other inmates who may not approve of
hearing my voice reading. Darnell told me, "There will not be
anybody bothering you. If they do, they will answer to me."
At that moment, I knew I had an angel in Darnell watching
out for me.

Darnell was in his fifties, and very worried that the judge
would sentence him to the twenty-years they were holding
over his head for trafficking methamphetamine; it would have
been a life sentence to him. By that time, I was strong in the
Lord, my faith was very strong, and I felt as if Darnell would
not go to prison. Over and over, I assured him that he would
not go to prison.

To back up my faith in the fact that Darnell would not go
to prison, I began a series of fastings. At first, I fasted three
days on and three days off, then, I expanded the fastings to
seven days on and seven days off. In a place like that, where
food is gold, it was not easy to keep the fasting secret, nor was
it easy to keep the other guys, who wanted extra food, happy
with me.

Glory to God, because He answered our prayers asking for Darnell not to go to prison. I saw Darnell working in public a few months after I was released from jail.

PERSECUTION

Despite the lights out curfew at ten o'clock each night, most of the inmates stayed awake talking or playing games. Then, they would go back to bed after breakfast to sleep until the noon meal. It became my habit to sit at the table after breakfast and read from the Holy Bible out loud, in a low voice.

One morning, as I was reading, a hotheaded bossy guy told me to shut-up from the second floor landing.

I always wore ear plugs due to the TV being played so loud, as well, I could better hear myself reading; thus, I did not have to read as loud. Therefore, I did not hear the guy until he raised his voice.

This guy was a fighter kind of guy, so no other inmate said anything to him until after the fact.

Once I heard him telling me to shut-up, I ignored him and kept reading. Before long, this guy came down the staircase to the table I was sitting at, and leaning over the table, he snarled, "I told you to shut-up!" I snapped right back with "I'm talking to Jesus!" In an aggressive voice, He said, "I don't care who you are talking to! I said shut-up!" He then reached out and tried to grab my Bible, but I slammed my hand down on it, and with authority, I aggressively said, "You don't tough the Word of God!" He backed away and turned to go back up the staircase; as he started up the stairs, he snapped, "If you don't shut-up I will send you to your Maker!" I happily shot back, "Good! I am ready to go!"

About that time, one of the other guys said, "Just turn on the TV, then, you will not be able to hear him."

A day or so later, one of the two Zero candy bars I had under my mattress was stolen. I had a sneaking suspicion that it was the same guy. I decided to take the other Zero candy bar that I had left and go taunt him by asking him if I could offer him a candy bar. Thus, I walked up to him and said, "Hey man! Do you want a candy bar?" He looked at the candy bar and then looked at me and snapped, "You better get away from me with that candy bar." I shot a half grin back at him, turned and walked away. Another guy standing there rebuked him for being a jerk to me. The bossy guy said, "He is accusing me of stealing a candy bar!" The other guy said, "No he was not! He was just trying to be nice to you!" Then, unfortunately, the two of them traded blows with their fists. I felt bad about the fight and went to the other guy to apologize. He said he was okay with it.

BIBLE STUDY AND MIRACLES

Darnell asked me if I would lead a Bible study with some of the other men in the bullpen. I agreed, we set a day and time, and he began inviting men. There were several men who attended, and the Bible study continued at least once a week after that.

A new man, name Jeff, came into the bullpen barely able to walk. When the nurse brought the medicine, he had to have help getting from his bunk to the bullpen door in order to accept his medicine. There were a few mornings where he could not even get up from his bunk and go get his medicine, causing the nurse to bring the medicine to him.

As well, his nephew, who was also in jail, would go get Jeff's food trays for him.

Jeff got to where he was walking a little better.

There was a shower on each floor with the better shower being on the top floor. Jeff would rather use the shower on the upper floor, therefore, he would walk up the flight of stairs taking one step at a time with his good leg, and dragging his bad leg up onto each step as he went.

My heart ached for Jeff to be healed as I watched him hobble up and down the stairs day after day. Many times, I wanted to go pray for him, yet I knew I had to wait for him to come to me for prayer.

The jailers moved us to a new bullpen, where the cells had doors. The cells had two bunks per cell; Darnell and I took a cell on the top floor.

After dinner, I enjoyed sitting in our cell because I could shut the door and take advantage of some quiet time.

One night, Jeff came up to the cell wanting to talk to me. He said he was a religious man at one time, attending church every Sunday. He told me of a time in his life when three of his family members lost their lives within about a three week period of time. Sadly, he said the deaths caused him to lose faith in God, and he quit attending church.

I consoled him the best I could at that moment, then, I saw an opportunity to pray for him. After I asked if I could pray for him, he agreed and told me of a sore that had come up on his forehead, right between his eyes. He told of how he could tell the sore was getting bigger because his eyeglasses rested on the sore each time he put the eyeglasses on his face. I asked if I could pray for his leg, to which he agreed. He said that he had surgery on his hip just days before he came into the jail, telling of how the doctors replaced the whole hip. We agreed in prayer for him to regain his faith, for the sore to be healed, as well for him to be able to walk better.

Within twelve hours later, I praised the Lord as I watched Jeff walk up and down the stairs repeatedly like a brand new man; his hip was healed!

A few days later, Jeff informed me that when he slid his eyeglasses on his face the next morning after we prayed, the eyeglasses never touched the sore, and that the sore was just about healed. We praised the Lord for the miracle.

Here is the best part. A couple of weeks before I was released from the jail, Jeff came and sat down at the table with me. He leaned over to me and quizzically said, "John. I need to ask you something. I don't know what this means. You know how a hip will pop sometimes when you get up and take off walking?" I answered, "Yes." He said, "My hip has started doing that now and again. Why is my hip doing that? The doctors put in a plastic hip, and it has not done that before." I exclaimed, "That means that God replaced your hip with a real hip!" Jeff agreed to that concept being his thoughts as well. We praised the Lord some more for His goodness, even with sex offenders inside a jail cell.

There were other notable miracles as well. As in a man who was in for allegedly kidnapping his girlfriend. After prayer for the truth to be heard, the charge was dropped when he went to court.

A young, cocky guy was booked into the jail. He was one of those types who had the looks, the girl, all the favor, and a prominent attorney mother who would do anything for him if she could. This guy would mimic and make fun of other less fortunate crippled people. This attitude from him bothered me.

One night, this guy came to our cell area and was talking with a couple of us guys. I piped up and said, "You should not make fun of less fortunate people like you do. I am praying for God to send you to a place that will teach you to respect other people." He laughed and commented to how he was just joking around when he made fun of other people.

Sometime later, he told of how his mother was able to get him placed into a one-year rehab facility that taught the Word of God, and how to be a better person. I laughed when I heard him tell what his sentence was to be. He did not think it to be very funny.

A young nineteen-year-old name Billy came into the bullpen. He was a hothead who could not control his temper at times.

Billy was devious in nature—he enjoyed picking fights, and stealing other people's things in order to cause trouble. The jailers kept him in 23 hour lockup most of the time because he could not gel within the inmate society without causing trouble.

As well, Billy would fight with the officers who attempted to control him when he got out of control. He would later win a two million dollar lawsuit against the jailers because they broke his arm during one such altercation.

Billy's hurtful attitude was not his fault. He was born a crack baby; his mother continued to shoot dope, allowing him to do the same as he grew into his teenage years.

I understood his problem; Billy was one of those children who was left to raise himself, while his mother stayed strung out on dope. He did not understand boundaries; he was a boy in a man's body.

I began talking to Billy about how to conduct himself as an adult. He was listening to me and actually practicing what he was being taught. Billy even worked hard to control himself, not picking fights, and leaving people alone so he could stay in bullpen society.

One day, Billy came to me and said, "John. I need you to pray for me." I asked him what he needed, and he told me that he wanted God to help him be a better person so he could get out and be productive in society. I told Billy that he needed to repent to God and ask for forgiveness before he could expect God to help him. I lead Billy in a sinner's prayer, and he went on his way.

My heart was broken one night. Billy was doing very well in not fighting with the other inmates. However, some of the other inmates did not like Billy because he was rambunctious, liking to horseplay most of the time. They wanted him to be taken out of the bullpen. Therefore, one guy picked a fight with Billy by calling him names like "Chomo" (a word that sex offenders are called when they are guilty of molesting a child; hence, "ch"—child, and "mo"—molester), saying that he had sex with children. Billy argued with the guy telling him, "I am not a chomo like you! I am in here on drug charges! They (the jailers) put me in here (protective custody, where the jailers put sex offenders) because of my age!"

I was sick at hearing the other guy badger Billy, and prayed for Billy to keep his cool. However, the other guy kept on and on until Billy got so mad, he ran down the stairs to pick a fight with the guy.

It did not take long for the jailers to show up and jerk Billy out of the bullpen.

I rolled over and cried tears of sadness because Billy was doing so well in keeping his attitude in check.

My sadness was short lived because the jailers did not keep Billy in lockup for very long. He was able to convince them that the fight was not his fault, but a conspiracy against him in order to get him removed from the bullpen. I continue having tears of joy.

The courts decided that a prison term was not fit for Billy. Thus, they cut him loose to some type of program that would help him, not just punish him. Praise God for His mercy.

GOD CHOSE THE FOOLISH

As you can see, God does great work in jail cells. In my opinion, the Spirit of God does more work in jails and prisons than He does in church houses across America. Why? Because, there is no room for pride in a jail cell. Sitting in a jail cell is just about the lowest place people can find themselves. In a jail cell, there is no place to look, but up.

Finding yourself in a jail cell is frightening, especially when you find yourself in a bullpen with 23 other people you just do not know.

However, there are just as many good people in a jail or prison, as there are sitting in the pews of a church house.

There is one other inmate I did not talk of. He was looking at life in prison because he got drunk, raped a woman, then, he burned the house down on top of her. He was a great guy in my book.

This guy did not talk to me much because he was afraid God would never forgive him for what he did to that woman. I spoke with him and told him that God loved him no matter what. He never said a word; he just nodded his head in an approving manner. He would not even attend the Bible study.

I never saw this guy lose his demeanor; he always kept his cool.

It is people as this guy who God will use to show His glory. Why? Because, this guy knows he is nothing. He knows that he is not worthy of God's mercy and grace.

Jesus Christ taught this parable: "And He (Jesus) also told this parable to some people who trusted in themselves, that they were righteous, and viewed others with contempt: 'Two men went up into the temple to pray, one a Pharisee, and the other a tax collector. The Pharisee stood and was praying this to himself: 'God, I thank You that I am not like other people—swindlers, unjust, adulterers, or even like this tax collector. I fast twice a week; I pay tithes of all that I get.' But the tax collector, standing some distance away, was even unwilling to lift up his eyes to heaven, but was beating his breast, saying, 'God, be merciful to me, the sinner!' I tell you, this man went to his house justified rather than the other; for everyone who exalts himself will be humbled, but he who humbles himself will be exalted.'" (Luke 18:9-14).

I, in seeing so much supernatural activity, get that way sometimes. I must also repent.

The Apostle Paul taught it this way: "For consider your calling, brethren, that there were not many wise according to the flesh, not many mighty, not many noble; but God has chosen the foolish things of the world to shame the wise, and God has chose the weak things of the world to shame the

things which are strong, and the base things of the world and
the despised God has chosen, the things that are not, so that no
man may boast before God." (First Corinthians 1:26-29).

In quoting one more Apostle: "Humble yourselves in the
presence of the Lord, and He will exalt you." (James 4:10).

A REWARD?

Some time about 2017, the same friend who asked me to
be involved with Kairos, said, "I have a motorcycle I want to
give you." My mouth fell open with chin bouncing off the
floor in amazement! The "faith jacket" was paying off again!
However, it was a while before I received the motorcycle.

I waited and waited for my friend to make arrangements
with me in order for me to take possession of the motorcycle.
In our crossings during Sunday school, and at Kairos ministry
weekends, we would talk about how he needed to get the
motorcycle out of his garage and into my hands, but it did not
happen.

After I was released from jail in July of 2018, I attended
Sunday school class and confessed to the class members of the
trial I had found myself falling into. The class was very
receptive, and equally forgiving. I was very humbled with
their love and compassion they showed towards me.

Finally, my friend made the arrangements, and I went out
and brought the bike home.

WHY THE FIRE?

Fire melts and consumes what is in its path, and what is
put in it. The Holy Bible teaches, "For the LORD, your God,
is a consuming fire, a jealous God." (Deuteronomy 4:24).

You are holy—set apart for a specific work of God. As
you progress in your relationship with God, He must remove
mindsets, attitudes, and unholy conduct from your mind and
body in order to be able to use you for His purpose. The
Apostle Paul said, "And we know that God causes all things to
work together for good to those who love God, to those who

are called according to His purpose." (Romans 8:28). Do you love God? Are you called according to His purpose? Then, ALL things are working together for your good.

The work God began in you, He will complete, not you. (Philippians 1:6). The measures and methods that He uses to "complete" that work is His business. He is the Potter and you are the clay. (See Jeremiah 18:1-12). When Jeremiah was a prophet of God, God's people were stubborn (Does this remind you of someone you know?). Because of my stubbornness, I know the feeling.

Thus, in order for God to prepare me for the coming ministry, God needed to put me in His fire and consume the alcoholism, in turn, consuming the sexual lust for the final time. God took it a step further and made it to where I would not want to go back to drinking alcohol by causing me to be labeled a sex offender. Am I ashamed of that, yes?

Is that who I am in God's eyes, no. I am the righteousness of God in Jesus Christ; that is what God created me to be.

Now, I can relate to those who are labeled sex offenders themselves. I know how they feel; I feel their pain, and their shame. However, through Jesus Christ, God is sending me to heal the brokenhearted, set at liberty the captives, to open the prisons of those who are bound, to proclaim the acceptable year of the Lord, also His coming day of vengeance, to give them beauty for ashes, the oil of gladness for sadness, as well, a garment of praise for their spirit of heaviness (Isaiah 61:1-3).

Maybe you think you are a vessel of God who is not worthy of anything except dishonor. I am here to tell you that you are being transformed into a vessel of God for honor. As the Apostle Paul taught: "Be diligent to present yourself approved to God as a workman who does not need to be ashamed, accurately handling the word of truth... Nevertheless, the firm foundation of God stands, having this seal, 'The Lord knows those who are His', and, 'Everyone who names the name of the Lord is to abstain from wickedness.' Now, in a large house, there are not only gold and silver vessels, but also vessels of wood and of earthenware, and some to honor and some to dishonor. Therefore, if anyone cleanses himself from these things, he will be a vessel for honor, sanctified, useful to the Master, prepared for every good work." (Second Timothy 2:15-21). Be diligent to show yourself approved to God. How do you "show yourself approved"? You fall, you get back up, you fall, and you get back up. You put your faith in your High Priest, Jesus Christ, whose blood was poured upon the mercy seat for your sins (Hebrews 4:14-16; chapter 9).

Jesus Christ was in the fire with the three Hebrew men (Daniel chapter 3). What was Jesus Christ doing while He was in the fire with the men? He was praying to the Father for them, telling the Father "these three men are Mine Father." (See Romans 8:34). If you are saved, you belong to Jesus Christ; He is in the fire with you, and you will come out not even smelling like smoke (Daniel 3:27). Jesus Christ will not lose any who the Father gave to Him (John 10:27-29).

God's holy fire is consuming YOUR desires; sanctifying you; purifying you; changing you to be made in the image of God's Holy Son, Jesus Christ.

NEGATIVE CONFESSION STRIKES AGAIN

As I sat in jail, I saw how I would not be able to complete the fifth semester of my college career. Therefore, I asked my mother to contact my degree manager and get her help in withdrawing me from college.

After that, I remember being very sad about having to withdraw from school. However, the "withdraw" began way back before I went to jail.

I was very afraid that I was too dumb to finish law school, much more, pass the Bar Exam. I even voiced my fears during class one day. The instructor was telling of how she was intimidated by the Bar Exam when it was her time to take it. I spoke up and fearfully expressed my fear in saying, "It will be a miracle if I even make it to the Bar Exam." Even then, the Holy Spirit was there in my ear saying, "You have the confession of your mouth." Eventually, I indeed gained the confession of my mouth.

THAT'S IT! NO MORE!!!

While I sat in jail, being a Christian was easy. However, I knew the time was coming when I would be forced back out into the world, facing the devil, and his temptations.

Life on the outside is difficult. There are so many pressures we must deal with. We must deal with the law, and obedience to it; employers, and obedience to them; family, and their needs; friends, and their demands. Inside the walls of a jail or prison, one just rolls over and goes to sleep in order to cope with the pressure. On the outside, there are so many avenues one can choose to follow in order to cope with the added pressure—alcohol, drugs, people, food, television, games, beer joints, movies, sex, music, and the list goes on and on.

I have never been able to deal with the pressures of life for very long periods of time. Usually, my pressure limit is about three months of battling life's issues and abstaining from any form of unrighteousness (which is the time frame I am at now), then, I can't help but cave in and have a drink of alcohol, or fall back into some form of sexual sin.

Thus, after I was released from jail on July 13th, I hit the ground running, trying to get my life back in order. The debt was so piled up against me that I just wanted to go to work and pull my name from the pit of hell that society held it captive in. I forgot of how close I became to Jesus Christ while I was in jail.

Before being jailed, I took care of the neighbor's lawn with trimming and mowing for him. I resumed this task after being released. One day, he offered me a beer to drink after I finished my work on his lawn. Although it would not have hurt his feelings in declining, I decided, "One beer will not hurt me". However, just as soon as I departed from his house, I stopped at a convenience store and bought a six-pack of beer to drink after I got home. The fight was back again.

I drank beer for about a month or so, then, I decided it was not worth it anymore. I have not had a drink of alcohol since about September of 2018, and I have no intentions of allowing that demon back into my life.

It took a little longer to get the sexual demon ousted out of my life than it did in getting the alcohol demon kicked out. Unfortunately, until November of 2019, I continued viewing things I should not have been looking at on the internet, and masturbating. I have not partaken of any unrighteous acts since November.

SNAKES

When I went to jail, I had a Filipino girlfriend who lived in the Philippines. She stayed with me during my incarceration. When I came out of jail, it did not dawn on me that I had some "special rules" to follow as a sex offender; I just focused on getting back into the game of life. Therefore, I kept the girlfriend until we broke up. Then, I acquired another Filipino girlfriend.

One of the rules of being a sex offender is that I can't have a girlfriend "with a child" without permission from the probation officer. I felt that love should trump the "rules".

Another rule is that I can't "maintain" a relationship with any minor under 18 years of age without permission from the probation officer. However, through one of my adult friends online, who lives in the Philippines, I carried on my friendship with her and her 16-year-old daughter, who is in college in the Philippines. I think of her daughter as my daughter; and I treat her as such. Why? Because, my oldest daughter, who I have not seen since she was three years old, is now a 16-year-old. I enjoyed the attention of a daughter, which my friend from the Philippines gave me. I encouraged her in her studies; warned her against having boyfriends; schooled her on modesty, and the like. I even mailed her a Holy Bible to read.

A part of my sentencing requires me to attend sexual counseling. One night, while I sat in one such group meeting, I spoke of having an "international girlfriend", to which, the counselor asked if I had disclosed that information to the probation officer. I admitted that I had not because I did not know it was a requirement. She brought the "special rules" to my attention. That night, I went home and read the "rules". Sure enough, I saw that I needed permission to have a girlfriend.

In seeking to rectify the situation, I informed the, then standing, probation officer. She agreed to meet my girlfriend by slideshow presentation via my laptop; her only concern was that my girlfriend has a five-year-old daughter, and was I having contact with the daughter. I informed her that my girlfriend was stationed in Saudi Arabia on a two-year work contract, while her daughter lived in the Philippines with her grandmother. With that, she still agreed to meet my girlfriend. I patiently anticipated the probation officer's approval.

That particular probation officer passed my supervision over to another woman, who in turn agreed to meet my girlfriend via the laptop presentation. My hopes were high.

The next thing I knew, the probation officer had filed a violation on me and asked a judge to issue a warrant for my arrest; also causing a motion to revoke the probation to be filed. They had stabbed me in the back with entrapment. Thus, I am currently awaiting the court's decision as to whether or not I will go to prison for violating the probation.

One of the requirements of probation is to take a polygraph test, every six months if passed, or every three months if failed. In believing I would get a "yes" or "no" answer from the probation officers concerning my girlfriend, I was totally honest (my character anyway) with the polygraph examiner on the first polygraph. This, in turn, emboldened the probation officer to file the violations. I am appalled at how the probation people stabbed me in the back. However, God is using them to destroy the flesh for His good, the flesh of bitterness, unforgiveness, sexual lust, alcoholism, and the "Judas kiss."

KARMA IS REAL

Some believe in karma, some do not. I do. For the Holy Bible teaches: "Do not be deceived, God is not mocked; for whatever a man (or woman) sows, this he (or she) will also reap." (Galatians 6:7). Jesus Christ Himself taught: "Treat others the same way you want them to treat you." (Luke 6:31). What goes around comes around. If you sow discord, strife, hurt, deception, or the like, you bring judgment on your own head.

That judgment does not necessarily come from God; it is just a natural law of the universe.

I have seen it happen over and over again; to me, and because of what someone else did to me. Let that stand as a warning. Treat others the way you want to be treated—love.

TAKE IT TO THE STREET!

As I have previously established, "…God… calls into being that which does not exist." (Romans 4:17). That means, God shows you what He has called you to do BEFORE you actually do it. Then, you have the responsibility to speak your future into existence just as God calls into existence what does not exist, yet.

Jesus Christ taught it this way: "Have faith in God." (Mark 11:22). Or, maybe you have heard this verse of Scripture said this way, "Have the God kind of faith." From my study of this verse over the past twenty years, and for me, this means to trust God, use the God kind of faith that He used when He created all things. You must "create" your world, with your mouth, based on what you believe God wants you to accomplish in this life.

For example, you may know that you have a music talent; God has called you to play an instrument, write music, and sing. However, you may not know the first thing about music, or how to carry a tune (I can't carry a tune in a five-gallon bucket!). So, you speak out of your mouth, "I believe God has called me to play an instrument, write music, and sing." Without knowing anything about music, you have just put your music career into motion with the words of your mouth. Yet, you have never played an instrument, written a note of music, or sung a tune. To me, that is the God kind of faith. Then, you acknowledge God in all your music career ways that you pursue, and He directs your paths. (Proverbs 3:6).

We see this truth from reading the context of the Scripture passages surrounding the verse of Mark 11:22. Before this verse, in Mark 11:12, Jesus sets the example for having the God kind of faith when He cursed the fig tree. One thing I have always marveled at is where the Holy Bible records, "...He (Jesus) found nothing but leaves, for it was not the season for figs." (Mark 11:13). What? It "was not the season for figs"?! Then why did Jesus Christ curse the fig tree if it was not the season for figs? Did not Jesus know this info? Yes, of course Jesus Christ knew this information. I believe He was setting a spiritual example for His disciples to follow, to show the power of our tongues. Jesus Christ was proving what the wisest king of the Old Testament meant when he penned Proverbs 18:21; life and death are definitely in the power of the tongue.

The next day, when Jesus and His disciples passed by the dead fig tree, Peter was astounded with seeing even the tree roots already dried up. Then, Jesus taught a lesson: "Have the God kind of faith Peter. Whatever you SAY, believe what you SAY will happen, and it will be granted to you." Jesus went on teaching about prayer saying, "Therefore, I say to you, all things for which you pray and ask, BELIEVE that you have received them, and they will be granted you." (Mark 11:24). I see no argument about that.

With that in mind. Along about 2015 was when God spoke the name of the ministry that He has called all of us to do— Take It To The Street Ministry. What are we taking to the streets? His healing power; the saving knowledge of Jesus Christ, and His soon return. Thus, God was calling things into being before I got to the actual point of them being; which is what He has been doing since 2000. As in 2004 with audibly saying, "I have called you to preach!" In 2007 with saying, "You will go worldwide and heal the masses." I am thankful for Estell and Stephanie, who signed on with the ministry name as undersigned incorporators of Take It To The Street Ministry Union—the ministry of Jesus Christ.

CURRENTLY

I have been praying in the Spirit on a consistent basis for the past three months straight. Things have steadily become much better on a spiritual level.

On December 31st of 2019, at midnight, I woke up to a presence of the Holy Spirit, as I have never experienced before; I have sensed Him in the room only a couple of times before, but nothing like this time. It was as if His presence was filling the whole room.

We talked for two hours straight. We discussed issues as in the sunglasses. I told Him that I was flat fed up with wearing these eyeglasses. He told me to "Keep the sunglasses close. Every time you get out of the bed, put them on your head. Keep the eyeglasses on the second shelf of the night stand and the sunglasses on the top shelf, within reach." That, to me, is crazy. However, I know it to be the Holy Spirit, because every time I wake up in the middle of the night and sit on the side of the bed, He reminds me of the sunglasses. That can only mean one thing—the 20/20 vision is very close to manifesting in these eyes.

The sunglasses are my point of contact for the faith in receiving the eyesight. One day, I will trade the sunglasses for the eyeglasses.

January 1st of 2020, I began the morning with an hour of prayer, praise, and confession of God's Holy Word.

Then, Dad took me out for breakfast in the wee hours of that morning. I argued with Dad, telling Him, "Dad! I don't have the money to go eat with. He calmly said, "You don't need any money son. I got the money."

While out to eat at 6 AM that morning, I bumped into Estell and his misses, who were in search of the same thing— breakfast. We pulled into the parking lot at the same time. I was not for sure it was their van, so I went on inside and found a seat. Sure enough, it was my trusting friends, Estell, Stephanie, and Estell III. They sat a table over and we discussed life and its exciting moments.

Estell has always respected me in that he "listens" to whatever is going on in my life. Estell knows just about everything there is to know about me. Yet, he accepts me— love.

After work, I come home and have an hour of prayer while a worship CD plays.

One day, as I drove home from work, I was having some issues, to which I was taking authority over in the spirit realm. As I spoke my demands, I felt as if I had the approval from my Father to take authority over the eyesight. Thus, I said, "I command 20/20 vision to come into these eyes! Now!" After I got home, I began the usual time of prayer. During these times, I always take off the eyeglasses and set them aside, wearing the sunglasses instead. I could see the blindness standing at the edge of the bed. In a vehement anger, I walked up to the blindness and shouted, "You must move and go to hell! In the name of Jesus! Because I am not backing down! I came to the throne for one thing, my eyesight! I am getting what I want, one way or another!" A few days later, I noticed that the blindness had indeed obeyed my command.

As well, I hit a deer with my luxury automobile, forcing me to buy a problem car (I call it my faith car). The motor developed a water leak from the area of a head gasket, behind one of the belt pulleys. In being ignorant of auto mechanics, there was no way I would be able to fix the problem myself, nor could I afford a mechanics repair bill. Therefore, I laid my hands on the engine of the car and vehemently said, "I don't care what stops you, but you are hereby stopped! In the name of Jesus!" The next morning, the water leak had stopped.

I then turned my attention to the brake master cylinder, which I replaced, and which was leaking; I told it the same thing I told the water leak. Although it has taken a little longer for the leaky master cylinder to stop leaking, my faith is working.

Finding a place to live is horrendous for a sex offender. We only have certain areas where we can live. With that in mind. One day as I was spending time in prayer, I got a message from my brother Estell who told me they were considering another place to rent and relocate. His reasoning was the fact that the property management were not taking care of the maintenance problems that he was complaining about. Becoming angry about the property manager (because I just can't pack and move at the drop of a hat), I prayed to God saying, "Please have the maintenance people come take care of their responsibilities!" Last word I got from Estell was that he could consider signing another lease because the maintenance people had indeed came and taken care of everything on the list but one item. I rejoiced for the answered prayer.

February 2nd of 2020 was a night for giving praise to Jesus Christ, because He healed some precious people.

Leading up to that night… I have worked at the same company since August of 2018. I went to work there about a month after I was released from jail in July of that year.

When I went to work there, I immediately bonded with a secretary name Gloria. It was as if I knew her from times past.

Gloria invited me out to her house so I could enjoy Thanksgiving dinner with her and her family. This gave me a great opportunity to meet her family, and spend some time with her husband, whose name is also John.

Towards the end of 2019, Gloria retired from the company; my heart was broke. I told her that I would come out and visit sometime. She did not hesitate in extending an invitation.

It took me a couple of months to keep my promise. Every time I saw Gloria visit the office, or thought about how I miss Gloria at work, the Holy Spirit would remind me of how I said I would visit her and John. Then, just about every Sunday of January, the Holy Spirit would say, "You need to go visit Gloria." I had some kind of excuse each week and would say, "I'll go next Sunday."

For some reason, I decided that Sunday February 2nd was the night to go visit. Just as soon as John opened the door to me, the Super Bowl of football was beginning. The Kansas City Chiefs were set to play the San Francisco 49ers in a match-up where the Chiefs had not won a Super Bowl in 50 years. Considering how I don't purchase any television programming, I felt it to be a blessing from the Father to be able to watch the Super Bowl at Gloria's house. We rooted for the Chiefs. After their near defeat, the team pulled out the win.

In the time that I have known Gloria, John has suffered from one ailment to another.

With that information in my mind, while on the way to visit, I asked my Father to give me the authority over any ailment that confronted me. He agreed. Thus, as the evening carried on, Gloria mentioned that her back was hurting, and it seemed as if it never stopped. I told her back to stop hurting. The attention turned to some cancer John said he was dealing with. Anger rose up within me because I hate cancer, and the devil knows it.

In the name of Jesus, I took authority over the cancer. After a short while, I could sense that the cancer was obeying the command. I told John that the cancer was leaving, adding that the pain leaving Gloria's back was evidence of the healing. Gloria agreed that her back did indeed feel better. John agreed that he believed every word I said because he had met people before, who walked in the power of God to heal.

I did the Father's will that night, and the biggest winner of the night was Jesus Christ.

THE END

The end of the end is near. Anybody who looks at the world with an honest eye can tell that things are just not right. If you can't see how bad the world is, study Scriptures from the Holy Bible as in 2 Timothy 3:1-5, Genesis 6 and 19, Matthew 24 and 25, and Luke 17:26-30. I pray that the Lord Jesus Christ will open your eyes to the truth so that you may not believe the lie of "Jesus Christ will not come in my lifetime." Jesus Christ will appear to those who wait for Him (Hebrews 9:28). Are you waiting for Him? Do you long for His return? Are you ready for the last great awakening? It's here!

If you are not saved by the Blood of Jesus Christ and going to Heaven when you die,

I encourage you to speak with someone who believes in Jesus Christ; find out what it takes to be saved.

The Gospel of Jesus Christ is simple. You hear about Jesus Christ; you believe what you hear about Jesus Christ; then, you confess with your mouth that you are saved by Jesus Christ. You will know whether or not you are really going to Heaven when you die. If you are not sure, get sure. We live in the dispensation of grace now. However, when Jesus Christ comes again, we will enter the dispensation of God's wrath.

There is no other way to live forever except by faith in Jesus Christ and His Blood.

Jesus Christ paid the ransom for your sin so that you could live forever with God the Father in Heaven. Just believe it.

Come to Jesus Christ and be forgiven. Don't be caught dead in your sin.

Peace to you.

CREDITS

My Mother. Thank you for the loving and directing memories.

Estell and Stephanie Kauffman. Thank you for your loving shelter.

Scripture taken from the NEW AMERICAN STANDARD
BIBLE®, Copyright© 1960, 1962, 1963, 1968, 1971, 1972,
1973, 1975, 1977, 1995, by the Lockman Foundation. Used
by permission. www.Lockman.org.

Scripture taken from the NEW KING JAMES VERSION.
Copyright© 1979, 1980, 1982, by Thomas Nelson, Inc. Used
by permission. All rights reserved.

The Free Encyclopedia, W. (2019, October 17). Billy Joe
Daugherty. Retrieved March 15, 2020, from
https://en.wikipedia.org/wiki/Billy_Joe_Daugherty

The Free Encyclopedia, W. (2020, February 2). Smith
Wigglesworth. Retrieved March 15, 2020, from
https://en.wikipedia.org/wiki/Smith_Wigglesworth.

Healing, R. (2020, March 3). ReceiveHealing.com. Retrieved
March 15, 2020, from
http://receivehealing.com/blog/89/why-doesnt-god-heal-
me/#more-89.

The Free Encyclopedia, W. (2020, March 10). John G. Lake.
Retrieved March 15, 2020, from
https://en.wikipedia.org/wiki/John_G._Lake.

Reads, G. (2020, March 3). Leonard Ravenhill Quotes (Author of
Why Revival Tarries). Retrieved March 15, 2020, from
https://www.goodreads.com/author/quotes/159020.Leonard_R
avenhill

About the Author:

I have had the pleasure of getting to know Mr. John Jackson over the years as both a friend and a confidant. He has become very nearly a member of our family over the years. We have laughed together, cried together, prayed together, learned together, prodded each other to get better. John lives a simple life that outwardly belies the intelligence and faith that guides it inwardly. His trust and faith in our Savior consistently amazes me while pushing me to question and strengthen my own. Although he and I lead very different lives, at least to look at, I have come to value what time I get with him very highly. I draw strength from his insight and courage from his immense faith. At the same time, he has expressed that he also draws strength from me which pushes me to become a better man so that I may have more to offer when or if he needs me to be there for him. His wisdom comes from very different experiences than mine and as such his perspective holds tremendous value when I need that outside perspective on something. John has become a trusted Prayer Warrior in my life and I love him like a brother. It has been, and will continue to be, my honor to have developed a relationship with my friend and Brother, John Jackson.

I love you man!

Estell Kauffman II

www.ingramcontent.com/pod-product-compliance
Lightning Source LLC
Chambersburg PA
CBHW021137090426
42740CB00008B/816